Why Be A Vegetarian?

Tarang Sheth
Tej Sheth

with a foreword by
David Jenkins, MD, PhD

Illustrations by Raj Bharadia

JAIN PUBLISHING COMPANY
Fremont, California

Library of Congress Cataloging-in-Publication Data

Sheth, Tarang, 1973-
    Why be a vegetarian? / Tarang Sheth, Tej Sheth; with a
foreword by David Jenkins; illustrations by Raj Bharadia.
        p.   cm.
    Includes bibliographical references.
    ISBN 0-87573-035-3 (acid-free paper: pbk.)
    1. Vegetarianism.   I. Sheth, Tej, 1973-   .   II. Title.
TX392.S444   1995
613.2'62—dc20   94-238710
                                                               CIP

Contents

Foreword

It is a pleasure to write a foreword to such a broad ranging and scholarly defence of vegetarianism. Though the book is scholarly, it will appeal to the general reader. It is not necessarily a book to be read from cover to cover in a single sitting. But its breadth guarantees that it will be picked up and studied on repeated occasions. It will be consulted frequently in the owner's life. The book is unique from three perspectives. First, it is comprehensive, dealing with man's possible dietary evolution in relation to plant foods and the implication of plant-food consumption on health, environment and the development of the humanitarian philosophy. Secondly, it is both studious and, at the same time, eminently readable. Thirdly, it is written by authors whose upbringing as Jains (strict vegetarians with a tradition of almost three millenia), raised in the midst of Western culture, allows them to challenge most effectively the lifestyle which we, in the West, regard as normal.

The reader will therefore find much in this book which is controversial. However, in an age concerned with global change, population explosion and pollution, many will feel that, as a species, we are obliged to make some changes in direction. This book provides ideas on major change that may be made with advantages for health and morals.

David Jenkins, MD, PhD, DSc
Professor of Nutritional Sciences, Faculty of Medicine,
University of Toronto
Director, Risk Factor Modification Center,
St. Michael's Hospital, Toronto

Acknowledgements

In the course of this project, we have been beneficiaries of the kind advice and support of many people. The first few books we read on the benefits of plant-food diets were generously provided by Mrs. Irena Upeniks. Her interest in teaching about the effects of diet helped set us on the path that led to this book. Profs. Alan Mendelson and Howard Aster have given us excellent advice and support. A publisher himself, Prof. Aster has been a trusted advisor about matters concerning publication. Our contact with him would not have been possible had it not been for the keen interest Prof. Mendelson took in our work.

For their insightful and critical comments at various stages of manuscript preparation, we express our gratitude to Ms. Susan Welstead and Prof. Mendelson. Their attention to detail helped immeasurably in making this book what it is. They have both offered their generous support since the start of this project. Prof. Sylvia Bowerbank and Prof. Harish Jain also provided criticism, identifying areas that needed strengthening.

We were very fortunate to have a scientist as distinguished and accomplished as Dr. David Jenkins write the foreword to this book. We are deeply indebted to him for his interest in our project and for his suggestions regarding the book's contents. It is fitting that Dr. Jenkins write the foreword to this book because it was participation in his mentorship programme that helped direct and shape the interest of one of us (Tarang) in nutritional science and also in a career in medicine. As a vegetarian himself, he has been an influential role model for us both. His insights not just into medicine, health, and nutrition, but also into cultural and religious history have been illuminating.

Mr. Mukesh Jain has been an accomodating and helpful publisher. He has patiently guided us through our first contractual publication. We would also like to thank Mr. Raj Bharadia for producing such wonderful illustrations.

Finally we would like to express our gratitude to our mother and father who have provided unwavering loving support since we began this project over four years ago through to this present publication. Their guidance, and the values they instilled in us, have enabled us to write this book with the dedication it required.

Preface

Why Be A Vegetarian? grew out of our first book, *The Case for Vegetarianism,* which was published in Fall of 1991. In the following pages, we endeavor to provide a comprehensive consideration of the implications of different human diets. A great volume of information has been published in the three years since our earlier publication. This book has also benefitted from our debate and discussion with numerous individuals and public audiences, through which we have had the opportunity to reexamine and expand our ideas. Over the past four years, our own understanding of the issues has penetrated deeper, and this book, we hope is reflective of this in its thoroughness and detail. We hope that it will serve both the general interest reader and those who wish to undertake further research in any of the broad spectrum of topics we have covered.

In this book, our discussion of diet revolves around the difference between plant and animal food. We feel that considering the matter of diet in these terms helps to clarify an important area of confusion that often surrounds debates about vegetarianism. Calling a diet vegetarian does not necessarily identify the level of animal products it contains. Those who are lacto-ovo-vegetarians still often eat considerable amounts of animal products. The same is true of lacto-vegetarians. By recasting the debate in terms of plant-food and animal-food, we can achieve a clearer understanding of the issues and more adequately address the question of what amount of plant-based and animal-based food we should have in our diet.

Our seventh chapter, "Philosophers, Shramans and Reformers," details the diverse history of vegetarianism amongst many different cultures. We think that vegetarian history, particularly that of Eastern cultures, is very useful to know because it shows that in some societies vegetarianism has been considered a standard practice. The information in this chapter, however, should not be construed as an argument by appeal to authority.

In this book, we have endeavored to provide a fairminded and measured treatment of topic. It is our hope that it will present readers with an opportunity to acquaint themselves with the wealth of information about the effects of human dietary choices and provide a basis for informed discussion and action.

Toronto, Canada
Fall, 1994

Introduction

Food is an integral and universal aspect of human existence. Like water and air, we cannot live for too long without its nourishment. The production and consumption of food are thus activities common to all peoples. Yet the food we eat is also very specifically defined by our cultural and religious heritage. As young children we are taught to eat and enjoy mostly those foods that are native to our tradition, since food is one of its defining characteristics. There is Mexican, Hungarian, Egyptian, Thai, a cuisine for every nationality. Historically, food habits have also been determined by religion. The Muslim must follow certain dietary restrictions, as must the Hindu, the Jew, and the Jain. Together, these cultural and religious factors have largely determined what people chose to eat.

In this book, we propose different grounds for making choices about our eating habits, based on the distinction between plant food and animal food. We examine diet, not in terms of culture and tradition, but in terms of the different types of foods that make it up.

Though people seldom think of their dietary choices in these terms, they constantly make implicit decisions of how much plant food and how much animal food to include. In North America, it is by far the most common practice to eat large quantities of animal foods, such as meat, poultry, fish, eggs and dairy products, with plant foods such as grains, vegetables, fruits, nuts, seeds and legumes playing a minor role in the diet. This eating pattern has often been called the meat-centered diet. At the other end of the spectrum are the vegans, or pure vegetarians, who eat only plant foods. Other patterns of plant-food/animal-food consumption include the

1

semi-vegetarians who eat no meat but eat fish and poultry, the lacto-ovo-vegetarians who eat eggs and dairy products and the lacto-vegetarians who consume dairy products but no animal foods. It is also important to mention that there is considerable variability in the amount of animal foods each type of vegetarian consumes. It is quite possible, that a lacto-vegetarian who drinks a large amount of milk will eat more animal products that a semi-vegetarian who eats chicken only occasionally.

In order to suggest a dietary choice based on a distinction between plant food and animal foods, we will contrast the implications of these foods in a number of key areas. First we will consider several topics related to personal health. Through an examination of the dietary evolution of the human species we will establish the relative importance of plant and animal foods in the human evolutionary diet. Then, we will examine present medical understanding of the contribution of diet to the major chronic diseases of our society.

Second, shifting from personal health concerns to the health of the planet, we will survey the impact of animal agriculture on the land, forest, water and energy resources of the global ecosystem. We will consider the implications of different diets on world food security and our ability to feed a growing human population.

Third, we will examine how animal foods are produced in the modern factory farm, considering some of the ethical arguments advanced in favour of a diet based exclusively on plant foods. To broaden our understanding of vegetarianism, we will also survey some of the important individuals and movements in the history of vegetarianism in Western and Eastern culture.

Finally we will examine the recommendations of nutritional authorities regarding consumption of plant and animal food.

As we take in turn the perspective of an archaeologist and evolutionary biologist, a physician, an environmentalist, a person concerned with animal welfare, a historian, and a nutritionist, we consider significant medical, environmental and ethical problems. But, these are not the only issues addressed in this book.

This book is also about more daily concerns, touching upon activities that we each engage in every day. It is about what we choose to buy on shopping trips, what we eat at our meals and what we choose to cook for friends and relatives. The discussion that follows is an attempt to show that these daily actions, which most of us seldom question, have wide-ranging implications. We hope to demonstrate that, by making food choices wisely, each of us can benefit our own health and have a positive impact on the world around us.

Origins

It is held that to go to the beginning of human history we must go back five or six million years to ancient Africa, when the forbears of apes, monkeys, and humans alike, existed on earth.[1] Living in an arboreal environment, these early primates had to adapt to the abundant challenges their surroundings created. To nourish themselves adequately, they had to collect food from a number of different sources, which were often far apart from each other. They lived as foragers, animals that collected a wide variety of fruits and leaves from trees and other vegetation growing in the forest. Their diet was predominantly, if not exclusively, based on these plant foods.[2]

The anthropoids, namely apes, monkeys, and humans, evolved from this common ancestor. Around five million years ago, the hominid line, to which modern humans belong, separated from its common lineage with apes and monkeys.[3] This divergence was brought about by the movement of early hominid from the forests, where other primates lived, to the savannas of ancient Africa.[4] The savanna was a new environment where seeds, fruits, and roots were in abundant supply. Hominid soon evolved more effective ways to make use of these plentiful food sources. The most prominent and distinguishing of these adaptations was a change from quadrupedal to bipedal locomotion.[5] This physical adaptation was accompanied by the invention of tools and their use in obtaining and preparing plant foods.[6]

It is important to note that human evolution from these earliest humans to modern *Homo sapiens* was not a linear progression of one species giving rise to the next. It is more likely that different species of early hominid coexisted, with one gradually out surviving the other. In addition, certain

5

branches of evolution from the early primate ancestor may have gone extinct without leading to a new organism to continue the evolutionary lineage.[7] Archaeologists have found a number of different types of fossil remains from early hominid. These are probably best thought of as sign posts in human evolution, giving snap shots in time of the stage evolution had reached. It may be a simplification to give these different types of hominid distinct names and treat them like distinct species, as they evolved very gradually, but it is useful in understanding the overall process taking place. At least four distinct groups of hominid have been identified, each appreciably different from the other but still sharing a significant number of their traits.[8]

The first genus that has been identified in the hominid family is *Australopithecus*, thought to have emerged in Africa around 4.5 million years ago. If you were to meet one of these early hominid today, he or she would stand upright and, with exception of an ape-like snout, would look remarkably human.[9] With a brain only slightly larger than that of an ape, *Australopithecus* was probably a fairly dim-witted creature. The fossil record indicates that *australopithecines* possessed large molar teeth that would have been well suited to a diet of tough plant-based material like that of their primate ancestors.[10] Hence, the diet of these early hominid was largely dependent on the fruits, roots and seeds they found in the African savanna.[11]

Another distinct species in human evolution came about two million years ago. *Homo habilis*, the name given to these hominid, identifies them as the first member of our genus. *Habilis* is Latin for "handy-man" or "tool-maker" and conveys the fact that *Homo habilis* was proficient at making and using various implements.[12] Mentally, this species gained considerably on the earlier *Australopithecus* and, physically, had lost some of the earlier ape-like features.[13] Studies of wear on the teeth of *Homo habilis* fossils reveal that they were predominantly fruit eaters.[14]

The next major change came with the evolution of *Homo erectus* around 1.5 to 1.6 million years ago. *Homo erectus*, as the name suggests, had fully adapted to the upright posture and stood over five feet tall on average. Members of this species had faces that looked much less ape-like than earlier hominid forms and much more like present-day humans.[15] Another distinctive change between *H. habilis* and *H. erectus* was a reduction in the size of molars and pre-molars, indicating a decrease in the amount of chewing required in the diet of *H. erectus*. Stone tools found with fossil remains may explain this change, as they suggest that these hominid were processing their food by removing portions that were difficult to chew.[16] Plant foods again constituted the vast majority of food consumed, and if any animal food was eaten, it was derived from scavenged carcasses from which remaining flesh might have been removed.[17]

The evolution of *Homo sapiens* from *Homo erectus* was well underway 300,000 to 250,000 years ago.[18] Modern humans, given the name *Homo sapiens sapiens*, emerged as a distinct species 35,000 to 40,000 years ago. It is thought that by this time, modern humans were the only species of hominid left on the planet.[19] Essentially possessing the same physical characteristics as humans do today, these people soon covered almost the entire world, either by replacing earlier hominid or by evolving from them.[20]

After a long period of evolution as an almost exclusively plant eating species, *Homo erectus* and then *Homo sapiens* were the first hominid to hunt for food.[21] The first evidence of human hunting is dated around 400,000 years ago and suggests that *Homo erectus*, at a late stage in its development, used tools to kill and butcher animals for food, a practice that was continued by *Homo sapiens*.[22] The relative contribution of hunting, and hence animal food, to the human evolutionary diet for both *Homo erectus* and *Homo sapiens* is important to establish. Some who have asserted that humans have been a predominantly hunting species base their evidence on the diet from the time of *Homo erectus* onward. According to this theory, humans stopped eating plant-based foods and began to eat increasing quantities of meat.[23]   This development is thought to have facilitated human mental development, since hunting is a more complex activity than gathering, requiring the stalking and capture of prey. By such reasoning, humans are considered to have evolved as omnivores, suited to, indeed, requiring, a large amount of animal food in their diet. This view of human evolution dominated the literature for quite some time, but it now appears that there is considerable evidence to doubt this construction of events.

The emphasis given to hunting in human evolution, an activity predominantly the preserve of men, underestimates the contribution of women to the food supply. Rosalind Miles notes:

> Of women's duties, food gathering unquestionably came top of the list, and this work kept the tribe alive . . . women regularly produced as much as eighty per cent of the tribe's total food intake, on a daily basis.[24]

By highlighting the importance of women in food collection, Miles and other scholars have helped to correct the popular view of humans, or rather of man, as a hunting species. Biological research on this period has also contributed to a different understanding of the diet of early humans. Studies of hominid teeth from the *Homo erectus* period reveal extensive wear and chipping, suggesting that the diet required considerable amounts of chewing. Human teeth are specialized for the grinding of tough food, an ability which resembles that of conventional herbivores. Our teeth are not the teeth of a meat-eating species.[25] In addition, an examination of present day gatherer-hunters indicates that, though a number have practiced some form of hunting, even today, the overwhelming majority of these people consume a predominantly plant food diet.[26] The !Kung San of the Kalahari desert provide an example. The !Kung live in a dry, woodland environment and they gather the nutritious mangetti nut as their primary food all year round. The remainder of their diet is selected from at least 85 other edible plant species. Brian Fagan, an archaeologist at the University of California, Santa Barbara, notes that the edible vegetable foods are so plentiful for the !Kung San, that they rarely have to eat anything but their favourite plant foods.[27]

Throughout human evolution, plant foods have been an easy and relatively safe source of nutrients, while hunting with tools has been a risky, potentially low-return activity.[28] Equipped with agile fingers and co-ordinated hands and eyes, early humans would have faced little competition in exploiting these plant-food sources. Indeed, the macronutrient composition of the typical gatherer-hunter society, that is 15-20% fat, 50-70% complex carbohydrate, and 15-20% protein, suggests a diet based very heavily on plant food.[29]

Although it has been suggested that an increasing reliance on meat as a high-energy food source directed the course of later human evolution, in particular that of the brain, it is important to note that the characteristics which distinguish humans from primates, namely upright posture, bipedal locomotion, thumb and index finger precision, and the expansion of brain power, had all developed before humans took up hunting.[30] Indeed, by the logic that argues that the energy density of meat made possible an increase in the human brain size, we would have to conclude that the world's purely carnivorous species should have become its most intelligent.

If animal foods were not necessary for human sustenance and if they entailed unnecessary risk or effort, why then did humans begin hunting? In all likelihood, the search for food in colder climates encouraged this development. Karl Butzer notes that "meat may have become a critical food source when hominid expanded out of Africa into the temperate zones where plant availability is seasonal."[31] Indeed, the first undisputed evidence of hunting is found in Terra Amata in Spain and in Lehringen in northwestern Germany, both relatively colder locales than the African savanna.[32]

Although the later human species, *Homo erectus* and *Homo sapiens*, took up hunting, there is little evidence to suggest that human anatomy and physiology changed to adapt to this development. In order to better understand the diet for which humans are evolutionary suited, researchers at the University of California, Berkeley, compared the human and chimpanzee digestive systems. The feeding habits of chimpanzees are almost exclusively herbivorous, with an estimated 94-98% of their diet coming from plant foods.[33] Their studies showed that the chimpanzee digestive tract bears considerable resemblance to our own, suggesting that our digestive system has changed little over the five million years it took for us to evolve to our present form.

The evolutionary design of humans as a plant-eating species can be further clarified by a comparison of humans with carnivores and herbivores. While carnivores have a short bowel to permit the quick expulsion of toxins, plant-eating animals have long bowels to allow for the slow digestion and fermentation of plant foods. Flesh-eaters have long, sharp teeth and retractable claws and jaws that open straight up and down. By contrast, plant-eaters have jaws that can rotate in a circular motion to allow for grinding and chewing by teeth that are mostly small and flat. Herbivores sweat through the skin while carnivores keep cool by breathing rapidly and dangling their tongues.[34] In all of these ways, humans are like other plant-eating mammals. Our physical characteristics, like our digestive tract, are clearly those of a predominantly herbivorous species.

From these physiological and anatomical facts, we can infer further information on the actual role of meat in the human evolutionary diet. If our bodies have not changed very much in their herbivorous design since the advent of hunting, then meat-eating could not have played a significant role in human evolution. Had meat-eating been important in evolution, humans would have evolved a more carnivorous digestive system. Since this has not occurred, we are led to conclude that in the diets of our closest ancestors, meat must have played at most a marginal role, allowing earlier humans to survive when plant foods were not available, but not forcing human evolution onto a carnivorous path.

Though capable of hunting, humans clearly have not evolved to be meat eaters. In cold climates where plant food was seasonal, an ability to hunt helped people to survive. Nevertheless, humans have not developed any of the physiological adaptations of other animals who rely heavily on animal food. The archaeological, anatomical, and physiological evidence we have discussed shows that hunting, though practiced to some degree by humans over the past 400,000 years, has been of minor biological importance. Since animal products have played only a limited role in the human diet, they have not exerted a strong enough selective force in evolutionary terms to cause humans to develop carnivorous biological adaptations. That our digestive system, as well as the rest of our anatomy, remains strongly herbivorous attests to the fact that humans have evolved as a plant-eating species. Though we cannot conclude that humans evolves as exclusive plant-eater, there is little doubt that humankind came into being sustained on a diet that was almost wholly plant-based.[35] And since evolution is a very slow process on the human time scale, our biological constitution has changed little over the 40,000 years that modern humans have been around.[36]

Although humans are not naturally suited to the regular consumption of animal products, meat plays a central role in the diets of a large proportion of people living today. Indeed, meat has acquired the status of a dietary staple in Europe, North America, and parts of Asia. This evolutionarily aberrant diet has its origins in the agricultural revolution which occurred in different parts of the world within the last four to five hundred generations. From around the 10th millennium to about the eighth millennium B.C., humans all around the world began to cultivate plant foods and domesticate animals. As agriculture gradually developed, the gathering and hunting way of life came to an end for the vast majority of human beings.[37] The agricultural revolution profoundly changed the sources of human food. From a predominantly gathering lifestyle, consuming a large variety of wild plants, humans adopted a diet based on staple crops. These were rice in South and South-east Asia, maize in Central America and Mexico, and cereals in Europe.[38] The diets of people in these areas of the world were based on carbohydrate-rich plant foods and a seasonal supply of fruits and vegetables.

The domestication of animals also marked the first time in our history that humans consumed the milk of other animals.[39] Although animals were kept, the peasant agriculturalist could scarcely afford to slaughter them regularly, and meat was eaten only very rarely.[40,41] In fact, only the wealthy could afford substantial quantities of milk, butter, meat and other foods from domesticated animals.[42] As a result, the diet of humans during this period, although markedly different in its sources, changed little in its actual nutrient content from that of the preceding gatherer-hunter one. The nutrient profile of the typical diet of agriculturalist times has been suggested as being 10-15% fat, 60-75% carbohydrates, and 10-15% protein, quite consistent with the evolutionary diet of our species.[43] Thus, despite the dramatic changes that accompanied the agricultural phase of our existence, the vast majority of humans continued to consume an essentially vegetarian diet.

After it began, the diet and livelihood of the peasant agriculturalist remained the way of life for almost all of humanity for thousands of years, until the 1800s and the dawn of the industrial revolution in Europe. This second drastic change in human society, occurring within the past seven or eight generations, profoundly altered not only the sources of our food, but the nutrient profile of our diet as well.

The industrial revolution made possible the first application of modern technology to agriculture and methods such as crop rotation and fertilizers were developed.[44] With advances in the science and practice of agriculture, food production increased dramatically. When mechanization entered the farming sector, with cutting machines, threshers, winnowers, and the like, grain production increased again. With large quantities of surplus grains, it was possible to cycle the nutrients through animals instead of consuming them directly. Soon animal products, such as meat, milk and butter, became much more widely available. Fuelled by the association of animal products with wealth and prestige that was developed during agriculturalist times, increasingly affluent people in the West steadily increased the numbers of animals they raised for meat.

The new-found agricultural productivity and growing meat supply that followed the industrial revolution had dramatic consequences. The human diet, which had been essentially vegetarian for the entire span of our evolutionary history, suddenly, in industrial countries, became heavily dependent on animal foods. Intake of animal protein, cholesterol, and saturated fat doubled and then doubled again. Statistics from the United Kingdom show that per capita intake of fat in grams per day increased from 25g in 1770 to 75g in 1870 and then to 145g in 1970, a 580% increase in just 200 years.[45]

As industrialization, wealth, and increased agricultural productivity have spread to other regions of the world, increased meat consumption has followed closely behind. During the 1980s meat consumption increased by 80% in Asia and nearly 30% in Latin America and Africa.[46] Indeed, gross national product figures and dietary patterns indicate that there is a very clear association between increasing wealth and meat consumption.[47]

Alan Durning and Holly Brough of the World Watch Institute note that during the past 50 years livestock industries have increased dramatically in many countries of the world. Soaring grain yields have made feeding animals on corn and barley relatively inexpensive, so that intensive, specialized meat, egg, and dairy farms have proliferated.[48] In only the last 40 years, the global number of cattle, pigs, sheep, and goats has nearly doubled, to four billion and the number of chickens has more than tripled, to 11 billion.[49] There are now three domesticated animals for every man, woman, and child on the planet. Occupying one-quarter of the earth's land mass, cattle, together with other ruminants, now eat more grain than all the people in the developing world put together.[50]

In 1990, meat consumption around the globe was four times higher than in 1950.[51] As a group, Americans ate 112 kg of meat per capita per year, the highest level in the world, with Canadians and Europeans not far behind. In fact, in the average North American's lifetime, he or she will eat 21 cows, 12 hogs, 14 sheep/goats, 900 chickens, and 11,275 eggs.[52,53]

Modern industrial societies are now characterized by this aberrantly high consumption of animal products. The nutrient profile, which had been roughly 10-15% fat, 60-75% carbohydrate, and 10-15% protein for hundreds of thousands of years, has, on an evolutionary time scale, instantaneously changed to 40-45% fat, 45% carbohydrate, and 10-15% protein.[54] Associated with the rise of animal product consumption, the consumption of dietary fibre, which is derived exclusively from plant sources, has plummeted. Fibre in the North American or European diet is as little as 10% its historical norm.[55]

One only has to put these recent developments in evolutionary perspective to see how distorted our food habits have become. The modern meat-based diet of industrialized human societies is a large and very recent divergence from the diet our species evolved to consume. If hominid evolution is represented as a 24 hour day, hunting, the active killing of animals for food, only emerged in the last couple of hours, between 9:30 and 10:30 pm. For the first 22 hours or so of their existence, humans have eaten a plant-food diet. That our digestive tract has changed little from when we diverged from chimpanzees 6 million years ago and that our physical characteristics are those of herbivores and not carnivores attest to this fact. The meat humans consumed in their diet was, until recently, incidental and therefore has not influenced our physiology or anatomy to take a more omnivorous or carnivorous form.

In the 24-hour model of human evolution, humans have consumed heavily meat-centered diets typical of modern industrialized societies, for only last four seconds of the last minute of the last hour! As Katharine Milton, professor of anthropology at the University of California at Berkeley has noted, the foods eaten by humans today, especially those consumed in industrially advanced nations, "bear little resemblance to the plant-based diets anthropoids have favored since their emergence."[55]

This change has been accompanied by a great cost, to human beings, to the environment, and to the animals raised for meat. Evidence is growing that many of the health problems seen in the industrially advanced, and increasingly in industrializing countries are due to a mismatch between the diet we now consume and that to which our bodies have adapted over millions of years of evolution. The environmental costs of a global meat industry that supports over 15 billion domesticated animals with immense quantities of food, energy, and water resources is becoming increasing apparent. And the stressful, highly unnatural conditions under which animals exist in modern factory farms are being revealed. In the next three chapters we shall consider each of these issues in detail.

Diet and Disease

We know from the study of evolution that the diet for which we have evolved is essentially vegetarian. Increasingly, medical and nutritional research suggests that there are many long-term problems associated with feeding our bodies a diet high in animal products. A growing body of evidence demonstrates that by mismatching our diet and our physiology, we are contributing to the epidemic of premature chronic disease in industrialized nations, where one in two men die of a heart attack, one in four people have high blood pressure, and one in 10 develop diabetes. In fact, seven out of 10 deaths in North America are due to chronic diseases.[1] Included among these are heart disease, diabetes, cancer, high blood pressure, kidney failure, rheumatoid arthritis, osteoporosis, calcium stones, and gallstones.

What is the link between diet and disease? Does increased animal product consumption contribute to the prevalence of these diseases? What is the nutritional basis for increased disease risk? What benefit does abstention from animal products offer in each of these cases? These are some of the questions we seek to answer in the following pages.

One way medical researchers investigate the link between diet and disease is by comparing the health status of different dietary groups. For example, a researcher would compare heart disease prevalence between meat-eaters and vegetarians. In the medical literature, meat-eaters are defined as people who consumes meat daily as part of their diet, following what is commonly called a "meat-centered diet." Those who abstain to varying degrees from animal products fall into three categories of vegetarianism. Lacto-ovo-vegetarians eat

17

eggs and dairy products, lacto-vegetarians eat dairy products, and vegans (often called pure vegetarians) eat no animal products at all. In the evidence we shall consider, one or more of these groups is used as a basis of comparison to meat-centered diets.

Further distinctions emerge from these definitions. Meat-centered diets contain higher total fat, saturated fat, and cholesterol and less dietary fiber than vegetarian diets. Protein is consumed in greater quantities in meat-centered diets, and most of this protein is of animal origin, whereas vegetarians consume less protein, mostly, if not entirely, of plant origin. Also, vegetarians consume more monounsaturated and polyunsaturated fat,* which are more abundant in plant foods.

Meat-eaters, of course, do eat plant-based foods. But the amount of plant-based food they eat is less than vegetarians. What researchers are really testing when they compare these diets, therefore, is the effect replacing meat with plant-based foods has on the prevalence and development of various chronic diseases.

Heart disease was first considered a major public health problem in the early 1900s.[2] By the 1950s, it had grown to become the leading cause of death in the Western world. In the United States, one in three people die as a result of heart disease; in Canada and the United Kingdom the death rates are similar.[3,4]

---

* The terms saturated, monounsaturated and polyunsaturated refer to the three types of molecular structures of fat. Saturated fats serve no nutritional purpose other than as an energy source. They tend to be hard and sticky. Butter and lard, for example, are almost entirely made up of saturated fat. Monounsaturated and polyunsaturated fats tend to be more liquid. For example, sunflower oil is high in both monounsaturated and polyunsaturated fat. The only types of fat the body nutritionally requires are three polyunsaturated fatty acids—linoleic, linolenic, and arachidonic—the rest serve as energy sources.

Like all chronic diseases, heart disease develops over time. Essentially, fatty deposits accumulate in the arteries feeding the heart muscle and lead to the narrowing of these blood vessels. Normally quite elastic, these vessels become harder as the deposits grow. Over the years the area through which the blood flows becomes smaller and smaller. This process is called atherosclerosis. It is possible that an artery, once it has narrowed and hardened significantly, will become completely blocked. Blood-flow through the artery will stop. Without blood flow, the area of the heart that received nutrients from the blocked blood vessel will no longer work. Often, the result is a heart attack, the most common and often fatal result of the atherosclerotic process. One of the first indications that heart disease might be related to diet came in the 1950s when three U.S. army doctors conducted autopsies of soldiers killed in the Korean War. Their study examined 300 U.S. and Korean soldiers, all of whom had appeared healthy at the time of their death. The doctors found that 77% of the American soldiers had developed heart disease to a significant extent. Among the Koreans, only five percent had any evidence of disease progression.[5]

The results were intriguing. The men in both groups had been young and very physically fit. Why, then, did the Americans have such a high prevalence of incipient disease? The answer, the doctors suggested, was to be found in the food each group consumed, the only major difference between the soldiers being that the Americans obtained their protein from meat, eggs, and dairy products while the Koreans got their protein almost exclusively from rice and beans.

Since the 1950s many such studies have compared the prevalence of heart disease among people who eat different types of diets. For example, scientists at Loma Linda University in California monitored a group of 25,000 vegetarians from 1960 to 1980.[6] Their purpose was to observe the risk of disease among vegetarians and then to compare this with overall U.S. statistics. They found that for men between the ages of 45 and 64 being a vegetarian reduced the risk of heart disease by over 60%. A similar study was conducted in Norway in 1991, where vegetarians were found to have one-half the rate of heart disease of the general Norwegian population.[7]

Diet and risk comparisons are also possible between countries. In one such comparison, researchers from Cornell University and the Chinese Academy of Preventive Medicine surveyed 6,500 people in China, where the diet is essentially vegetarian. They found that the prevalence of heart disease among this group was one-fifth that of a comparable portion of the U.S. population. Again, the difference was attributed to the plant-based diet of the lower-risk group.[8]

Why does a meat-based diet double or even triple the risk of heart disease? The answer lies in the types of nutrients meat-eaters consume, and at the same time in the types of nutrients vegetarians get more of by following a plant-based diet. Dr. T. Colin Campbell, director of the China study, notes that the Chinese eat much less saturated fat, cholesterol, and animal protein than do North Americans. In addition, Chinese people consume greater amounts of vegetable protein and much more fiber, as much as three times more, than North Americans do on average.[9]

Most people are aware that the consumption of high levels of saturated fat and cholesterol is an important cause of heart disease. Many studies have been conducted to establish this association.[10,11,12] The significant problem with meat and other animal-based foods is that they contain large amounts of these substances. In fact, dietary cholesterol comes only from animal products.[13] At its worst, a high-fat North American diet can exceed the maximum recommended intake of cholesterol by over 450%.[14] And saturated fat is also present in abundant quantities.

Fortunately, as much as 60% of the cholesterol we eat passes straight out of our bodies. But the 40% that remains enters the blood stream through the intestines. Since the body manufactures its own cholesterol to digest saturated fat, meat-based meals translate into high levels of cholesterol and saturated fat circulating in the blood stream.

Cholesterol deposits itself in the linings of arterial walls, starting the process of atherosclerosis. The more cholesterol in the blood, the more likely it will be deposited and the faster plaque will build up on the artery's walls. Saturated fats also play a role in this process. Since they are sticky, solid substances, they accelerate the build up of plaque. Remember, this process does not begin at 45. The young, healthy soldiers examined during the Korean war could not have been more than 25 years old and had already formed deposits in their arteries. Heart disease is a gradual process that occurs largely without noticeable symptoms.

Given the importance of blood cholesterol levels, a group of scientists at Harvard University compared 73 male and 43 female vegetarians with corresponding non-vegetarians to assess the benefits of abstaining from meat. Led by Dr. Frank Sacks, the team reported that vegetarians had only 68% of the blood cholesterol levels of meat eaters. In addition, the level of low-density lipoprotein (LDL) cholesterol, or "bad" cholesterol, was 39% lower in vegetarians.[15] These results are not surprising, of course, given the foods in which saturated fat and cholesterol are found.

While the dangers of these substances is now widely accepted, there is growing evidence to suggest that animal protein also accelerates heart disease. One study which points to the negative effects of animal protein was conducted in Japan, where researchers at the University of Tokushima School of Medicine studied the relationship between diet and heart disease in 12 regions of the country. They found that an increased intake of animal protein was associated with an increase in heart disease risk, a relationship that was independent of the other variables studied.[16]

If cholesterol and saturated fat are dangerously excessive in meat-based diets, what about the nutrients vegetarians get more of in their diets? In fact, two dietary constituents found abundantly in a vegetarian diet, namely vegetable protein and dietary fiber, provide protection against heart disease. Research shows that vegetable protein is likely to lower blood cholesterol levels when substituted for animal protein. Researchers at the University of Western Ontario replaced animal protein in the diets of healthy young women and found a 10% reduction in blood cholesterol levels over a period of four weeks.[17]

Medical research also indicates that eating plenty of fiber lowers cholesterol levels. Although some controversy in this area persists, the Canadian Ministry of Health and Welfare, in its *Nutrition Recommendations*, notes that there is now considerable evidence that eating a diet high in dietary fiber can reduce blood cholesterol levels.[18] One such study, conducted by researchers at Harvard School of Public Health, monitored 1,000 people over a period of 20 years. After this long period of observation, the researchers concluded that a greater consumption of foods containing dietary fiber lowered the risk of coronary heart disease by 40%.[19]

A recent addition to this body of research, conducted by Dr. David Jenkins and colleagues at the University of Toronto, was one of the most scientifically thorough yet conducted. In this study, patients were placed on low-fat vegetarian diets which were very high in dietary fiber. At the conclusion of the four month trial period, cholesterol levels in the patients' bloodstreams declined by five percent, despite the fact that they had been previously eating a low-fat diet.[20] In addition, the study identified soluble fiber, found in legumes, beans, and oat bran, as being more beneficial than insoluble fiber, which is found in whole-grain breads.

To decrease saturated fat, cholesterol, and animal protein, and to increase vegetable protein and fiber, one has to cut down on animal foods and increase plant-based foods in one's diet. This is for the simple reason that plants contain absolutely no cholesterol and animal protein, and are also very low in saturated fat. Animal foods contain no dietary fiber, and, of course, no vegetable protein. In short, those nutrients which can cause heart disease are found almost exclusively in animal based foods and those which protect against heart disease are found in plant foods. Avoiding heart disease through nutrition, therefore, means becoming a lot more vegetarian in the foods we eat.

This fact would also suggest that a plant-food diet might be used as part of a treatment for heart disease. If it tilts the balance away from progression of disease, then might it not also help people who already have the disease? This question was investigated by Dr. Dean Ornish of the University of California, San Francisco School of Medicine. In the late 1980s, Dr. Ornish conducted a year-long trial with a group of 28 patients, all of whom had advanced stages of heart disease. Stopping their medications, Dr. Ornish placed them on a low-fat vegetarian diet and motivated them to stop smoking and engage in moderate exercise and stress management. Another group of 20 patients continued their regular treatments during the same period of time and were used as a basis for comparison. At the conclusion of the year's trial, the degree of atherosclerosis, or plaque buildup, in the patients' blood vessels was measured using angiography, the most accurate way to assess progression of heart disease. What Dr. Ornish's research team observed was unprecedented in medical history.[21] While every one of the regular-care patients' has suffered a worsening of their heart disease condition over the one-year period, 82% of the patients on the vegetarian diet and other lifestyle modification programmes showed a regression in the blockages of their arteries—without the use of any form of medication.[22] The lifestyle treatment, in other words, had begun to reverse the heart disease process.

Since this study was published in the British medical journal the *Lancet*, it has received widespread recognition. Together with the other evidence on heart disease and nutrition, it suggests quite conclusively that a vegetarian diet can help prevent, and even reverse, heart disease.

Cancer is the second leading cause of death in the Western world. In the United States, all forms of cancer combined account for one-quarter of American deaths.[23] Yet cancer remains a mysterious disease. It is not known when it will strike or who will develop it. There is no known cure. Though treatments using drugs and radiation can destroy cancer cells, there is no guarantee that the mutant cells will not come back. There are several hypotheses concerning the cause of cancer. Certain chemicals are known to be carcinogenic. Lung cancer is very definitely associated with smoking. And diet also plays a role.

The importance of diet was suggested by dietary and disease prevalence comparisons across countries. The United States, which has the world's highest per capita meat consumption, has the world's highest rate of colon cancer. In India, Japan, or China, on the other hand, where meat is eaten infrequently, if at all, the incidence of colon cancer is less than one-fifth that of the United States.[24,25] Diet was again implicated when Japanese women who follow Western-style, meat-based diets were found eight times more likely to develop breast cancer than Japanese women who followed a more traditional diet of plant foods.[26] These statistics, among many others, have led some leading scientists to suggest that up to 40% of cancers in men and up to 60% of cancers in women are attributable to diet.[27]

Investigating this possibility, researchers in Japan studied over 120,000 men above the age of 40, comparing those who ate a vegetarian diet and did not drink or smoke with those who ate meat, drank alcohol, and smoked. They found that the meat-eating group had five times the risk of developing cancers of the mouth, pharynx, esophagus, and lung, and were twice as likely to develop cancers of the stomach, liver, and colon. Although smoking and alcohol consumption were certainly involved, Dr. T. Hirayama, who wrote the study report, noted that a meat-based diet played an important role in each of these cancers.[28]

It is thought that meat-eaters are at an elevated risk for some cancers because of their increased consumption of fat and decreased intake of fruits and vegetables. Evidence that consumption of fat is important in cancers of the breast, prostate, rectum, and colon is plentiful. Studies of population groups throughout the world show that death rates for both breast and colon cancer are related to per capita fat intake.[29]

In 1990, researchers from Harvard Medical School published a study regarding the intake of meat, animal fat, and colon cancer.[30] They had monitored a group of over 88,000 women over a six-year period and collected data on the food they ate and on the incidence of colon cancer amongst them. Commenting on the results, the authors noted that:

> Of the 61 foods we examined for relation to risk of colon cancer, the strongest association was with beef, pork, or lamb eaten as a main dish; women who reported daily consumption had two and one-half times the risk of those who reported eating such meals less than once a month.

The researchers concluded that a higher consumption of meat and fat from animal sources increases the incidence of colon cancer.

The weight of accumulated evidence has led a number of health agencies to similar conclusions. Over a decade ago, the National Research Council noted that:

> [there is] convincing evidence that increasing the intake of total fat increases the incidence of cancer at certain sites, particularly breast and colon, and conversely, that the risk is lower with lower intakes of fat.[31]

In recognition of the danger high-fat diets pose, the World Health Organization notes that for the danger from fat to be reduced, current consumption levels would have to be halved, from 37% of total calories to less than 20%.[32]

An insufficient amount of dietary fiber also plays an important role in the development of cancer, specifically colon cancer. Pioneering work on this link was done by Dr. Denis Burkitt, a physician who first popularized the benefits of a high-fiber diet. He suggested that high rates of colon cancer may be caused by the virtual absence of dietary fiber, found only in plant foods, from the Western diet. In a remarkably dedicated career, Dr. Burkitt spent many years measuring the size and consistency of human stool samples in Africa. He found that the fecal material of African tribespeople, who consume a high-fiber diet, was much larger and less rigid than the characteristic North American stool sample. He hypothesized that fiber was essential in the diet because it sped the transport of fecal matter through the intestines. Whereas it may take only a day for a high-fiber vegetarian meal to make its way through the intestinal tract, the food of a meat-eating person, typically low or lacking in fiber, can take three or more days. Dr. Burkitt suggested that, in the relative absence of fiber, cancer-causing substances can become concentrated in the stool and, because of the slow transit time, are left in extended contact with the bowel wall, thus increasing the likelihood of tumor formation.[33]

Since Dr. Burkitt first published his ideas more than 20 years ago, a considerable amount of research has been conducted to investigate this hypothesis. Recently, Swedish scientists investigated dietary causes of colon cancer and reported that the high-fiber content of a vegetarian diet was the primary cause for a lower rate of colon cancer among people abstaining from meat.[34] In their 1992 report, the researchers also noted that switching to a lacto-ovo-vegetarian diet led to a decrease in the presence of potential cancer-causing substances. The Harvard study of meat, fat, and colon cancer also found that dietary fiber exerted a protective effect against the development of cancer.[30]

Vegetarians are also at a lower risk for most cancers because they tend to consume greater quantities of fresh fruits and vegetables in comparison to people eating non-vegetarian diets. The World Health Organization reports that a relationship has now been established between a high consumption of fruits and vegetables and a lower risk for cancers of the lung, colon, prostate, rectum, mouth, stomach, cervix, and esophagus.[35]

The importance of fruit and vegetables has been highlighted by the Physicians' Committee for Responsible Medicine, a physicians' group based in Washington, D.C.[36] The group suggests that vitamin C, found in citrus fruits and many vegetables, may lower risks for cancers of the esophagus and stomach. It also blocks the conversion of nitrates into carcinogenic nitrosamines in the stomach.

Vegetables are important, not only because they are low in fat and high in fiber, but also because they contain a number of cancer-fighting substances. Carotenoids, the pigments that gives fruits and vegetables their dark colors, have been shown to help prevent cancer. Dark green and yellow vegetables contain beta-carotene, which also helps to protect against lung cancer and may help to prevent cancers of the bladder, mouth, larynx, esophagus, breast, and other sites.[37]

Vitamin C and carotenoids help the body fight cancer because of their effect on free radicals. Free radicals are a sort of mutant class of molecules and are thought to play a role in the development of cancer. Vitamin C and carotenoids are antioxidants, which means that they help retard the action of free radicals, and, consequently, help protect against cancer.

In an article reviewing the evidence that fruits and vegetables lower cancer risk, Dr. Regina Ziegler of the National Cancer Institute in Maryland wrote:

> Low intakes of vegetables, fruits, and carotenoids are consistently associated with an increased risk of lung cancer . . . studies suggest that vegetable and fruit consumption may reduce the risk of certain other cancers.[38]

In addition to the effects of low fat, high fiber, and high intake of fruits and vegetables, there are other factors in a vegetarian diet which may help in the avoidance of cancer. A study conducted in Germany indicated that vegetarians had twice as many active natural killer cells as meat-eaters. Natural killer cells are specialized white blood cells that attack and neutralize cancer cells. The researchers had also noted that carotene was higher in vegetarians. From their investigation, they concluded that these two factors might be part of the reason why there is a lower cancer risk in vegetarians.[39] Other explanations of the protective effect of a vegetarian diet have also been suggested, including a decrease in cancer-associated bacterial enzymes excreted in the stool[40] and the increased potassium intake in vegetarian diets.[41]

As in the case of heart disease, the evidence suggests that if we become substantially more reliant on plant-foods in our dietary practice, we lower our risk of cancer. As Dr. Walter Willet, director of the Harvard University colon cancer study notes, moderate red-meat intake is certainly better than large amounts, but it is quite possible that no red-meat intake is even better.[42] In the case of reducing cancer risk, the balance must shift from high animal-fat foods to those low in fat and rich in fiber, including particularly fruits and vegetables.

Adult-onset or non-insulin-dependent diabetes mellitus (NIDDM), another highly prevalent chronic disease, is a disorder which prevents the body from fully using glucose derived from carbohydrate foods. People afflicted with this disease, suffer from a high level of glucose in the blood, which can lead to a number of serious complications of the eyes, nervous system, and kidneys. In the United States, an estimated 7% of the adult population, or nearly 10 million people have this disorder.[43]

It has been well established that the major determinant of NIDDM is obesity. In fact, approximately 80% of people with diabetes are obese. Research indicates that the rate of NIDDM is almost doubled when a person is moderately overweight and can be more than tripled if the person is obese.[44] Thus, against diabetes, the first protection of a vegetarian diet is that eating low-fat food decreases the likelihood of becoming overweight.[45]

But, additionally, following a plant based diet appears to provide an protective benefit simply by virtue of its higher plant volume. Evidence for this is found in a study of over 25,000 Seventh Day Adventist vegetarians in the United States. This group was monitored for the development of chronic disease over a period of 21 years. At the conclusion of this period, the researchers found that the vegetarian group had only half the cases of diabetes that would be present in a typical non-vegetarian American population of the same sex and age distribution. The importance of these results would be diminished if other factors, such as lower body weight or more physical activity, accounted for the lower rate of diabetes in the vegetarians. But, accounting for these factors did not change the results. This team of scientists, led by Dr. Snowdon of Loma Linda University in California, thus found that a vegetarian diet, in and of itself, can lower the risk of diabetes.[46] It is, in fact, now recognized in the medical community that the diet of those persons who have NIDDM should follow the principles of a lactovegetarianism.[47]

A vegetarian diet, along with regular exercise, can better control and sometimes even eliminate diabetes. Because vegetarian diets are high in fiber and complex carbohydrates, glucose is released more slowly into the blood stream after a typical vegetarian meal. Complex carbohydrates take longer to breakdown and fiber, particularly soluble fiber, further slows this breakdown process. When glucose is released slowly, the body does not have to produce as much insulin, the hormone that takes up glucose. The cells of the pancreas that produce insulin do not have to work as hard, and they are more effective in regulating glucose levels in the blood. Since diabetes worsens as these cells become exhausted, a vegetarian diet helps to better manage the diabetic condition. One of the earliest indications that following a vegetarian diet results in lower blood pressure came in 1926. A U.S. scientist fed meat to lacto-ovo-vegetarian college students and observed increases in both systolic and diastolic blood pres-

sure.[48]   Since then, more than 20 studies of the relationship
between diet and blood pressure have concluded that vegetarians have lower blood pressure than meat-eaters.

In one of these, Dr. Frank Sacks of Harvard University
studied the blood pressure of 210 men and women following
a vegetarian diet in the greater Boston area. Their mean
blood pressure was lower and the increase in blood pressure
with age was less than that usually found in Western populations.[49]   Another recent study investigated blood pressure
levels in two religious communities, the Seventh Day Adventists (vegetarian) and the Mormons (non-vegetarian). Australian scientist Dr. Ian Rouse, who conducted the research,
reported that the prevalence of high blood pressure was 10%
in the Mormon population and only one to two percent in
the Seventh Day Adventist population.[50] These numbers
contrast sharply with those of the whole U.S. population.
According to the National Health and Nutrition Examination
Survey conducted by the U.S. Department of Health and
Human Services, more than 40% of the U.S. population between the ages of 45 and 54 had some degree of high blood
pressure, and this increased to 60% for those between the
ages of 55 and 64.[51]

Dr. Rouse and co-author Dr. Lawrence J. Beilin reviewed
evidence on the diet and blood pressure link, noting that:

> there is now convincing evidence from epidemiological
> studies and dietary interventions that a lacto-ovo-vege-
> tarian diets . . . result, on average, in lower levels of
> blood pressure than do omnivorous diets.[52]

A lower blood pressure can be very beneficial in a number of ways. According to the World Health Organization, an
increase of 7.5 millimeters of mercury in diastolic blood
pressure, if sustained over a long period of time, can translate
into a 46% increase in heart disease risk and a 44% increase in
risk   .[53]   Lower blood pressure places less strain on
the heart and lessens the complications of kidney failure and
diabetes.

Vegetarianism helps to avoid high blood pressure because it provides a diet which is low in sodium (salt) and high in potassium. Livestock animals, like all animals, including humans, consume both minerals, but tend to retain sodium and excrete potassium. Conversely, plants retain potassium over sodium. As a result, flesh foods are high in sodium and low in potassium while plants have a low sodium/potassium ratio.

At present, the amount of sodium an individual consumes is thought to play a role in the development of hypertension. Studies of nutritional trends indicate that the problem of high blood pressure is uncommon in regions of the world where people eat diets low in sodium and high in potassium.[54] In addition, a large-scale, multinational study involving people in 32 different countries, called the Intersalt Study, determined that increasing intake of salt had a significant effect on the rise in blood pressure with age.[55]

Investigating the role of potassium, scientists from Australia conducted a study which suggested that the higher content of this mineral in the vegetarian diet may contribute to blood pressure differences.[56] Their findings were supported by results from the Intersalt Study, which indicated that potassium and magnesium (also found in abundance in vegetarian diets, but often deficient in meat-centered diets) seemed to play a role in limiting the rise of blood pressure.[55]

There may be factors in addition to sodium and potassium which affect blood pressure, since recent studies suggest that the high amounts of fiber and magnesium in the diets of vegetarians are also responsible for their lower blood pressure.[57] While the role of individual nutrients is still being sorted out, there is little doubt that the overall effect of a vegetarian diet is beneficial for blood pressure.[52]

In fact, in a number of scientific investigations, the adoption of a vegetarian diet after life-long meat consumption has been shown to reduce blood pressure. In a 1986 research trial in Western Australia, 59 hospital employees were divided into three dietary groups. One group ate meat consistently throughout the experiment, another group ate a vegetarian diet for six weeks and then switched to a meat diet, and the third group ate the meat diet first and then switched to a vegetarian diet for the second six week period. The researchers reported that during the vegetarian diet phase blood pressure fell on average five percent and rose the same amount when the meat diet was resumed.[58] Director of the study, Dr. B. M. Margetts, concluded in her report that switching to a vegetarian diet may bring about a worthwhile drop in blood pressure.

The roles of saturated fat, cholesterol, sodium and fiber in heart disease, cancer, diabetes, and high blood pressure have often received significant attention. But, in the importance devoted to these aspects of meat-based diets, the story on animal protein has remained largely untold. Once regarded as the primary virtue of meat, few people are aware that diets high in animal protein have been strongly linked to kidney failure, osteoporosis and the formation of calcium and gallstones, ailments which are all common in meat-eating societies.

Kidney disease results from a failure of kidneys to perform their filtration function. A high incidence of kidney disease has been consistently related to a high-protein diet.[59] One study that helped to establish this relationship was conducted by Dr. M. J. Wiseman and colleagues in 1987. This research group measured how hard the kidneys were working in 18 vegans, 16 lacto-ovo-vegetarians, and 18 omnivores. Omnivores ate significantly more total protein and protein of animal origin than the other two groups. The kidneys with the most strenuous purification task were in the meat-eaters, whose high protein consumption dramatically increased the workload on their organs.[60] This difference in kidney workload was attributed to differences in diet.

There is a simple physiological link between high protein consumption and a heavy workload for the kidneys. Protein in excess of the body's daily requirement is metabolized and eliminated through the urine. In a high-protein diet, the concentration of these protein-derived wastes is high and the kidneys have to work harder to remove it. The body cannot store protein, so all protein in excess of daily requirements must be eliminated. As a result, a diet high in protein strains the kidneys. Dr. John Harvey Kellogg, the inventor of the breakfast cereals, wrote that "an ordinary mixed diet of even moderate meat-eaters requires of their kidneys three times the amount of work in elimination of nitrogenous wastes than is demanded of flesh abstainers." He added that "while the kidneys are young they are usually able to bear this extra burden so that no evidence of injury appears; but as they become worn with advancing age they become unable to do their work efficiently."[61]

Osteoporosis is disease of aging and involves the loss of bone tissue density, mainly through calcium depletion. Bones become brittle and more prone to breaks. With the increasing elderly populations of Western nations, the incidence of osteoporosis is on the rise. The National Hospital Discharge Survey of 1986 in the United States found that eight percent of patients over 65 admitted to hospital had had an osteoporosis-related bone fracture.[62] By the age of 90, one-third of women and one-sixth of men in the U.S. will have had hip fractures. In 12-20% of cases, the fracture or its complication will be fatal; half of those who survive will need long term nursing care.[63]

Like most of the chronic diseases discussed above, the prevalence of osteoporosis varies widely around the world. There is, for example, a 20 times higher rate in the United States than there is among South African Bantu.[64] The popular view that osteoporosis is avoided by calcium intake would suggest that the Bantu, on average, consume much more calcium than Americans do. In fact, the opposite is true. The Bantu consume much less calcium than Americans. Their diet, primarily vegetarian in nature, is made up of mostly whole cereals, including abundant, fiber-rich maize and only a little milk.[65] In general, populations in developing countries appear to be less at risk from osteoporotic bone fractures than those in developed countries, despite consistently lower calcium intakes.[66]

Based on such evidence, the World Health Organization has concluded that "it is by no means certain that calcium intake is the key feature determining bone density and bone loss in adult life."[66] In challenging the idea that a calcium-rich diet is beneficial, Dr. D. M. Hegsted of Harvard Medical School writes that "there are no data available to demonstrate that high calcium intakes do, in fact, help prevent osteoporosis."[67]

What, then, is the cause of calcium depletion? A diet high in protein is likely to be involved since the body uses calcium to process excess protein. We have already noted that protein consumed in excess of daily requirements must be excreted. Increased protein consumption will inevitably increase calcium loss from the body. When protein is consumed in excessive quantities on a daily basis for many years, the body begins to leach calcium from the bones, where it is most plentiful.

A more likely reason for the Western world's high rates of osteoporosis, therefore, is the high amount of protein in typical western diets. The U. S. Department of Health and Human Services documented that Americans typically consume one and a half to two times their daily protein requirement.[68] Dr. Hegsted notes that studies in different countries show that osteoporotic hip fractures and protein intake are positively related. Indeed, it is well established that developing countries with lower osteoporosis rates, have much lower levels of protein consumption.[66]

The long-term result of the calcium-leaching of a high-protein diet was well illustrated by a 1979 study in which vegetarian and meat-eating women were examined for evidence of osteoporosis at the age of 65. While both groups consumed a similar number of calories daily, the vegetarians consumed less protein and less calcium on average than the meat-eating group. The scientists found that while the vegetarians had lost 18% of their bone mass, the meat-eaters had lost 35% of theirs.[69,70] Part of the reason why vegetarians had

lost less bone mass maybe due to the fact that vegetable protein, which constitutes the bulk of the protein vegetarians
consume, helps to conserve calcium, since it requires less
calcium in metabolism than does animal protein.[71]

Nonetheless, it is widely recommended that to avoid
osteoporosis, one should consume large amounts of calcium,
particularly by drinking milk. Though this well-intended advice attempts to remedy calcium loss, it could, in fact increase
bone depletion since dairy products are also high in protein.
Commenting on the ongoing studies of the relationship between osteoporosis and a direct rich in protein, Dr. Hegsted
writes, "It will be embarrassing enough if the current calcium
hype is simply useless; it will be immeasurably worse if
the recommendations are actually detrimental to health."[67] A
successful approach to forestalling osteoporosis will likely
involve reducing the high intakes of protein which underlie
this debilitating illness.

Like chronic kidney failure, the formation of calcium
stones is related to excessive consumption of animal protein.
A calcium stone begins as a tiny mineral deposit in the kidneys and can grow quite large over a number of years, often
to more than an inch in diameter. Stones too large to pass out
with the urine can get lodged in the urinary tract, where they
cause a great deal of pain. There is at present no cure for
stones that do not pass on their own, though sometimes physicians can use medical techniques to help in this process.

Evidence of the link between calcium-stone formation
and a high animal-protein diet was found by a British
research group which discovered that, among men, "those
who recurrently formed calcium stones ate more animal protein than normal subjects, and single stone formers had animal
protein intakes which were between those of normal men and
recurrent stone formers."[72] This evidence suggests that there is
a parallel relationship between the amount of animal-protein
consumed and the frequency of calcium-stone formation.

The researchers also reported that a high intakes of animal protein caused a significant increase in three of six main

urinary risk-factors for calcium-stone formation and that the overall relative probability of forming stones was markedly increased by a diet high in animal protein. Vegetarians, on the other hand, were characterized by a relatively low probability of forming calcium stones.

Another study carried out by the same research team shows that increasing one's intake of animal protein increases the risk of calcium-stone formation. The scientists increased their subjects' regular level of animal protein consumption by adding 5 ounces of fish to their daily diets. Five ounces of fish contains about 34 grams of animal protein, an amount roughly equivalent to the amount by which the average non-vegetarian exceeds the daily recommended intake. The study's results indicated that supplementing one's diet with this amount of protein increased the risk of forming calcium stones by up to 250%.[73] This evidence has led to recommendations in medical journals stating that calcium-stone formers should be advised to avoid an excess of animal protein[74] and that repeat calcium stone formers should seriously consider adopting a vegetarian diet.[72]

Like calcium stones, gallstones are a very common problem in North America. Roughly 10 per cent of the continent's population has at least one gallstone, and more than a million new cases are reported each year. In fact, autopsy studies show that 20 percent of all American women have gallstones when they die.[75]

Gallstones form in the gallbladder, which is the body's reservoir for bile, used to digest fats. Like kidney stones, gallstones also begin with a small deposit which grows as material solidifies around it. If the stones cause a great deal of pain, they have to be removed surgically, sometimes with the entire gallbladder.

Several studies suggest that diet plays an important role in the development of this illness. Drs. F. Pixley and J. Mann of the U.K. studied the dietary intake of 121 women with gallstones, finding that gallstone frequency was 11.5% in vegetarian women and 24.6% in non-vegetarian women. The researchers suggested that the high saturated-fat and animal-protein content of the non-vegetarian diet contributed to the higher incidence.[76]

A very large study conducted by researchers at the Harvard School of Public Health found that vegetable protein, usually the main, if not sole, protein eaten by vegetarians, has a protective effect against the formation of gallstones. In a survey of 88,837 middle aged women, the scientists attempted to draw correlations between the intake of different nutrients and the incidence of gallstone formation. The group at the lowest risk was found to consume the most vegetable protein. Additionally, the *less* vegetable fat one ate, the more likely one was to form gallstones.[77]

Thus, the research indicates that vegetarians, by consuming little saturated fat and little, if any, animal protein, and by deriving most of their fat and protein from vegetable sources, place themselves at low risk for this highly common and painful illness.

Rheumatoid arthritis is a painful deterioration of the joints. While not much is known about the actual cause of the disease, some interesting evidence has surfaced about its connection to diet. In North America and Europe, both regions of high animal-product consumption, the prevalence of rheumatoid arthritis is much higher than in a nation such as Japan, where the consumption of animal products is lower.[78]

A study done by Dr. J. Kjeldsen-Kragh of Oslo, Norway, tested the effect of a vegetarian diet for one year on 27 people with rheumatoid arthritis. For comparison, another 26 people with the condition followed their normal omnivorous diet for the same period of time. In the 10 measures by which the severity of rheumatoid arthritis was assessed, the vegetarians improved significantly in every one, while the meat-eating group improved in only one measurement. Dr. Kjeldsen-Kragh and colleagues concluded that:

the benefits in the vegetarian group were still present after one year, and evaluation of the whole course showed significant advantages for the vegetarian group in all measured indices. This dietary regimen seems to be a useful supplement to conventional medical treatment of rheumatoid arthritis.[79]

This large body of evidence showing the healthful benefits of a vegetarian diet and the detrimental effects of a meat-centered diet has prompted researchers to launch a large-scale long-term study of the *overall* health of vegetarians compared to meat-eaters,

In Germany, beginning in 1976, vegetarians were recruited from all regions of what was then the Federal Republic of Germany. After two years of recruitment, 1,904 participants were enrolled in the study. The majority of them (61%) were strict vegetarians or vegans, who consumed no foods of animal origin. Of the 858 men and 1,046 women composing the vegetarian group, 89% had followed their diet for more than five years.

The first results from the study were reported after five years of follow-up, during which time scientists kept track of the vegetarians' health status. By the end of the five-year period, based on age and sex proportions and national averages for lifespan, 219 deaths were expected to have occurred. Only 82 people had died.

Mortality for all causes was lower. The group had only 20% of the expected rate of heart disease, and only 55% of the expected rate of cancer, while showing significantly fewer deaths from diseases of the respiratory and digestive system and virtually no deaths from cancers of the colon, rectum, prostate, and breast. The evidence was fairly conclusive: vegetarians suffered from fewer diseases and were a healthier, longer-living group.[80]

In summary, meat-centred diets are characterized by high total fat, saturated fat, cholesterol, animal protein and total protein consumption and low dietary fiber consumption compared to vegetarian diets. Protein is consumed in greater quantities in meat-centered diets, and most of this protein is of animal origin, whereas vegetarians consume less protein, mostly, if not entirely, of plant origin. Also, vegetarians consume more monounsaturated and polyunsaturated fat, which are more abundant in plant foods.

If we assess the cumulative effect these different patterns of nutrient consumption have on human health, a clear trend emerges. High total fat, and in particular saturated fat (mostly of animal origin), in the diet increases the risk of heart disease, cancer, diabetes, and high blood pressure. Fats of animal origin increase the risk of colon cancer. Animal protein increases blood cholesterol levels, accelerates kidney disease, advances osteoporosis, and leads to calcium stones and gall stones.

Dietary fiber, on the other hand, protects against heart disease, cancer, diabetes, and high blood pressure. Complex carbohydrates help in the management of diabetes. Vegetable protein helps to lower cholesterol and slows osteoporosis. Vegetable fats help to protect against calcium stones. And vegetarian nutrition is generally beneficial for high blood pressure and arthritis.

The evidence is fairly conclusive that a diet high in animal-based foods increases the risk of the major chronic diseases of our society. Conversely, a diet based on plant-foods is clearly associated with lower, and in some cases much lower, risk for disease. It is now known that eating a meat-centered diet is an unhealthy and life-shortening practice. Mismatching our diet and physiology has indeed had dramatic consequences.

From a health perspective, a positive aspect of diet-induced risk is that it can be changed. Other factors, in addition to diet, can cause these chronic diseases. Genetics plays a role in some diseases and environmental factors, such as exposure to radon or pollutants, are believed to contribute to the cause of cancer. Most of these diseases are also part of the natural aging process. Unlike these factors, dietary risk can be directly affected by determined personal action.

In deciding what to eat for lunch or dinner, what to have for a snack, what to cook for a dinner party, we can each minimize our risk for the premature onset of these diseases. There is no complex and expensive technology needed and no highly trained specialist need be consulted. As the evidence clearly shows, our decisions, accumulated over time, can have dramatic effects on our health. Although seven out of 10 people die of chronic diseases in North America, we each have the capability, by changing the food we eat, of decreasing our chances of being one of them.

A plant-food diet is the optimal dietary choice for preventing disease. Not only does it reduce the risk for chronic disease, but cutting animal-food out of one's diet has also been proven as a viable treatment for several chronic diseases as in Dr. Dean Ornish's study, which for the first time reversed the heart disease process without drugs or surgery through a pure vegetarian diet. A vegetarian diet is recommended treatment for diabetes, and has been suggested for treating high blood pressure, kidney disease, rheumatoid arthritis, calcium stones, and gall stones. As Dr. T. Colin Campbell, the director of the China Health Study, notes, we are essentially a vegetarian species and our health is put at risk by eating meat and other animal products. While it is certainly true that eating the occasional hamburger is unlikely to be any more threatening to our health than smoking the occasional cigarette or pursuing other indulges of our modern lifestyles, the scientific evidence indicates that the progressive elimination of animal foods and increasing reliance on plant-foods is a very important strategy for those who want to maximize their health.

Plants, Animals and the Planet

Through agriculture, industry and other activities, humans effect the environment in two ways. First, they remove resources and energy from the environment to produce food and other goods. Early agricultural societies, for example, used the resources of the soil and lakes to grow crops which could be harvested and eaten. Second, humans cause the release of waste and garbage into the natural environment. In the case of agricultural societies, organic waste was the end product of farming.

Since human societies do not reuse and recycle most of what they consume, our activities deplete the environment. In spite of this, the environment was not threatened by our activities as long as the earth was given time to replenish the resources we used and to remove the wastes we produced. For most of human history, this was possible. Our population had been small and widely distributed and our technology, whether stone tools or ox-drawn ploughs, was limited in its scope and capacity. As a result, our impact on the earth over the millennia of human evolution and cultural development was minimal, on a global level, until about 200 years ago.[1]

The situation changed dramatically with industrialization. Applying the ingenuity of science to industry and agriculture, we were able to produce more efficiently and in much greater quantities. The tools and techniques we developed greatly intensified the rate at which we used the planet's resources.[2] With the industrial revolution, we entered a phase of human existence unprecedented in the amount of energy and resources we consumed and we have, in the process, essentially outstripped the ability of the earth to maintain an ecological balance.

After 200 years of increasingly intensive industrialization, we are now beginning to realize how rapidly we have depleted our resources. For the first time, the complete exhaustion of many of the planet's resources is in sight. Over the past two centuries, human beings have removed 6,000,000 square kilometres of forest from the earth's surface. Most of the primary-forest cover of Europe and America is gone and forests in the developing world are disappearing at an accelerating rate. Intensified agricultural production has accelerated the process of soil erosion so that the sediment load created by eroded soil has risen threefold in major rivers and by eightfold in smaller, more intensively used ones. The human demand for water has grown exponentially and withdrawals of water from the world's lakes and rivers has increased from 100 to 3,600 cubic kilometres per year. The rising consumption of energy has depleted two-fifths of known fossil fuel reserves and is now using 40% of our most elemental source of energy, the energy from the sun made available by green plants.[3]

At the other end of the process, waste is being produced at a rate far in excess of the earth's ability to process it. In 200 years, human activities have more than doubled the amount of methane in the atmosphere and have increased carbon dioxide levels by over 35%. Industrial processes have released thousands of chemicals that have polluted the air, soil, fresh water, and oceans. The accumulation of these pollutants in the biosphere poses a growing threat to all life on the planet.[3]

The consumption of resources and production of wastes is highly concentrated. More than 80% of global consumption occurs in industrial nations, where affluence is the greatest, while most of humanity lives on a minimal level of subsistence in developing countries. Thus, the wealthy 20% of the human population places a far greater burden on the earth's collective resources and waste capacity than the rest of humanity.

This disproportionate burden is particularly apparent in the resources used and waste created by a diet high in animal products. The production of animal foods is many times more resource-intensive and wasteful than the production of plant foods. The ecological burdens of animal farming arise from both technologically intensive livestock production methods, such as chicken and pig feeding houses and cattle feedlots, and from "low-tech" methods such as ranching and pastoralism. In terms of resources, modern animal agriculture accelerates land degradation and deforestation and greatly increases our demand for water and energy. In terms of waste, through the release of methane, manure, fertilizers and other chemicals, it contributes to pollution problems on a global scale. Because of its far-ranging impact on the earth, the raising of meat for human consumption is foremost among the human activities that are undermining the sustainability of life on the planet.

Yet, despite all the resources appropriated by agriculture, millions of people go hungry. Although, much of the global grain harvest is fed to livestock, a tenth of humanity lives without enough food to eat. In this chapter, we will examine the ecological ramifications of the livestock industry in terms of resource consumption and waste products as well as how the high volumes of animal products in the diets of the wealthy contribute to world hunger.

The appetite for meat among the world's wealthy has appropriated vast tracts of land. Cattle currently graze over one-quarter of the earth's surface.[4] In fact, cows use more of the earth than humans do. To feed the world's meat-eaters, the earth now carries a global cattle population of 1.3 billion animals.[5] This population of cattle has greatly exceeded the ability of the land to support it, leading to severe resource problems including overgrazing of fertile grasslands and land degradation.

When there are too many cattle on the land, the shrubs and grasses that cattle like to eat are devoured much faster than they can grow back. These plants are weakened and eventually die. In their place, plants that cows don't find palatable gain an advantage and begin to spread. The new-comers anchor the topsoil poorly, leaving it vulnerable to trampling hooves. The relentless pounding of cattle feet on the soil compacts the fertile upper layer and thins out the vegetative cover. Compacting disturbs the natural water cy-cle so the land becomes drier and less water-absorbent.[6] Under these conditions, wind and rain take their toll and pre-cious topsoil dries up and erodes away. When topsoil is no longer available, shrubs, grasses and other vegetation recede and a once-fertile land becomes more and more like a desert.[7]

This process of land degradation and desertification is widespread, affecting all areas where cattle graze, from Sub-Saharan Africa to the American West. The United Nations Environment Programme (UNEP) estimates that 73% of the world's grasslands are at least moderately desertified, having lost more than 25% of their ability to grow vegetation. In the United States, grassland and pasture account for 25% of the country's land mass.[8] The World Resources Institute estimates that only one-third of this grassland is in good con-dition, while two-fifths is in poor or very poor condition.[9] Most of America's grasslands and pasture are concentrated in the 11 western states, where 43% of the land area is leased by the government to private ranchers. These individuals are charged a nominal fee, subsidized by the taxpayer, for each cow they graze on the land.[10] Surveying the damage done by raising cattle on this land, Jeremy Rifkin has concluded that "the impact of countless hoofs and mouths has done more to alter the type of vegetation and land form of the American West than all the water projects, strip mines, power plants, freeways, and subdivision developments combined."[11]

Despite the large amount of land already used by cattle, cattle ranchers have continued to expand their domain, carv-ing into vast tracts of virgin forest. Earlier this century, much of the temperate forests of United States and Europe was cleared to create land for crops, pasture, and range for use in the production of meat, and recently, forests in tropical coun-tries have come under the same pressure. Increased livestock production has taken its toll most extensively on the forests of Latin America.[12] Today more than 40% of the Central American rainforests has been cleared to expand cattle ranching for the export of beef. In South America from 1973 to 1988 more than half of the 750,000 square kilometres of forest burned down were used to create range for cattle.[13] The fires that are set to clear this biologically diverse land are so large that they are visible from outer space.

The use of rainforest land for cattle grazing is, however, short-lived. Indeed, no land is as ill-suited to extensive livestock rearing as the land of former rainforests. Trees serve as vital links in the water and nutrient cycles of the rainforest, absorbing most of the rainfall. When this tree cover is removed, the underlying soil is not longer protected from the pounding rain and it rapidly loses critical nutrients. Grass for cows does not grow on this land for long and is quickly replaced by weeds and shrubs. Silt from the eroded lands washes into oceans, where it often buries and kills coral reefs. Most pasture obtained by rainforest destruction is abandoned within a decade of its first use for land newly carved from the forest.[14]

For this short period of productivity, ranchers and the meat consumers they serve sacrifice a vast treasure of biological diversity. Although tropical rainforests cover only seven percent of the earth's surface, they are home to over 50% of the earth's species. Biologists Christopher Uhl and Geoffery Parker have calculated that each hamburger produced from rainforest land consumes 55 square feet of the forest.[15] In a typical area of the forest, this space would be home to 60-foot-tall tree, hundreds of saplings and seedlings, and thousands of insects and would be used by dozens of bird, mammal, and reptile species. In sum, thousands of organisms inhabit and use the area of forest destroyed to produce just one hamburger. For each of the past 25 years that Central America has been deforested to create room for cattle, a thousand species have been forced into extinction.[16] A large portion of the beef raised in Costa Rica, Brazil, and other Latin

American countries is exported to the United States.[17]   The
imported beef is cheaper and leaner than anything produced
domestically, but it also comes at an enormous price—the
destruction of one of the last bastions of biological diversity
and natural wonder left on the earth.

Water is another natural resources increasingly threatened by animal agriculture. After centuries of taking abundant water supplies for granted, we are now entering a period of water scarcity. The global budget of water is rapidly
being exhausted, and by some estimates, demand will exceed supply by the year 2000.[18] The level of water consumption in most parts of the world is unsustainable, and often
involves drawing on stocks of ground water more quickly
than they can replenish themselves. As our demand for water approaches the limits of our resources, many areas of the
world, including northern China, North Africa, Mexico, much
of the Middle East, and parts of the western United States
face the possibility of chronic water shortages in the years
ahead.[19]

In North America, intensive animal agriculture, based in
feedlots, consumes a large portion of water resources. Just to
grow the grain needed to feed the livestock raised in factory
farms, farmers in California use one-third of all the water consumed in the state. The Ogalalla aquifer, which the beef
feedlot center of the U.S. relies on for water to irrigate crops,
is now severely depleted.[20] In addition to irrigation, water is
used to clean the insides of slaughterhouses and at many
other stages of the meat-production process. When all these
uses are considered together, animal agriculture consumes
one out of every two gallons of water used in the United
States.[21] Domestic uses, meanwhile, account for less than five
percent. In a special issue on water, William Graves, editor of
National Geographic, observed that it can take 1,000 gallons
of fresh water to produce one eight-ounce steak.[22] In metric
terms, each kilogram of beef requires 3,000 litres of water to
produce. Although it would take the better part of a year's
worth of showers for the average person to use 3,000 litres of

water, he or she would only have to eat half a dozen hamburgers to use the same amount.

While the threat of water scarcity is only beginning to dawn on us, the world has already felt the shock of fossil-fuel scarcity during the 1970's. Although efforts were taken to reduce our use of fossil fuels in the immediate aftermath of the oil crisis, they have since subsided. Reliance on fossil fuels has continued to grow in all human activities, and agriculture is no exception. It accounts for nearly 25% of the fossil fuel used in North America and animal agriculture, in particular, is one of the most profligate users of fossil fuels. The production of meat in intensive conditions depends on grains grown with the extensive use of fertilizers, irrigation fuel, machinery, herbicides, and insecticides.[23] Raising livestock animals themselves requires fossil fuels for transportation and machinery. All these factors add to the energy bill for meat.

Consider the following comparison of the energy efficiency of a representative plant foods and animal foods based on the research of David Pimentel, an agricultural energy expert at Cornell University. The energy efficiency of food can be calculated by dividing the calorie energy obtained from the food by the fossil-fuel energy required to grow or raise it. A high number indicates an energy-efficient food, while a number less than one means that more energy is put in than is actually received back. Among a representative group of plant foods, the energy efficiency ranges from 1.4 for peanuts to 6.4 for alfalfa. In fact, all plant foods have an efficiency greater than one. They give us more energy than we invest in producing them. Since most of the calorie energy in plants comes from the conversion of sunlight by the plant itself, with plant food we get something for nothing.

When we compare the efficiency of plant food with animal food, we see a staggering difference. The energy efficiency of a representative group of animal foods ranges from 0.045 for chicken to 0.01 for beef. Even the least energy-efficient plant food, peanuts, is 30 times more efficient than chicken, the most energy-efficient animal food.

Calculations based on protein content yield similar comparisons. It takes two calories of fossil fuel to raise one calorie of soybean protein, but 78 calories of fossil fuel are needed to raise one calorie of beef.[24]

Thus, the amount of fossil fuel energy required by one's diet is clearly a reflection of how much meat one eats. A non-vegetarian who eats 3,300 kcal of food energy a day indirectly consumes 33,900 kcal of fossil fuel energy, while a vegan eating the same number of calories requires only 9,900 kcal of fossil fuel energy. The fossil fuel energy intensity of a meat-based diet is so high that if we fed everyone on earth the meat-based diet of the United States all the world's known petroleum reserves would be exhausted in only 15 years.[25] Already, the enormous oil endowment of the United States is more than half gone. The United States' domestic production peaked in the late 1960's and its oil demand is increasingly being met by imports.[26] In the world as a whole, oil stocks are a fixed, non-renewable resource. The more efficiently we use them, the longer they will last.

Unfortunately, the intensive resource consumption characteristic of the meat industry is coupled with large quantities of waste production, including gases such as methane, solid materials such as manure, and a variety of chemicals. Some of these wastes contribute to the greenhouse effect. The greenhouse effect is the trend of warming worldwide caused by the accumulation in the atmosphere of gases that admit sunlight, but trap heat, and thus function like the windows of a greenhouse. The climate change that may ensue from the greenhouse effect is considered by many scientists to hold major implications for life on the planet. The warming produced may melt the polar icecaps, swell our seas, drown coastal cities, and dramatically change worldwide weather patterns.[30]

Methane, which is believed to be a major contributor to the greenhouse effect, is emitted in enormous quantities by livestock. Because of this fact, atmospheric scientists consider cattle to be a major contributor to global warming problem.

Every day, each domestic ox releases 400 litres of methane which translates into a total of nearly 80 million tonnes each year in North America alone.[27] On a global level, livestock account for 40% of the methane emissions.[28] Animal agriculture also contributes to the release of other greenhouse gases, including carbon dioxide, through the use of fossil fuels, and nitrous oxides, from manure and fertilizer.[29] Thus, intensively raised livestock are a significant factor in the emission of methane, carbon dioxide, and nitrous oxides, three of the gases that cause the greenhouse effect. With the global cattle population still rising, they are likely to play an even larger role in global warming in the coming decades.[31]

The concentration of animals in factory farms through intensive husbandry practices has created a manure problem of tremendous proportions. Intensive animal-raising produces malodorous and damaging manure at an astonishing rate of 250,000 pounds per second in the U.S.[32] Manure has become a major environmental problem in the Netherlands, Belgium, and France as a result of intensive animal-raising activity. In these countries, nitrates and phosphates from animal manure have saturated the soil and contaminated the water in many areas. Ammonia from animal manure adds more to acid rain in these parts of Europe than cars or factories.[33]

Since animals raised in factory farms are removed from the land, their manure cannot be used as fertilizer; instead it accumulates as waste. Thus, where once natural manure fertilized the land, artificial fertilizers have to be used. The manure wasted by American enclosed-feeding operations could replace an estimated 12% of the nitrogen, 30% of the phosphorus and 30% of the potassium that U.S. farmers apply to their land in chemical fertilizer.[34,35] The intensified use of fertilizers necessitated by factory farming compounds the water-polluting effects of unrecycled, wasted animal-manure. Water pollution from these sources contributes to the killing of flora in rivers and fresh-water lakes, destroying their biological vitality. Assessment by the Environmental Protection

Agency in the U.S. suggests that a third of the stream miles and almost half of the lake acreage have been polluted to the extent that they can no longer be used by people to drink.[36] The water pollution resulting from animal raising, including manure and fertilizer run-off, has been estimated to account for more of this damage than all municipal and industrial sources combined.[37]

We have seen that, by eating animal-food, a small proportion of human society contributes to land degradation, the destruction of rainforests, and the unsustainable use of water and energy. We have also seen that animal agriculture plays a significant role in the global greenhouse effect and is a major contributor to water pollution in many industrial countries. The ecological woes caused by meat-eating do not, however, end here. The growing demand for meat among the world's wealthy has contributed to food scarcity and world hunger.

The high animal-product diet typical of industrial countries requires that large amounts of cereal grains be fed to animals. In order to raise enough meat to satisfy the appetites of the world's meat-eaters, a great deal of grain must be produced. In fact, in the United States, animals raised for meat consume 70% of the grain, 80% of the corn, and 90% of the soybean grown in that country.[38] On a global basis, roughly 40% of the world's grain, especially corn, barley, sorghum, and oats is fed to livestock. Most of the feed usage, or 83% of the global total, is concentrated in industrial countries. Indeed, grains consumed indirectly through meat by the quarter of the world's population who live in developed countries is almost equal to the total of the cereals eaten directly as food by the remaining three-quarters of the world's consumers.[39] This appropriation of food crops by meat consumers is not limited to developed countries; it has dramatically affected agriculture in the developing world as well. As wealthy people in these countries augment their meat consumption, more and more grain is being diverted to the mouths of animals.

Until the early 1960's, the developing world was a grain exporter. But by the late 1970's, it was importing grain, a change largely precipitated by a growing meat-consuming class. In 1981, 75% of the imports of corn, barley, sorghum, and oats into developing nations fed animals.[40]

The increased consumption of animal products among the affluent in developing nations deprives the world's poor even further, since it causes a further increase in the share of global farmland devoted to producing crops for animal feed. In Mexico, for example, from 1960 to 1980, the percentage of grain used for animal feed quadrupled from five percent to 20% of the total. At present, while 22% of Mexico's people go hungry, livestock consume 30% of the country's grain.[41] Taiwan is an example of a country where the explosive growth in meat consumption made a formerly self-sufficient country dependent on the import of food crops. In Taiwan, meat and egg consumption has increased by 600% since 1950. To meet the demand, Taiwan went from exporting grain in the 1950s to importing 74% of the animal feed it used in 1990.[42] This is a picture repeated across the developing world. As livestock industries have taken hold and meat consumption has increased, grain requirements have grown dramatically. The massive global consumption of meat by a growing global class of wealthy consumers causes direct competition between meat producers and the world's poor for the global grain harvest. And, sadly, it is a contest that the world's rich are winning.

While vast amounts of grain continue to be fed to animals, over 75% of the human population can barely feed itself. Almost 500 million people are severely malnourished and 15 million children die each year from starvation and related illness, 41,000 every day.[43] These 500 million people, representing 10% of the earth's population, cannot afford even a minimum diet for good health and normal activity. Famine relief offered by rich nations reaches some people in some situations, but it does little to alleviate the bulk of quiet, grinding, daily hunger among the poor.[44]

The contest for the world's grain resources, in which these people are losing competitors, will increase in the future. In the years ahead, the pressures of decreases in crop-yields, growth in population, and expanding industrialization in developing countries will continue to mount. The growth in population is particularly daunting. As the end of the millennium approaches, humanity continues to add more people to the planet to be fed. The pressure of population growth on supplies of food is already being felt in Latin America and Africa, which have seen a decline in their ability to produce sufficient cereal grains. During the 1980's, 25 of the 43 African nations and 17 of the 23 Latin American nations saw a drop in their per capita food grain production.[45] The United Nations projects that the world population, currently at 5.4 billion, will reach 6.3 billion by the year 2000 and actually double by 2050.[46] There is no precedent in human history that even comes close to approximating the population pressures we will experience in the next 10 to 20 years.[47] In the next two to four generations, if the affluent continue to eat diets high in animal products, world agriculture will be called on to produce as much food as has been produced in the entire 12,000 years since agriculture was invented.

Is such a food-production increase possible? It has happened before. Through the Green Revolution and other technological advances, harvests have been increased all over the world. This was achieved through a ninefold increase in fertilizer use between 1950 and 1984, tripling of irrigated areas in the same period, and the use of chemical insecticides, herbicides, and fungicides. Between 1950 and 1985, world grain production rose from 600 million metric tons per year to over 1,800 million metric tons per year.[48] It is estimated that the artificial fertilizer and pesticides account for as much as 50% of world agricultural production.

However, the gains made by the Green Revolution are unlikely to be duplicated. World harvest levels have not increased significantly since 1984. Further increases in fertilizer application have produced marginal returns and are not likely to dramatically improve the current status. In the future, environmental exigencies such as soil erosion, waterlogging, salinity, and deforestation will further decrease the land available for cultivation and may actually lower yields or at least make further increases considerably difficult to achieve.[49] Already, millions of acres of land have been withdrawn from food production because of erosion and other environmental problems. Though the pressures on global food security continue to mount, there is no new technology on the horizon to solve our problems.[50]

To feed humanity in the future, we cannot simply continue to produce more of the same, in the same way. Energy, land, and other biological resource limitations will make it impossible to provide the growing world population with even minimal nutrition requirements while an affluent minority eat meat-based diets. The food necessary for the future is not likely to come from increased production; adequate amounts of food for everyone must come from redistribution. We must, therefore, turn our attention to the food currently being fed to animals. Cycling the nutrients in grain through animals before they are eaten by human beings is a very wasteful process. The majority of the energy input is expended by the animal in its daily metabolism, leaving only a fraction stored in its body to be eaten as meat. Feeding grain to livestock requires an average seven kcal input for one kcal generated.[51]

Because of their nutrient-intensity, animal foods require much more land to produce than plant foods. The land acreage required to produce 20 kg of protein (enough for one adult for one year) from animal-food sources varies between 3 for chickens and 6 for beef. For plant food, the land required to produce the same amount of protein varies from 0.25 acres for beans to 0.7 acres for potatoes.[24] The most efficient animal-food, chicken, requires four times as much land to produce as does the least efficient plant food, potatoes.

Food plants are more efficient because of their position in the food chain. Plants are referred to as primary producers because they are at the bottom of the food chain. Herbivores and vegans who consume these foods directly for all their nutritional requirements make efficient use of the energy in plants. Carnivores and meat-eaters are one stage higher on the food chain. By cycling their nutrients through animals first, they waste up to 90% of the energy and nutrients in the original food. Agricultural scientists Maarten Chrispeels and David Sadava have calculated that 14 people eating a strictly vegetarian diet can be supported by one hectare of land. Because of the inefficiency of meat production, that same hectare could support only four or five people who get half their calories from animal products. As scientists Chrispeels and Sadava note:

> The large amounts of animal protein now consumed by most people in technologically advanced countries are nutritionally superfluous and are a drain on the global reserves of staple foods.[52]

If all of humanity lived on a vegetarian diet, the world's available farmland could feed 15 billion people. Though people often retort that less meat eaten among the rich will not help feed the poor, the connection between a hamburger eaten in North America and hunger in the developing world is, in fact, quite direct. Since grain is bought and sold on a global market, the logic of the market is constantly deciding how much grain each country will use and how it will use it. In the global marketplace, whether wheat produced in Australia will be fed to people in Ethiopia, pigs in Russia, or sheep in the Europe is a choice that is constantly being made.[53] Relative affluence has become one of the greatest determinants of how world food supplies are allocated. Thus, demand for meat among the world's rich inevitably reduces the supply of grains and cereals to the world's poor.

At present, even a modest decline in the consumption of animal products among the more affluent could help relieve pressures on the earth's agricultural ecosystem.[54] When someone eating a regular North American diet converts to vegetarianism, they free up enough land to feed 10 other people on plant-food diets.[55] The main obstacle to the more efficient use of farmland is the demand for meat among the world's rich.

This demand for meat is created in part by each and every meat consumer. The choices we individually make about what to eat for breakfast, lunch, and dinner have a role in the global problems of ecological devastation and hunger. A diet high in animal-products costs dearly in terms of the resources it consumes and the wastes it produces. Meat production accounts for 50% of North America's water use and 25% of its fossil-fuel consumption, one-quarter of the earth's land use, and is a major force behind the destruction of the tropical rainforests. Factory farms also play a significant role in the greenhouse effect. Manure and fertilizer run-off from animal agriculture is the major contributor to the pollution of North America's lakes and rivers.

The meat eaten among the world's wealthy uses more of the global grain harvest than goes to all of the people in developing countries. This is a very distorted distribution of food in a world where starvation is still commonplace. Because of the limits on agricultural production, it is not possible to expect humanity to be fed if people in industrialized nations continue to eat the amount of meat they do. The development aid and famine relief we send will do little in the long term if the rich continue to feed much of their food to animals first. It is a matter of simple justice that sufficient calories, protein, vitamins, and minerals be available for each person so that he or she has the opportunity to achieve a full and satisfying life. We each have a role in ensuring this right for our fellow human beings.

Since the phrase "think globally, act locally" was first coined by French thinker Jacques Ellul, it has become the motto of the environmental movement. By using this slogan, we recognize that although the environmental problems we now face are of a planetary scale, each of us, through our own actions, can make a difference. Empowered with an awareness of the impact of animal food, we are all able to make our decisive contribution towards ecological sustainability and an end to world hunger.

Animal Farming

The demand for animal food among the world's wealthy has changed the way livestock is raised. In earlier times, animals were used to plough fields, provide transportation, and perform other labor-saving tasks. Working on small plots with only a few animals, farmers developed close associations with their cattle, pigs, and chickens. Since they were important to farming life, they were only occasionally slaughtered.[1]

As industrialization increased the demand for meat, animal agriculture changed in a fundamental way. Farmers sought to raise animals specifically to supply the growing markets for animal products and became full-time producers of meat and dairy products. Over time, small animal farms tended by individual farmers were replaced by industrial factory farms owned and operated by large corporations. Large amounts of capital were invested in an effort to make animal-raising more efficient, to save land and labor, and to increase profits.[2]

Since the value of animals in the meat market is largely determined by their gross weight, farmers were motivated by profit to automate and mechanize the raising of animals and to develop ways to achieve greater weight-gains through short cuts and cost-saving methods. These considerations provide the logic of modern animal factory farms. Because of their relentless push for lower costs, factory farms have largely taken over animal agriculture in North America, forcing smaller, traditional farms out of business. Factory farming is most extensive in the U.S., where agribusinesses produce 95% of the nation's eggs and 90% of its pigs.[3]

One of the first propositions of the factory approach was that free-roaming animals were a wasteful and expensive use of land. As a result, methods were developed that focused principally on the confinement of animals into smaller spaces. Movement and interaction with other animals, the basic elements of existence in the natural environment, began to be sacrificed. Gradually, the cage and pen sizes shrank, until, in some cases, there was not room enough for the animal to turn around. To further improve the efficiency of flesh production, many aspects of the animals' lives were controlled and manipulated. Grains and other foods were added in large quantities to the animals' natural diets of grasses and other roughage. Antibiotics and hormones were added to the feed in order to accelerate growth artificially. And when the powerful, unsatisfied instincts of the confined and manipulated poultry and pigs drove them to attack each other, the factory farmer responded by debeaking chicks and cutting the tails off young piglets. By employing these industrial approaches, factory farms managed to produce high volumes of meat at low cost.[4]

While factory farms, with their industrial efficiency, may have been a profit windfall for their owners, they have been a nightmare for animals. In the factory management approach, many trade-offs compromise the welfare and freedom of animals for the sake of financial gain. In the words of animal scientist Dr. Marian Dawkins,

> Profits in agriculture are not made by setting up conditions in which each individual animal is maximally productive, or even maximally healthy . . . Economies of space, for example, putting more hens into a battery cage, may lower individual productivity, but enable a larger number of animals to be kept in the same area. This may more than compensate for the losses on each individual.[5]

Thus, the welfare of individual animals, so important to the prosperity of small farmers, was readily compromised in large-scale farming enterprises, because other costs, such as machinery and the maintenance of large buildings, became

more important. Using confinement, artificial feed supple-
mentation, and other techniques, factory farmers have, in
their relentless search for productivity, consistently sacrificed
animal welfare. Consequently, animals are subjected to an
extremely high level of stress that is demonstrated through
psychological and physical diseases and high death rates.
The constant crowding, noise, and abuse in factory farms is a
world apart from the tranquil natural environment of early
farming life.

The chicken was the first animal to which factory farming
technology was applied. At present, over seven billion chickens are raised and killed each year in North America.[6] Although originating in North America, the practice of factory
farming has spread rapidly to other industrial countries and it
is now catching on in developing nations such as China and
Brazil.[7] Factory chicken production occurs on both broiler
farms, which produce chicken meat, and layer farms, which
produce eggs and it begins at the hatcheries.

A hatchery consists of long, low-height multiplication
buildings. They confine birds producing eggs for hatching in
massive incubators.[8] If the hatchery is producing chicks for
layer farms, only females are kept. Once the egg in the incu-
bator hatches, the sex is determined and, if it is male, the
chick is killed. In fact, every year some 250 million chicks are
killed at this early stage of the process. The chicks may be
crushed or exploded in special chambers or they may be simply piled up in plastic bags and left to suffocate. The remains
of these chicks will often be ground together with unhatched
and partially hatched eggs into a mush that is added to the
factory animals' feed.[9]

Chickens used for meat production are called broiler
chickens. Upon their entry into the windowless buildings of
broiler farms, all aspects of their lives are controlled to
achieve maximal growth at minimal cost and time. Each
broiler building houses up to 80,000 chickens, providing
approximately 20 square centimetres per bird.[10] For the first

two or three weeks, the young birds are subjected to near-constant bright light in order to get them to eat more often. Periodically, the light is turned off for two to three hours to simulate a night cycle and convince the birds that they have slept. As the birds get larger, the crowding and noise intensifies. To lessen the resulting agitation and aggressive behavior, the birds are kept in total darkness until they are fat enough for slaughter.[11]

On the egg farms, chickens are even more closely confined. To minimize the space required, each cage houses three or four birds, and rows of cages are stacked upon each other. In these cages, the feathers and skin of egg-layers become ragged, bruised, and blistered because of continual friction with the wire mesh walls, while toes and toenails become entwined in the wire mesh floors. Inclined so that the eggs will roll out immediately when laid, the floors of these cages save labor for the farmer, but aggravate the effect of the mesh on the birds' feathers and feet. Because of their cages, the birds have almost no feathers left by the time they are taken to be killed.[12]

Factory farmers also attempt to alter the cyclical laying pattern of chickens. After each laying cycle, birds naturally undergo a moult period during which their bodies replenish nutrients that are used in the strenuous process of egg production. The farmer will often attempt to reduce the time between laying periods by accelerating the moulting phase. This is done by subjecting the birds to food deprivation and other extreme forms of stress. The deprivation causes chickens to quickly stop producing eggs, after which they can be fed so that they begin the next laying cycle. Mortality rates as a result of the forced moulting tend to be high, up to four times the regular loss during laying periods.[13]

In factory cages, the animals' natural combative instincts are aggravated by the stress of crowding. Cage confinement prevents weaker birds from fleeing from stronger ones; consequently, the stronger birds, lacking any verification of their superiority, will continue to fight the weaker ones. The inability to establish instinctive hierarchies can lead to cannibalism in the stronger birds, which, disoriented by the crowding and noise of the battery cages, peck, kill, and eat the weaker animals. Although cannibalism among chickens is caused by crowded cages, factory farmers do not address the problem by enlarging the cages they use. Rather, they attempt to reduce the ability of chickens to eat each other. When chicks are only two or three days old, their beaks are cut off by a hot knife. In industry literature, the practice is made to seem analogous to cutting off a finger nail, but a more accurate comparison would be cutting off a finger. Along with the hard covering of the beak, a very soft, sensitive tissue is also cut off and left exposed by this painful process.[14] Once their beaks are removed, chickens can no longer preen or defend themselves. In spite of this, the practice of debeaking has become routine at layer farms.

In cattle production, intensive husbandry techniques vary according to whether beef, milk, or veal is being produced. Most beef cattle spend the first few months of their lives on a range, in comparative freedom and in the company of their mothers. By the age of eight months, however, the calves enter the factory farming system and their lives are directed towards one objective—gaining weight as cheaply and as quickly as possible. The calves are transferred to feedlots, small, flat, fenced fields that can hold up to 100,000 cows and leave as little as 17 square feet per animal.[15] Although shade and shelter areas are frequently available in natural conditions, they are not a feature of crowded feedlots.[16] The crowded conditions prevent free movement, so that all energy intake is used to increase weight.

Faster weight gain is also promoted through a high-calorie feed consisting of corn, soy, and other supplements.[17] Although they get fat faster eating this food, cattle are not suited to such energy-rich diets. Grass and roughage constitute the natural diet of cattle and they have been equipped with four stomachs to digest the bulk. The switch to grain,

soy beans and other energy-rich foods causes a change in
stomach bacteria. Since the maximum amount of food is
forced as rapidly as possible through the cow's metabolic system, the system becomes overloaded and is pushed to the
point of breakdown. This disruption often results in a painful
condition called acidosis, in which the acidity of the cow's
stomach is thrown out of balance. Acidosis is the cause of
rejection for 90% of the liver that does not pass government
inspection in the U.S.[18] Diets for cattle in feedlots can be even
more unnatural than grain and soy beans. Sawdust, newspaper, cotton trash, cardboard boxes, feedlot bedding,
peanut hulls, condemned carcases, and dried blood are all
frequently used in factory cattle feed. Even ordinary cement
dust has been used as a feed additive because it produces
weight gain 30% faster than regular feed.[19]

Confining animals in feedlots and replacing their natural
food with grain and other materials are, of course, directed at
increasing farmers' profits. The variety of methods employed
on feedlots enable farmers to triple the natural weight-gain
rate of cows, bringing them to slaughter three times faster
than before.

Factory farms raise about half of America's dairy cattle.
Dairy cattle are usually held in long, dark confinement
barns, where rows upon rows of steel stalls house 200 to 300
animals. In some barns, cows are herded to a separate area at
milking time, but, in others, the cows never move and porta-
ble milking machines are brought to their stalls. Cows are
milked by an automated system of rubber cups, plastic tubes,
and vacuum pumps that extracts the milk and pumps it into a
refrigerated tank.[20] Under factory conditions, it is not just the
milking system that is mechanized. The cows themselves are
treated as if they were machines, with every aspect of their
biology manipulated to increase efficiency. One area in
which this efficiency is sought is in the amount of milk removed each day from dairy cattle. Under natural conditions,
a nursing calf would suck small amounts of milk from the
udder throughout the day and, by continuously replenishing

the little bit removed, the cow keeps the udder full. The mechanized tubing on factory farms, however, completely removes all of the milk in the cow's udder two or three times a day. The increased metabolic stress induced by this demand can cause a variety of diseases, including ketosis in which the cow breaks down its own tissue to make milk.[21] The dairy industry clearly did not have the cow in mind when it created the jingle "milk does the body good."

Another goal of dairy efficiency is to create a steady year-round flow of milk. This is accomplished by impregnating a cow a month or two after each calf is born. When the 10-month nursing period ends and milk production dries up, the farmer will not have long to wait before a new calf is born, and the cow is producing milk again. Through this system, the cow will spend almost all its six years of life in pregnancy.[22] At the end of this time, the flesh of dairy cattle is too poor for use in anything but hamburger. The five or six calves which will be born during the cow's lifetime are removed within two or three days of birth to save their mother's milk for the humans who will later drink it. These calves may be shipped to feedlots, sold to veal producers or kept by the dairy.

Those calves that end up in veal factories are the least fortunate of all. Consumers of veal, and the gourmet chefs who prepare it, demand pale and tender flesh. Healthy calves, allowed to eat roughage and wander the fields freely, do not produce veal. Veal is only produced in the most unnatural conditions. To obtain the prized white flesh, veal calves are fed an iron-deficient liquid diet containing milk, fat, sugar, starch, and other additives. Though the calves gain weight quickly, they remain weak and anaemic.[23] Unable to obtain iron from their food, the animals try to satiate their craving for iron by licking their own urine or the iron fittings on their stalls. The stall in which the veal calf is confined soon after its birth is too small to allow the calf to move or even turn around. Thus, veal calves live out their short lives unable to eat properly, completely confined, and denied contact with other animals. Within four months of their birth, they are sent to slaughter. Farmers might like them to weigh more, but the calves would likely sicken or die if they were kept much longer.

The factory farming approach to pig-raising begins with confinement as extreme as the veal stall imposes. In pig farming, the confined space is called a "gestation crate," and it is used to house sows during their four-month pregnancies. The dull and boring life in gestation crates makes agitation common among these pregnant animals. To reduce the aggression that would otherwise result, factory farmers maintain complete darkness in the barn except during feeding. The animals are fed only three times a week to prevent weight gain and ensure that they do not outgrow their crowded cages.[24]

Upon the birth of the piglets, the mother and her offspring are moved to a farrowing crate, where they are kept with hundreds of other animals. The confinement and confusion of smells and sounds often prevents the pig from recognizing its own offspring. The mother can step or sit on its own piglet without even noticing. It is estimated that nearly 20% of piglets are crushed to death in this way.[25] For the piglets which survive, confinement allows them continuous access to their mother's milk and denies their mother any relief or respite. Once these piglets are weaned, the sow will be impregnated again. A factory sow averages 2.5 litters a year. After four to five years of constant pregnancy, the sow is slaughtered.

Once they are separated from their mothers, the piglets are moved to battery cages located in buildings where feeding, watering, and manure removal are fully automated. Automation saves labor, allowing one farmer to manage six to eight thousand animals.[26] Fed diets rich in nutrients and chemicals, eight to 10 piglets are kept in each square-meter cage until they are fat enough for slaughter. These cages are poorly suited to the anatomical structure of the pigs. The wire-mesh floors, for example, cause tremendous pain because they are not soft enough to give under the protruding front of the pigs' hard hoofs. Lesions develop on their feet, their backs become misshapen, and the animals become lame.[27]

The crowding and understimulation give rise to psychological problems which pigs display through repetitive motions, aggression and, particularly, by biting at each other's tails. To reduce tail-biting, factory farmers remove the pigs' tails and castrate males soon after they are born. Removing these parts of a pig does not, of course, solve the real problem. The pigs are still unable to find outlets for their powerful instinctual urges. Without the freedom to escape from or otherwise acknowledge the superiority of stronger animals, the weaker pigs are under constant attack. They sometimes become so fearful that they do not move, even to eat, and thus die of starvation.[28]

Over two-thirds of the pigs raised in the U.S. live in total confinement. Although pig-rearing is the most recent area of factory farming, the trend towards larger and more intensive units is growing. Between 1980 and 1986 the percentage of pigs raised under intensive conditions nearly doubled, to 70%.[29]

Intensive husbandry practices have proliferated widely in the past 40 years. The majority of livestock in North America now live in factory-style conditions characterized by extreme confinement. Throughout their lives, these animals experience monotony and boredom. They become frustrated, restless and agitated. This psychological state leads to repetitive behaviours, such as continuous biting on the cage wire, hysteria, or aggression against other animals. Research has confirmed that many of the behavioral problems of factory farm animals are a direct result of intensive husbandry practices and that these problems disappear when factory conditions are alleviated. In poultry, for example, it has been shown that overcrowding and the inability to form stable social groups, lead to aggression and cannibalism. Among cattle, reduced personal space and the frequent interaction with strange animals, a common feature of crowded feedlots, can lead to intensified social aggressiveness. Factory cattle often engage in tongue rolling, a behavior that is symptomatic of boredom. Among pigs, the inability of weaker animals to submit to stronger ones leads to excessive aggression. Bar biting and other repetitive behaviors frequently observed in factory pigs have been shown to be the result of boredom, crowding, and unstable social groups.[30] In younger animals, these problems are aggravated by forced separation from their mothers soon after birth, and by the physical mutilation they must undergo, such as the debeaking of chicks and the tail-docking and castration of piglets. The shock of these treatments even kills some of the young animals. That these problems are endemic to factory farming is a clear reflection of the neglected welfare concerns of domesticated animals in modern livestock conditions.

The behavioral problems of factory animals are one aspect of their existence under intensive husbandry conditions. Another hardship is disease. Indeed, the nature of disease in domestic animals has changed dramatically since factory farming was introduced. In the words of agricultural engineer David Sainsbury:

> In almost every country of the world livestock production is becoming increasingly intensive. The momentum of the change has been so great that it would not be untrue or unkind to say that it has been instrumental in presenting the veterinarian with problems that have outstripped his knowledge. The disease pattern has tended to change radically. Instead of being presented largely with diagnosable and preventable or treatable disease, the tendency has been for the occurrence of chronic, insidious, and complex groups of disease.[31]

In pigs, respiratory disease caused by the dust and fumes of manure is common. Pigs may also succumb to procrine stress syndrome causing them to literally drop dead when mixed

with unfamiliar animals during transfers. Chickens in crowded broiler barns will suddenly leap in the air, squawk, and fall
over dead, killed by an affliction called, for lack of a better
name, "flip over syndrome." Mortality from this disease has
been found to be particularly high in the biggest and fastest-
growing birds. It has also been linked to factory conditions of
constant lighting and crowding stress.[32] These new afflictions
provide additional evidence that factory farming is causing
unnatural stress to factory animals. Their mortality is already
unnaturally high. The U.S. government estimates that the
death prior to slaughter ranges from 20 to 40% among pigs,
from 15 to 40% among cattle, and from 15 to 25% among
chickens.[33]

   In an attempt to lessen the spread of disease and reduce
death rates, farmers prop up the immune systems of factory
animals through antibiotics. In fact, as disease prevalence
and death rates increased under factory conditions, antibiotics became an integral part of the factory management
approach, a vital technology that allowed farmers to keep
large numbers of animals crowded together without a large
proportion of them dying of illness.[34] As each new antibiotic
was released for human medical use, it was also exploited in
the livestock industry.[35] At present, 55% of all the antibiotics
manufactured in the U.S. are fed directly to animals. The
National Academy of Sciences estimates that 70% of the beef
cattle and veal calves and 90% of the pigs raised in the U.S.
consume penicillin, tetracycline, and other antibiotics as a
part of their daily feed regimen. Thus, the majority of Americans who eat meat will also have a constant intake of these
powerful drugs. No one has determined what the implications of low-level, long-term antibiotic consumption are.[36]

   The attempt to use antibiotics to alleviate factory-
induced disease has been implicated in the increase in bacteria resistant to these antibiotics. Bacteria mutate and breed
under conditions of habitual antibiotic use. These mutants
are resistant to the effects of antibiotics and can transfer this
resistance to other bacteria, some of which may be harmful to

humans. When such resistant bacteria infect humans, the antibiotic to which they are resistant will no longer be effective in treating the infection.[37] Concerns about preserving the effectiveness of antibiotics led the United Kingdom and a number of other European countries to ban their use in livestock feed and to require all antibiotics to be used only with veterinary prescriptions. Similar measures have not been adopted in North America. Until such bans are enacted, factory farmers will continue to squander medicinal agents that have been vital in fighting human disease.[38]

The industry also attempts to improve production outcomes by other chemical means. Growth hormones such as bovine somatotropin (BST), made by recombinant DNA technology, allow growth rates to be rapidly increased in colds. Although concern has been raised about the long-term dangers such biologically active compounds may pose to human health,[39] the BST hormone has recently been approved for use in Canada and the United States. Dr. Samuel Epstein, a professor at the University of Chicago, has expressed grave reservations about the use of hormones of this type.

> Over the last forty years we have paid such a terrible price for refusing intelligently to assess the risks of new technologies before leaping into them. We have too often perturbed natural systems for short-term gains, but with disastrous long-term consequences. And quite apart from science, I feel instinctively that it is a terrible mistake to interfere with anything so delicately poised as the endocrine system, with so little information about where it is leading us.[40]

For some time now, such interventions have been used by factory farmers to manipulate the reproductive processes and the genetic make-up of farm animals. In breeding companies across the world, advanced fertilization technology and genetic engineering have been employed to develop "super animals." Today, chickens produce 10 times the number of eggs their ancestors did and cows produce 25 times their body weight in milk each year. Still the industry aims to intensify the use of genetic engineering. In the words of Richard Gowe, director of the Animal Research Institute of Agriculture Canada, "we are trying to breed animals without legs and chickens without feathers."[41] Despite the many advances in biology and medicine, our knowledge of biological systems is still limited. We also know very little about the long-term consequences of the biological techniques being used by factory farmers to increase the output of meat and dairy products.

In response to concerns about animal health under intensive husbandry conditions, the industry often points to the incredible increases in productivity that have been achieved, suggesting that productivity is a bona fide measure of health. Yet, as we have pointed out, the productivity of factory farms is really due to the use of drugs, physical mutilation, and environmental manipulation. If farm animals were healthy in and well suited to intensive husbandry conditions, then such treatments obviously would not be necessary.

Is the practice of factory farming ethically justified? Factory farmers seem to think so, but a growing number of observers question the right of humans to treat animals the way we do.

The prevailing attitude towards animals in western society is reflected in the thinking of western philosophers, many of whom distinguished between humans and animals to the detriment of the latter. Cartesianism, a philosophy developed by René Descartes in the 17th century, perhaps goes the farthest. Descartes, often called the father of modern western philosophy, emphasized the importance of reason as the distinguishing element between humans and animals and insisted that animals lacked the ability to think in abstract terms as humans can.[42] In many of his writings, he went further, denying animals feeling, sensation, and drives. So convinced was he of this view that Descartes wrote, "if there were machines with the organs and appearance of a monkey or some other irrational animals, we should have no means of telling that they were not animals."[43] Cartesianism suggests, therefore, that animals are unfeeling, unsuffering objects for human use and establishes a clear dividing line between humans and all other living animals. Working under these assumptions, factory farmers are able to justify their treatment of animals in inhumane ways. The Cartesian philosophy and other similar perspectives on the rights of animals provide an ideology that sustains animal exploitation in factory farms.[44]

The concern of animal rights advocates is to encourage a reexamination of the fundamental premises that made factory farming philosophically acceptable. Early advocates of the view that animals could suffer and should be humanely treated were often motivated by personal experience and expressed themselves in passionate and persuasive prose. Montaigne, a French essayist who died a few years before Descartes was born, was greatly moved by the pain and suffering inflicted on animals. On the assumption of human superiority that underlay this treatment, he wrote:

> Presumption is our natural and original disease. The most calamitous and fragile of all creatures is man, and yet the most arrogant. It is through the vanity of this same imagination that he equals himself to a god, that he attributes to himself divine conditions, that he picks himself out and separates himself from the crowd of other creatures, curtails the just shares of other animals his brethren and companions, and assigns to them such portions of faculties and forces as seems to him good. How does he know, by the effort of his intelligence, the interior and secret movements and impulses of other animals? By what comparison between them and us does he infer the stupidity which he attributes to them?[45]

Objective proof of the nature of mental experiences in animals which Montaigne described remained elusive for many centuries. In the absence of evidence, humans presumed that a large difference existed between other animals and themselves. Pain, sensitivity, awareness, and the entire spectrum of emotions were assumed to be exclusively human experiences and hence, the Cartesian view was successfully sustained over alternative views such as that of Montaigne.[46] In recent years, however, evidence from the scientific study of evolution, ethology, anatomy, and other fields has led to a revision of this view and greatly strengthened the argument that animals are conscious, feeling beings.

Although there is no way to determine scientifically what an animal is actually feeling or experiencing, scientists have identified the pathways within the brain that play a role in sensation, perception, cognition, and emotion. They have isolated chemicals and studied behavioral mechanisms that closely correlate to specific emotional states.[47] Serotonin, for example, is a chemical in the brain that is known to counter human depression. Depressed people are often found to have elevated levels of this chemical in their brains because it is not effective in its intended action. But this chemical is also present in the brains of other animals where it is believed to mediate depression in a similar manner. It is, therefore, now scientifically acceptable to study depression and other emotional states, formerly believed to be exclusively human, in rats and other lab animals.[48]

The results of this scientific research has far-ranging implications for our perception of mental experiences in animals, prompting a revision of formerly secure boundaries between human and non-human animals. As animal behaviorist Donald Griffin has noted:

> It is no more anthropomorphic, strictly speaking, to postulate mental experiences in another species than to compare its bony structure, nervous system, or antibodies with our own . . . The prevailing view implies that only our species can have any sort of conscious awareness that, should animals have mental experiences, they must be identical to ours, since there can be no other

kind. It is this conceit which is truly anthropomorphic, because it assumes a species monopoly of an important quality. This attitude resembles, in many ways, the pre-Copernican certainty that the earth must lie at the centre of the universe.[49]

Griffin highlights the fact that mental experiences in animals are likely to vary considerably in sophistication. Although research into animal behaviour and other areas continues, current evidence suggests that mental experiences are widespread, at least among multicellular animals, but differ greatly in complexity. Although nobody would deny that the capacity for reason is most highly developed in humans, it is clear that many of the emotional states previously believed to be limited only to humans are present throughout the animal kingdom. In short, there is no rigid line of demarcation between human and non-human animals. There are, in fact, many gradations in the ability to suffer and feel emotion.[50]

Several arguments for animal rights have been advanced which are based on the understanding that animals have feeling and the capacity to suffer. These approaches, like Montaigne's, reject the Cartesian view and attempt to challenge common assumptions about animal suffering and animal rights. Peter Singer, in his book *Animal Liberation*, argues that animals deserve consideration equal with humans. He argues from a utilitarian position, a moral perspective that seeks to secure the greatest good for the greatest number. The main concern for utilitarians is, according to a classical advocate, Jeremy Bentham, that "the question is not, 'can they reason?,' not 'can they talk?,' but 'can they suffer?'" Since animals suffer, we must expand our consideration to include them. Singer argues for abstention from all animal foods because of the pain inflicted on animals in factory farming.[52]

Another argument for a plant-food diet on the basis of animal rights is put forward by Tom Regan in his *Moral Basis of Vegetarianism*. Regan argues that we are obligated to follow a principle of non-injury and thus have an obligation not to cause pain. Pain and suffering are, of course, inherent in meat-raising and meat-eating. The animals raised for meat have their natural instincts frustrated and their physical and psychological systems subjected to constant stress. To the extent that we eat the flesh of animals, we help create demand for it. On the basis of the unjustifiable pain to which animals are subjected and the routine killing that meat requires, Regan argues that vegetarianism is an ethically warranted practice, and that the onus is, in fact, on of those who eat animal foods to establish justification for the suffering inflicted on animals by their dietary practices.[53]

Non-vegetarians, as consumer of the products of modern factory farms, implicitly consent to the raising of billions of feeling animals as if they were machines and, of course, to their slaughter. Clearly for some, these facts do not pose a moral dilemma. Assuming that animals are indeed like machines, some people, following in the intellectual tradition of Descartes, feel that they should not be accorded any rights. But, is the view that animals are non-sentient really tenable? As we have shown, the notions of animals as machines is steadily being undermined by modern science. Much evidence now suggests animals share many of our mental processes, that they can experience anger, frustration, and joy, that they can get depressed and feel happy. The understanding of animal minds provided by the various disciplines of biology may help us to rethink the ethics of factory farming. There are various ways we can grapple with this issue, a few of which we have discussed in this chapter. But, for some, the most convincing grounds for respecting animal rights may arise out of a critical reexamination of personal experience.

While chickens, pigs and cattle are slaughtered by the billions, it is ironic to see loving care given by many in our society to other mammals and birds, such as budgies, dogs, and cats. Pet owners, who often value their animal as a member of the family, would balk at the thought that it was a machine. And yet similar animals, no less feeling and alive than cats or pigeons, are treated with abominable cruelty and raised for the dinners of these same people. What is the reason for this double standard? Perhaps a greater awareness of the conditions under which animals are raised will prompt a reexamination of meat-eating among those who treat some animals which such admirable compassion.

Sensitivity to the suffering of animals and a principled objection to their slaughter has motivated vegetarians for centuries. Henry S. Salt, an ardent British vegetarian of the 18th century, formulated his own vision of how the human diet would be shaped by an awakening of compassion for non-human animals:

> Vegetarianism is the diet of the future, as flesh-food is the diet of the past. In that striking and common contrast, a fruit shop side by side with a butcher's, we have a most significant object lesson. There, on the one hand, are the barbarities of a savage custom—the headless carcasses, stiffened into a ghastly semblance of life, the joints and steaks and gobbets with their sickening odour, the harsh grating of a bone-saw, and the dull thud of the chopper—a perpetual crying protest against the horrors of flesh-eating. And as if this were not witness sufficient, here close alongside is a wealth of golden fruit, a sight to make a poet happy, the only food that is entirely congenial to the physical structure and natural instincts of mankind, that can entirely satisfy the highest human aspirations. Can we doubt, as we gaze at this contrast, that whatever intermediate steps may need to be gradually taken, whatever difficulties to be overcome, the path of progression from the barbarities to the humanities of diet lies clear and unmistakable before us?

Philosophers, Shramans and Reformers

Vegetarianism has been preached and practiced for thousands of years. Those who think conscientious abstention from meat is a recent development are often surprised to learn that a meatless diet has been advocated by many different individuals and groups of varying religious, cultural, and geographic origins for almost three millennia. In the next few pages, we shall endeavor to give you a sense of this diverse global vegetarian tradition.

The earliest recorded practice of vegetarianism in the West is based on beliefs in a mystical Golden Age among the Greeks of 1000 B.C. In this idealized period of time, humans were thought to have lived in harmony with animals, contentedly eating a simple vegetarian diet. Because the Greeks strongly believed that what had happened in the past was better than the present, vegetarianism was practiced by a number of people throughout the Greek period in an attempt to conjure an age of perfection similar to that of the Golden Age.[1] Later in Greek history, a group called the Orphics helped to establish philosophical justifications for vegetarianism. Opposed to the indulgent lifestyle practiced by many Greeks around 700 B.C., the Orphics advocated a simple, serene lifestyle. A meatless diet was necessary because it was thought to purify the soul of unnatural and hedonistic influences. This idea, that vegetarianism is associated with purity, recurs throughout vegetarian history.

Pythagoras, the famous mathematician and philosopher who lived in the sixth century B.C., was influenced by the Orphic tradition. In addition to his well-known mathematical pursuits, Pythagoras was a religious leader and founded a religious community of considerable importance in ancient Greece. Though he left no writings of his own, Pythagoras is known through the works of his religious followers, the Pythagoreans, as a vigourous advocate of a vegetarian lifestyle. He was the first person in recorded Western history to lay down a comprehensive philosophical justification for not eating meat. Pythagoras believed in the doctrine of the transmigration of souls, that the souls of animals could be reborn as humans and vice versa. This conviction proscribed meateating for fear of eating a deceased distant relative or friend.

Vegetarianism was also an essential part of what Pythagoras considered to be a natural and hygienic lifestyle. He believed that vegetarian food was essential to maintaining a balance of the humors, elements which the Greeks believed governed human well-being. The purity of the Pythagorean diet remained renowned for centuries after Pythagoras' life. In 1743, Antonio Cocchi, a fellow of the Royal Society of London, gave a lecture on its merits:

> The Pythagorean diet consisted of the free and universal use of everything that is vegetable, tender, and fresh . . and which requires little or no preparation to make it fit to eat, such as roots, leaves, fruit, and seeds.[2]

Pythagoras's ethical and practical reasoning gave him strong conviction in his meatless diet. When speaking to meat-eaters, Pythagoras did not hesitate to point out the error he saw in their ways. One of his eloquent pleas is thought to have been as follows:

> Oh, my fellow men, do not defile your bodies with sinful foods . . . The earth affords a lavish supply of riches, or innocent foods, and offers you banquets that involve no bloodshed or slaughter; only beasts satisfy their hunger with flesh . . .

The contribution of Pythagoras and his followers to vegetarianism in Greece and later in Europe led to his widespread recognition as the founder of conscientious vegetarianism in the West.

In addition to this noteworthy thinker other classical philosophers, including Empedocles, Ovid, Seneca, and Plutarch advocated a meatless diet. During their time, it was common in Rome to slaughter large numbers of animals and feast on their flesh. The excesses of this custom likely strengthened the commitment to vegetarianism among these philosophers. Seneca wrote:

> I shall admire you only when you scorn not plain bread, when you have persuaded yourself that herbs exist not for other animals only, but for man also—if you shall recognize that vegetables are sufficient food for the stomach into which we now stuff valuable lives.[3]

Groups within the Judeo-Christian tradition have also promoted a vegetarian diet. Though in the minority, Jewish vegetarians maintain that their religion has a distinct vegetarian outlook. A common inspirational source for Jewish vegetarians comes from the Hebrew Bible. In Genesis 1:29 it is written that on the sixth day of creation,

> God said, look to you I give all the seed bearing plants everywhere on the surface of the earth, and all the trees with seed bearing fruit; this will be your food.[4]

Meat-eating, however, is not forbidden by Judaism. Jews are permitted to eat flesh that is killed by a kosher slaughter or *Shehitah*. It is felt that this technique minimizes the animal's suffering. Jewish vegetarians, on the other hand, fail to see the kindness in any form of slaughter and many believe that God's "Thou shalt not kill" commandment should encompass all animal life, not just humans.[5] In addition, foods of animal origin are often seen in the Jewish tradition as capable of inducing passion. Consequently, meat is associated with the "animal" aspect of human nature. Samson Raphael Hirsch, a prominent 19th-century German rabbi, subscribed to this view, noting that:

Anything which makes the body too active in a carnal direction brings it nearer to the animal sphere, thereby robbing it of its primary function, to be the intermediary between the soul of man and the world outside. Bearing this function in mind . . . , one might come to the conclusion that the vegetable food is the most preferable, as plants are the most passive substance; and indeed we find that in Jewish law all vegetables are permitted food without discrimination.[6]

Similar considerations provide motivation for Christian vegetarians. While, the majority of contemporary Christians also eat meat, a number of outspoken individuals and movements in the Christian tradition have advocated vegetarianism.

Early Christianity appears to have shown considerable support for a meatless diet. Colin Spencer, a historian of vegetarianism, notes that before St. Augustine in the third century A.D., there were numerous Christian thinkers who lived on a frugal diet without meat. Titus Flavius Clement, founder of the Alexandrian school of Christian theology, was one such person. He paid particular attention to the violent nature of meat-eating. Writing in the second century A.D., Clement observed that it is unnatural for life to depend on death, and that it is inhuman to fatten oneself on cattle.[7] He wrote:

But those who bend around inflammatory tables, nourishing their own diseases, are ruled by a most lickerish demon . . . It is far better to be happy than to have a demon dwelling with us, and happiness is found in the practice of virtue. Accordingly, the apostle Matthew partook of seeds, and nuts, and vegetables, without the use of flesh.[8]

These early advocates shared many of the views of Mani, who founded a religion called Manicheanism in 226 A.D. Unlike the prevailing Christian ideas of the time, the Manicheans gave full equality to women and were committed vegetarians. Furthermore, the Manicheans were firm believers in non-violence and would not kill any creature, no matter how small. Interestingly, their ideas bear striking resemblance to those of the Jains and Buddhists of India, and some have speculated that Mani had met with Jains and Buddhists and heard of their ideas through traders.[9] Manicheanism spread over Asia Minor and to the east and west. Mani appears to have modelled himself on St. Paul, the early propagator of Christianity, and spread his teachings as widely as possible. Mani's message was well received by the people to whom he preached and he left behind a sizable community at the time of his death. But despite its early success as a rival to the dominant Christian tradition, Manicheanism's following gradually lessened and eventually died out completely.

Montanus, who founded the Montanist Church, an unorthodox Christian teacher who shared some of Mani's ideas. The Montanists regarded a vegetarian diet as an essential part of an ascetic lifestyle, serving to purify the soul. Among early vegetarian monastic orders, the Benedictine Order, founded in 529 A.D., is perhaps the best known. St. Benedict, its founder, advocated simplicity in diet, preaching that "nothing is more contrary to the Christian spirit than gluttony."[10] Much later, in the middle of the 17th century, the Trappist monastic order went through a reformation process under the leadership of its abbot, Armand Jean de Rance. From that time until the late 1960s, Trappists uniformly abstained from eating any flesh food, including eggs.

A number of passages in pre-Christian texts also advocate a meatless diet. For example, the *Essene Gospel of Peace*, painting an unconventional portrait of Jesus as vegetarian, quotes Jesus as saying:

> And the flesh of slain beasts in a person's body will become his own tomb. For I tell you truly, he who kills, kills himself, and whosoever eats the flesh of slain beasts eats the body of death.[11]

The largest modern Christian vegetarian church, with its members numbering around two million worldwide, is that of the Seventh Day Adventists. Founded in 1842, the movement established its first headquarters in Battle Creek, Michigan, in 1855. Among Seventh Day Adventists, the practice of vegetarianism is inspired by the beliefs of their group's founder, Ellen White.[12] She believed that the body should be regarded as God's temple and that, as a result, any abuse of the body would also be a violation of God. With this principle of purity in mind, she denounced meat consumption.

One of the more famous members of this group was Dr. John Harvey Kellogg, the inventor of breakfast cereals. Kellogg received his medical degree in 1875 and thereafter was active in health advocacy and teaching. In accordance with the principles of Adventism, he maintained a consistent dedication to a diet comprising fruits, nuts, and grains and regarded this diet as the natural one for humans. Implementing these beliefs in his medical practice at the famous and influential Battle Creek Sanatorium, Dr. Kellogg insisted that all his patients consume a meatless diet. For this purpose, a number of vegetarian substitutes for animal foods were developed, including the soyburger and soy milk, items which are quite popular among North American vegetarians today.[13]

Philosophical support for vegetarianism in the West is evident in the writing of a number of noted modern philosophers, poets, and scientists, each of whom have made a significant contribution to conscientious vegetarianism. Leonardo da Vinci (1452-1519) was likely the first of these. He is widely remembered as a remarkable Florentine painter and inventor. Born and raised on a farm near Anchiano in Italy, da Vinci became acquainted with a large variety of animal life. Compassion for animals, developed during this early part of his life, was probably the main motivating factor for his meatless diet. He is reported to have said:

I have from an early age avoided the use of meat, and
the time will come when men such as I will look
upon the murder of animals as they look upon the
murder of men.

A confirmation of da Vinci's vegetarianism is provided by a
letter written from India to Guiliano de Medici, da Vinci's
patron and close friend, by Andrea Corsali, a Florentine trav-
eller and acquaintance of da Vinci. Corsali met and was im-
pressed by a particular community in India whom he called
"Guzzarati." These people, he writes, "do not feed upon anything that contains blood, nor do they permit among them
that any injury be done to any living thing, like our Leonardo
da Vinci."[13]

Although, the British poet Percy Shelley (1792-1822)
lived in a period of Western history when vegetarianism was
rarely practiced, he wrote a number of books and essays ar-
guing in favor of a vegetarian diet. Shelley observed that:

The change which would be produced by simpler eating
habits on the political economy is sufficiently remarkable. The monopolising eater of animal flesh would no
longer destroy his constitution by devouring an acre at a
meal. The quantity of nutritious vegetable matter consumed in fattening the carcass of an ox would afford ten
times the sustenance. It is only the wealthy that can, to
any great degree, even now, indulge the unnatural craving for dead flesh, and they pay for the greater licence of
the privilege by subjection of supernumery disease.[14]

Evident in Shelley's views are concerns about the environment, food security and health which remarkably anticipate
the convictions of many modern vegetarians.

Charles Darwin (1809-1882), whose theory of evolution
set the framework for the biological sciences, was a committed vegetarian. Darwin's work established the human species
as a branch of primate evolution further evolved than apes

and chimpanzees but bearing many similarities to them. Darwin noted that these animals were vegetarians and concluded, based on the similarities between these primates and humans, that humans ought to be vegetarian as well. But his thoughts carried him beyond anatomy. Darwin also thought that there were many commonalities in mental experience between humans and the higher animals. Anticipating the results of modern scientific study, Darwin believed that animals could feel pain, suffer from boredom and have the desire to be loved. Thinking that animals were thus endowed with a number of "human" characteristics, Darwin felt is was wrong to slaughter them for food.[15]

The American philosopher Henry David Thoreau (1817-1862), author of the famous work *On Walden Pond*, advocated a lifestyle of simplicity. He spent a portion of his life living in isolation on the banks of Walden Pond, speculating on the nature of human existence. On vegetarianism, he once wrote:

> I have no doubt that it is part of the destiny of the human race in its gradual development to leave off the eating of animals as surely as the savage tribes have left off eating each other when they came into contact with the more civilized.

Leo Tolstoy (1828-1910), the Russian writer, observed that "while we ourselves are the living graves of murdered animals, how can we expect ideal conditions on earth?" Vegetarianism was, in his view, essential to moral progress. Tolstoy's position in favour of meatless living advanced the practice of vegetarianism in Russia in the later part of the nineteenth century.[16]

George Bernard Shaw (1856-1950), the famous Irish playwright who wrote works such as *Pygmalion* and *Arms and the Man*, once simply summed up his commitment to vegetarianism by saying, "Animals are my friends, and I don't eat my friends." After he adopted vegetarianism at the age of 25, Shaw was regularly warned by doctors that it would kill him. Forty years later, when asked if he had ever returned to those same doctors to rub it in a little, he replied, "I would have, but they all passed away years ago." Shaw lived to be 94 years old.[17,18]

Of all the noted modern vegetarians in the West, Albert Schweitzer (1875-1965) carried his conviction the furthest. He had a deep-seated reverence for all life, a conviction born out of a very poignant childhood experience. As a young boy growing up in Germany, Schweitzer and other children used to try to kill birds with sling shots. He was initially as remorseless as his peers when the birds were hit by their stones. As time wore on, however, he became increasingly sensitive to the birds' suffering. When his turn to shoot came, he would miss the birds intentionally and soon gained the inner strength to cease the practice altogether. Later in life, as his awareness of the plight of animals grew, his compassion for their suffering grew as well. Eventually Schweitzer refused to kill even the ants in his cabin, choosing to feed them with grapefruit juice instead.[19]

Albert Einstein (1879-1955) is well remembered as a brilliant physicist whose theory of relativity revolutionized our understanding of the physical universe. Less well known is the fact that Einstein was also a vegetarian. Widely acclaimed as one of the most powerful minds of the 20th century, he became popular for his views on human relationships, the economy and other non-scientific subjects. Regarding vegetarianism, Einstein suggested that "nothing will benefit the health and increase the chances for survival of life on Earth as the evolution to a vegetarian diet."

Continuing in the tradition of conscientious vegetarianism founded by early Greeks, these modern Western thinkers expounded ethical and compassionate arguments against the practice of meat eating. Standing against the strong current of popular wisdom and practice, they vigorously objected to the needless suffering and slaughtering of animals brought about by those who eat meat. They possessed a keen awareness of where their food came from and at what cost it was wrought. Reflecting on this, Henry S. Salt, a 19th-century British humanitarian, wrote:

> I found myself realizing, with an amazement which time has not diminished, that the "meat" which formed the staple of our diet, and which I was accustomed to regard like bread or fruit, or vegetables—as a mere commodity of the table, was in truth dead flesh—the actual flesh and blood of oxen, sheep, swine, and other animals that were slaughtered in vast numbers.[20]

Our journey through the vegetarian heritage of the East begins in India. Of all the regions of the world, India is unique because it has the strongest vegetarian tradition. The history of Indian vegetarianism is a rich mingling of ideas among the religions native to the subcontinent. The effect of this dialogue has been common advocacy of vegetarianism by Jains, Hindus, and Buddhists alike, though sometimes with varying strictness of practice. The milieu from which this remarkable cultural tradition has grown is unusual because of its deep-rooted advocacy of non-violence and respect for all forms of life.

The teachers of this ancient philosophy are the shramans, sadhus, and sannyasins. Jainism and Buddhism are shramanic religions, and the monks and nuns of both religions, called shramans, live their lives as homeless mendicants, spending most of their time in meditation and teaching. In the Hindu tradition, a sadhu in one who gives up worldly life at a young age, and a sannyasin is one who seeks spiritual growth after fulfilling all familial obligations. What unites all of these holy men and women of India, is that, as perhaps the earliest environmentalists and animal rights advocates, they taught a philosophy and way of life that was based on an intimate awareness of the living, breathing world.

Of all the vegetarian groups in Indian society, Jains are the most strictly committed to a vegetarian lifestyle. The ancient religion of Jainism has a unique position among world religions in that it has never permitted the eating of animal flesh. The unwavering commitment of the Jains is rooted in the principle of *ahimsa*, or non-violence. In accordance with this principle, Jains seek to minimize the harm they do to other living beings and extend the maximum possible compassion to all forms of life, whether plant, insect, or animal.

Faced with the necessity of eating to survive, Jains recognize that they must take the lives of other living beings. In order to minimize harm to sentient life, Jain thinkers devised a scale of senses which ranks life according to its ability to suffer. On this scale, animals, possessing five senses and the ability to fear and sense pain, are ranked at the top while plants, possessing only the sense of touch are ranked at the bottom. Jains consider it logical, therefore, that to minimize suffering they should eat a pure vegetable-based diet. Vegetarianism provides Jains with a way to enact the principle of *ahimsa* on a daily basis and thus holds a central place in the Jain way of life.

The first Jain monk to leave India was Gurudev Shri Chitrabhanu. An eloquent spokesperson for the philosophy of reverence for life, Gurudev Chitrabhanu expressed his view on meat-eating at the World Vegetarian Congress at The Hague in 1971 by saying:

> He who wishes to attain spiritual sublimity must take food which is pure and untainted with blood. It is the food we take that sustains the body and it is the body that houses the mind and the mind which gives form to our thoughts. If the body is sustained by meat and other food which are the product of violence and bloodshed, how can you expect your mind to generate thoughts which are pure and noble?[21]

The Indian religion with the largest following, Hinduism, also advocates a vegetarian diet. The rationale behind vegetarianism in the Hindu religion lies in philosophical speculation about the relation between the food we eat and our frame of mind. These ideas are recorded in the *Bhaga-vad Gita,* a poetic Hindu scripture. According to the *Gita,* all food can be classified as being of three types: *satvic, rajasic* and *tamsic. Satvic* foods are foods in the "mode of good-ness" and include fruits, vegetables, wheat, sugar, and rice. *Rajasic* food are food in the "mode of passion" and include salty, bitter, overly spiced or sour foods as well as onions and garlic. *Tamsic* foods are food in the "mode of darkness" and include, in particular, meat and alcohol. In the words of the *Gita* such food is "stale, unsavory, putrid and spoiled."[22,23]

Furthermore, each food type is associated with one of three personality types.[24] *Satvic* food engenders knowledge and happiness. It is associated with various virtues such as a love of truth, holiness, faith, as well as compassion and char-ity. *Rajasic* food brings about a passionate and active dispo-sition. Such people are industrious and seek gain, but may also be inclined to be unforgiving and at times unhappy and covetous. *Tamsic* food, associated with a dark or wicked dis-position, engenders sloth and ignorance. It is believed that a person who eats such food will grow sinful, sensual and will be unable to properly manage his or her own affairs. Conse-quently, Hindus eat only food of the first two types, attempt-ing to maximize *satvic* food, but permitting *rajasic* food. *Tamsic* food, and therefore meat and most other animal prod-ucts, is strictly avoided. Vegetarianism, according to Hindu-ism, cultivates reverence, spirituality, and compassion.

Mahatma Gandhi (1869-1948), perhaps the greatest modern exponent of non-violence, was an ardent vegetarian. Gandhi was born and raised in the Kathiawar region of the province of Gujarat. Kathiawar, often considered the holy land of western India, is a place characterized by an intermin-gling of Hindu and Jain ideas and practices. Gandhi's earliest influences were drawn from this environment where non-violence and vegetarianism were considered normal.[25] Though a vegetarian since birth, Gandhi had at one time ex-perimented with meat eating. In his autobiography, Gandhi writes that as a boy, he was always thin and weak. He once went to a burly schoolmate for advice on how to get bigger. The boy encouraged Gandhi to eat meat, convincing him that animal flesh was the solution to his diminutive physical stature. Determined to get bigger, the Mahatma went with his friend to a secret place where he began chewing some goat flesh. That night he dreamed that there was a helpless goat braying inside him, crying out to be let free. Revolted by the image, Mahatma Gandhi was shaken by what he had done and never thought of eating meat again.

Although this revulsion provided the Mahatma with the motivation not to eat meat, he became a firm conscientious objector to flesh consumption after reading Henry Salt's book *A Plea for Vegetarianism*. Gandhi considered this to be a momentous event in this life, after which he no longer remained content just to follow a vegetarian diet, but felt compelled to advocate it to others. Indeed, the strength of his conviction, and the powerful example he made of his own life, inspired many of his fellow Hindus to uphold their vegetarian tradition, despite increasing western influence on India.

Gautam Buddha (563-453 B.C.), the founder of Buddhism, sought an alternative to the asceticism of Jainism and the dominant Hinduism. Buddhism thus came to be known as the *Madayana* or middle path. Like Jains, Buddhists are believers in the principle of *ahimsa*. The Buddha was overwhelmed by the suffering he saw to be an unavoidable part of life, and he was himself a vegetarian. His views are expressed in the *Lankavatara sutra*:

> How can the bodhisattva (Buddhist aspirant), who wishes to treat all beings as though they were himself, eat the flesh of any living being? The bodhisattva, desirous of cultivating the virtue of love should not eat meat, lest he cause terror to living beings.[6]

Despite this fairly clear doctrine, some Buddhists, including some monks, began to eat the flesh of animals when it was killed for them by another person. In response to this trend, the Buddhists scriptures have specifically noted that it is not proper to eat meat, regardless of the source. Some confusion remains amongst Buddhists, and today, while many Buddhists are vegetarian, a significant number are not. The scriptures, however, leave no doubt as to the authentic Buddhist position:

> But it [meat] is nowhere allowed in the *sutras* as a legitimate food. All meat-eating in any form or manner and in any circumstances is prohibited, unconditionally and once and for all.[27]

Among the more famous Buddhists is Ashoka, an Indian emperor of the third century B.C. Born in the Mauryan lineage, Ashoka ruled over a vast empire, ranging over the whole Indian subcontinent with the exception of the southern tip. Ashoka's conversion to Buddhism was prompted by his shocked reaction to the death and destruction caused by one of his military conquests. After his conversion, he attempted to govern India according to the precepts of Buddhism. The new Buddhist policy was soon spread throughout the empire's domain by a series of edicts engraved on rocks and pillars, many of which can still be found today. One refers to the transition that took place in animal slaughter after Ashoka adopted vegetarianism:

> Formerly in the King's kitchen several hundred thousand animals were killed daily for food; but now at the time of writing only three are killed—two peacocks and a deer. Even these animals will not be killed in the future.[28]

Ashoka's empire stands out in history because it was the first and thus far only state of any sort that avowed a non-violent policy. It is difficult for the modern mind to imagine what the years after Ashoka's conversion would have been like. Though it is unlikely that the empire was completely transformed into the non-violent and tolerant image Ashoka had in mind, the fact that the emperor and his administration advocated compassion for animals to all of its citizens and that vegetarianism was encouraged and also practiced by the powerful in society is remarkably unique. Ashoka's empire and its non-violent policies survived almost two generations after his death, and in fact, after this era of Buddhist imperial rule, most Indians became vegetarian in their dietary practice. The Ashokan empire also marked the high point of Buddhism on the Indian subcontinent.

When Muslims and Turks invaded India between the 10th and 12th centuries A.D., Buddhists were widely persecuted. As refugees, they fled central India to the south to Sri Lanka and to the northeast through the Himalayas. Sri Lanka became a flourishing Buddhist kingdom and successive royal families were all devout Buddhists. In the 11th century, Buddhism became established in Tibet and in the 17th century in Mongolia. It is thought that a small Buddhist community had existed in Thailand since the time of Ashoka. In the 11th century, when the country was unified, Buddhism was made the main religion. From Thailand, Buddhism also exerted influence on present-day Malaysia. The religion reached north Vietnam by the third century AD and flourished there, and when Korean monks returned from China in the sixth century A.D. with the precepts of Buddhism, it soon became the religion of the ruling elite. Buddhism influenced the large civilizations of China and Japan early on, and there is evidence that Buddhists were present in China from as early as 50 A.D. and reached Japan in 538 A.D.[29] Thus, although Buddhism originated in India, it has exerted a greater effect on the religious development of other Asian countries, where today vegetarianism is practiced by large numbers of Buddhists.

The importance of Buddhism is particularly evident in China where it became the major religion of all classes of society. More than 30,000 temples had been built by the end of the sixth century A.D. Although the vegetarian tradition in China can largely be ascribed to Buddhist influence, the native Taoist religion also suggested that people should abstain from meat.[30] The basis for the Taoist position was not reverence for life, but a belief that meat upset the body's harmony.

Due to support for Buddhism amongst a number of China's emperors there are stories of great vegetarian feasts and bans on the slaughter of animals during Buddhist holy periods. One emperor, I Tsung, is reputed to have led a Buddhist procession, the path for which was dotted with large pavilions, donated by wealthy families, at which vegetarian foods were given to the clergy and lay people.[31] As a result of this rich tradition, Chinese cuisine developed delicious and varied vegetarian dishes. In fact, the traditional Chinese diet consists almost entirely of foods of plant origin, including grains, legumes, vegetables and rice.[32]

Buddhism also exerted a strong influence in Japan. But even before it arrived, there were various imperial injunctions against the consumption of meat, particularly beef. The cow, the Japanese felt, did its duty by bearing and raising calves and labouring at the plough. Since the animal was respected for its faithful service, it was considered wrong to eat its flesh or drink its milk.[33] When Buddhism did arrive, the Japanese developed their own indigenous versions of its teachings, such as Zen Buddhism, a form which has recently gained popularity in the West.[34] The Zen Buddhists attempted to stop the eating of fish and chicken in Japan and were quite successful. The traditional Japanese diet includes rices and vegetables and offers a wide array of vegetarian dishes.[35]

The Japanese vegetarian tradition remained very strong throughout all social classes until the beginning of the 20th century.[36] In recent years the consumption of meat in Japan as well as in other Asian countries has begun to rise. As affluence spreads, consumption of meat and dairy products has followed close behind. In many Asian nations, vegetarianism has begun to lose ground to the growing popularity of animal foods.

And yet, even as these changes occur in Asia, many people in North America and Europe, which have been for a long time predominantly meat-eating societies, are beginning to seriously question their meat-eating ways. Considering convincing arguments concerning health, the environment, and animal welfare, large numbers are adopting a vegetarian diet. In fact, in the United States, it is estimated that there are currently 12 million vegetarians and that every week 20,000 more people give up meat.[37] In the United Kingdom, where vegetarians number in excess of 15 million, approximately 30,000 people turn vegetarian a week and the membership of the British Vegetarian Society has grown rapidly. And subscriptions to *Vegetarian Times*, a U.S. magazine, have doubled in the last five years to 170,000.[38] These people constitute the newest and perhaps one of the most energetic movements in the ancient and varied vegetarian tradition.

Plant-Food Nutrition

In the years before the health advantages of a plant-food diet were recognized, concerns were often raised about its nutritional adequacy. It was commonly believed that a meat-based diet provided an easy way of obtaining all daily dietary requirements and that people who ate few animal products or none at all would generally have difficulty in meeting their nutritional needs. Convinced of the merits of meat, many people believed that a vegetarian diet could not supply sufficient amounts of a variety of specific nutrients. These were often those nutrients found in high concentrations in animal products, including protein, iron, and calcium. People interested in becoming vegetarian were frequently asked questions by concerned family and friends: Can you really get enough protein from a vegetarian diet? What about iron, is it not a problem? Should you not worry about calcium? In this chapter, we shall explain how perceptions of the nutritional inadequacy of vegetarian diets arose and address some common questions. As you will see, special concern over specific nutrients among vegetarians is quite unnecessary.

Many of the perceptions of nutritional inadequacy among vegetarians were formed when thinking among nutritional scientists was much different than it is today. As a measure of this change, we will consider an abbreviated history of nutritional recommendations to the public made through the Food Guide. A tool commonly employed for public education in meal planning, the Food Guide reflects the view taken by government nutritional authorities on the right selection of foods for a healthy diet. Ever since its conception, the make-up of the Food Guide has been the subject of much debate. The Food Guide currently in use was dramatically redesigned in recent years, but there are well-substantiated arguments for even more significant changes.

The first Food Guides, formulated in the U.S. in the 1920s and '30s, aimed at avoiding nutrient deficiency in the population. Certain nutrients, particularly protein, were targeted to be of concern. Books such as *Meat Three Times a Day*, which focused on protein deficiencies and urged consumers to eat more meat, were published and widely read. In an attempt to ensure that the protein requirement was met, the U.S. Department of Agriculture advocated a 12-food-group classification in which three food groups were animal products. In this climate of preoccupation with protein, nutritional scientists raised concerns about vegetarianism. Vegetable protein was viewed as inferior, and vegetarians were cautioned that they would require special awareness to overcome the nutritional deficiencies of plant food.[1]

The early Food Guide designs also reflect an ignorance of the importance of diets low in fat and high in fibre. In the Canadian Food Guide, for example, butter was placed in the breads and cereals food group.[2] Nutritionally, these foods have nothing in common and the classification of them together in one group is unjustified. In later years, American nutrition authorities gradually reduced the number of groups in the Food Guide until, in 1956, there were only four food groups left. Intense lobbying pressures from livestock and dairy industries ensured that two of the four groups in this scheme were animal products, an even greater share than in previous designs.[3] In this form, the four food groups were fruits and vegetables, beans and cereals, meat, and dairy. Consumers were encouraged to eat equal amounts from each group, and the guide was accordingly shaped into four equally sized squares.

Scientific research, however, eventually forced a reexamination of this Food Guide design. A recommended daily intake was specified for an increasing number of nutrients. Many of the nutrients being added were available only from plant foods. Since the Food Guide in use was heavily biased in favor of animal products, those who followed it faithfully would routinely fail to meet many of these recommended daily intakes. This fact was documented in a study conducted in 1978 which showed that only nine of the 17 Recommended Daily Allowances (RDA's) could be obtained if one followed a diet constructed according to the Four Food Groups guide. Such a diet would typically lack sufficient Vitamin C, found in fruits and vegetables, and Vitamin E, folacin, magnesium, and zinc, all of which are found in dark-green leafy vegetables.[4] The Four Food Groups, therefore, were making it difficult for North Americans to satisfy their requirements for several vitamins and minerals predominantly available from plant foods.

The preoccupation with animal foods as exemplified in the Food Guide was failing consumers in another critical area. North Americans were eating too much saturated fat and cholesterol and not enough dietary fibre. In 1988, the U.S. Surgeon General's *Report on Health and Nutrition* stated that although malnutrition remained a problem for some Americans, "for most of us the more likely problem has become one of overeating—too many calories for our activity levels and an imbalance in the nutrients consumed along with them." The main conclusion of the report was that "overconsumption of certain dietary components is now a major concern for Americans . . . the disproportionate consumption of foods high in fats, often at the expense of foods high in complex carbohydrates and fibre that may be more conducive to health."[5] In short, North Americans were eating too many animal products and not enough plant foods—too much butter and not enough bread.

The importance of nutrition in the development of major chronic diseases was increasingly being realized and nutritional recommendations to the public finally began to catch up. In the late 1980s, the American Heart Association, American Cancer Society, United States Department of Agriculture and National Cancer Institute all recommended a major shift in the American diet. Unaminously, they suggested that Americans eat less fat, particularly saturated fat, increase their consumption of complex carbohydrates and fibre through breads, cereals, and other starchy foods, and increase the quantity and variety of fruits and vegetables in their diets.[6]

It was recognized that the old four food groups were limited in their ability to promote such dietary change and, in 1992, Canada and the U.S. adopted revised food guides. In Canada, the Food Guide was converted to a rainbow, with the outer and largest strip representing breads and cereals, the second one representing fruits and vegetables, the third one representing meat and alternatives and the smallest inner strip representing dairy products.[7] Americans adopted a inverted pyramid, placing similar emphasis on fruits, vegetables, and grains. The reduced prominence of animal products in the revised Food Guide raised alarm among beef producers in the U.S. Under pressure from their powerful lobby, the U.S. Secretary of Agriculture tentatively withdrew the pyramid design just before its scheduled release date in June, 1991.[8] Not much of a scientific case could be made against the long-overdue changes contained in the Guide and it was eventually released to the public. According to the pyramid Food Guide, people should eat five to 10 servings of grains, five to eight servings of fruits and vegetables, two to three servings of dairy and two to three servings of meat and alternatives, which include legumes and nuts. Followers of the new Food Guide were urged to think of chicken, fish, and other animal foods as side dishes and legumes, grains, and vegetables as the main courses.

Although the revised Food Guides signal a clear shift in thinking among legislative organizations about what North Americans should be eating, they have not sufficiently addressed the issues of dietary fat, cholesterol, and lack of fiber, that are so significant in the development of heart disease, cancer, and other chronic diseases.[9] For example, the revised Food Guide classifies beans and meat in the same food group, implying that the consumption of these dramatically different foods is somehow equivalent and interchangeable. According to the Food Guide recommendations, the meat and alternatives servings could be met with either eggs or beans. Although both foods are high in protein, beans contain no cholesterol or saturated fat and are high in fibre. A person who consistently avoids eggs would eliminate a major source of cholesterol in his or her diet. But these factors are not considered in the Food Guide revisions.

The failings of the recently revised American and Canadian Food Guides are addressed in a dietary plan called the "New Four Food Groups" proposed by the Physicians' Committee on Responsible Medicine, a Washington-based physicians' group. The New Four Food Groups have been endorsed by many leading researchers in the nutrition field, including Dr. T. Colin Campbell of Cornell University and Dr. Denis Burkitt, the pioneering fiber researcher. In this scheme, the four food groups are legumes, fruits, vegetables and grains. For the average adult, a healthy diet would include five servings of grains, three servings of legumes, three servings of vegetables, and three servings of fruit. Since all the foods in the four groups are healthy, there is no warning to eat particular foods in moderation. Animal products are considered only as an optional part of the diet and are placed in the same category as vegetable oils, alcoholic beverages, and nuts. The design of the New Four Food Groups suggests that ideal human nutrition will likely consist of a diet similar in composition to that of our evolutionary ancestors, and hence entail the virtual elimination of all animal products.[10] In designing their plan, the Physicians' Committee for Responsible Medicine has drawn on clinical and epidemiological evidence which suggests that the ideal fat intake should be much lower than the one currently recommended by public health agencies. Because the process of change among major public health agencies is gradual, the organization's founder, Dr. Neal Barnard, predicts that the New Four Foods groups will not be accepted by public agencies for another 30 to 40 years.

Although nutritional authorities will likely be slow in accepting the New Four Food Groups, they have already revised their views on vegetarianism. The seismic shift in nutritional opinion that has occurred in recent years has cast vegetarianism in a new light. Summarizing research experience in the area of vegetarian diets, Australian scientist Dr. Beilin wrote:

> It is clear from numerous studies by the authors and others that, in comparison to omnivores, vegetarians eat substantially more whole grain cereals, vegetable oils, polyunsaturated margarine, fruits, vegetables, and vegetable protein. This dietary pattern results in a greater intake of dietary fibre, polyunsaturated fats, Vitamin C, Vitamin E, . . . potassium, magnesium, and calcium and lower intakes of saturated fat, cholesterol and protein.[11]

It has also been shown that vegetarians have a higher mean intake of thiamin, riboflavin, Vitamins A, B, and D than non-vegetarians.[12,13] Where formerly authorities regarded vegetarian diets with suspicion, they now offer endorsement. In 1988, the American Dietetic Association stated that "vegetarian diets are healthful and nutritionally adequate when appropriately planned."[14] Moreover, it recognized that "it may be easier, as well as more acceptable, for some individuals to meet the Dietary Guidelines for Americans by following a vegetarian diet rather than a non-vegetarian diet," pointing to the fact that "vegetarian diets that are low in animal foods are typically lower than non-vegetarian diets in total fat, saturated fat, and cholesterol, an important factor in risk reduction for heart disease and some forms of cancer." On questions of protein and other deficiencies, the American Dietetic Association recognized that "vegetarian diets do not have any special nutritional requirements."

The history of food guidance shows the dramatic change in the expert opinion on a vegetarian diet, once regarding it as a questionable alternative and now seeing it as a desirable ideal. In spite of this change, concerns are still raised about the availability of certain nutrients in a vegetarian diet, particularly protein, iron, and Vitamin B12. Naysayers routinely wave these suspicions about in an ill-informed attempt to counter the considerable evidence in favor of vegetarian nutrition. We shall briefly discuss these topics in order to put to rest any persistent reservations about the nutritional adequacy of a diet free of animal products.

When concerns about the protein adequacy of vegetarian diets were first raised, meat was believed to offer a superior-quality protein because all essential amino acids were contained in a single serving of meat. Since it was believed that plant food contained incomplete protein, vegetarians were urged to combine their foods to ensure sufficient protein intake. The view that plant protein is incomplete is only sustainable if different foods are studied in isolation. It is, however, very misleading to consider only individual foods, because a pure vegetarian diet will include many different sources of protein that ensure nutritional adequacy.[15] Indeed, Health and Welfare Canada[16] now recognizes that "vegetarian diets have an overall protein quality, in terms of the amino acids they contain, that seems generally comparable to that of the mixed Canadian diet." In addition, authorities such as the American Dietetic Association acknowledge that the amino acid profiles of protein from a mixture of grains, legumes, vegetables, seeds, and nuts eaten throughout the day complement each other without the need to specifically combine proteins. No special care is required whether the diet includes animal products or not. Indeed, it would be quite difficult for a vegetarian eating enough calories and a balanced diet *not* to meet the required intake of protein.

In recent years, the debate about protein quality has, in fact, reversed. There is a growing awareness of the perils of excessive protein consumption revealed through recent studies linking high protein intake to osteoporosis and kidney failure, and high intakes of animal foods in general to heart disease and other chronic afflictions. Some scientists argue that plant food is superior to animal food as a protein source, because it provides an adequate supply of essential amino acids without excess protein and saturated fat and without any cholesterol.[17]

Since sources of iron are abundant in a vegetarian diet, vegetarians usually have a good iron status.[18] Iron is commonly obtained from such sources as dark-green leafy vegetables, iron-fortified cereals, whole grains, lentils, chick peas, raisins and other dried fruit.[19] In addition, the higher levels of Vitamin C in vegetarian diets improve the absorption of iron from food.

Vitamin B12 is produced by bacteria. Humans have traditionally obtained it from the food on which B12-producing bacteria live. The requirement is so minute that, in earlier times, dirty root vegetables would have contained enough B12 to satisfy the body's needs. However, because of modern food processing and hygiene, vegan diets no longer contain an adequate source of vitamin B12. Although B12 deficiency is very rare in vegans, people pursuing a vegan diet should ensure that they supplement their diet with B12.[20] Vegetarians who consume some animal products will receive an adequate supply through this source.

In addition to protein, iron, and B12, concerns are sometimes raised about zinc, calcium, and other minerals. However, vegetarian populations show no gross mineral deficiencies.[21] In a well-balanced and varied vegetarian diet, the problems of deficiency are rarely encountered, and the healthy benefits of a diet low in fat and cholesterol and high in fibre, fruits, and vegetables are easily seen.

In planning a vegetarian diet, variety is the key. It is not likely that people reducing the amount of animal products in their diet will be able to eat a sufficiently varied diet by simply cooking vegetables the way they have been used to. They may need to learn new recipes that allow them to cook vegetables as main courses and not as side dishes. Those becoming vegetarian can take comfort in the fact that the traditional diets of many cultures and civilizations have been primarily vegetarian. As the many vegetarian cook books now available will reveal, there is a wide variety of food available to the vegetarian cook.

A Matter of Choice

Although vegetarianism has had a long and diverse history, the justification for a plant-food diet has perhaps never been stronger than it is today. Tracing human evolution from our origins as primates reveals that we are naturally suited to a diet that is overwhelmingly constituted of plant foods. Like our nearest evolutionary relatives, we are essentially a herbivorous species, and have been so for most of our existence. Even after the agricultural revolution, the amount of animal products in the diet remained very small for most people. It was only after productivity and wealth increased dramatically through industrialization that the majority of people in our society were able to eat meat on a regular basis. At present, animal products provide more than half the calories in the average North American diet, a level that is a dramatic divergence from our evolutionary past.

Not surprisingly, this aberration has had dramatic consequences for our diet and health. The rise in dietary saturated fat, cholesterol, and animal protein and the decline in fruits, vegetables, and dietary fiber, that have accompanied increased animal-product consumption have been implicated in heart disease, cancer, diabetes, high blood pressure, and numerous other prevalent chronic diseases. From the perspective of health alone, we should drastically reduce the amount of animal food we eat, whether it be from meat, fish, chicken, or dairy products. This realization is gradually altering recommendations put out by nutritional authorities. A Food Guide that once encouraged us to eat equal amounts of plant and animal foods has recently been replaced by one that encourages us to eat much more plant food. In time, this limited change may well be replaced by a "New Four Food

Groups" guide presently endorsed by many leading nutritional scientists. This guide suggests that our optimal diet would
consist of grains, vegetables, fruits, nuts, seeds, and legumes.

The decision to choose our diet according to such
guidelines would benefit not only our own health, but the
health of the planet as well. As considerations of resource
consumption and waste production reveal, the ecological
cost of animal foods is enormous. Single servings of meat
consume many times more land, water, and energy and generate far more waste than nutritionally equivalent amounts
of plant food. As our awareness of ecological issues grows,
many of us are increasingly willing to undertake "environ-
mentally friendly" initiatives such as recycling or composting.
To act more extensively and effectively on the ecological
problems we face, we must also drastically reduce the
amount of animal food in our diet.

As a result of the resource intensity of a diet high in
animal products, the conversion of the average North American meat-eater to vegetarianism frees up enough land to feed
10 other people on vegetarian diets. In an era of increasing
pressures on food security and declining growth in agricultural yields, a redistribution of the global grain harvest from feed
for animals to food for humans is essential.

In response to these medical and environmental concerns, many chose to become semi-vegetarian, lacto-ovo-
vegetarian, or lacto-vegetarian. But, it is also important to
note that if we choose to continue to eat animal products
at some level, even milk and other dairy products, we will
continue to contribute to the practices of factory farming.
The conditions in industrial animal raising are characterized
by confinement, crowding, noise and aggression. These
highly artificial and manipulated environments cause considerable stress to the animals they contain; stress which can
reasonably be considered to cause suffering not much unlike
that felt by humans animals.

The decision to eliminate animal products completely or
only to simply reduce the level of animal products is a per-

sonal one. But, as the evolutionary, health, ecological, and animal welfare perspectives suggest, the progressive elimination of animal foods yields many benefits. Whether we are meat-eaters, lacto-ovo-vegetarians, or lacto-vegetarians, by taking steps towards a plant-food diet, we each directly contribute to our own health, to the health of the planet, and to the welfare of non-human animals. We become kinder citizens of planet earth, seeking to live a life orchestrated to the rhythms of the world around us.

Notes/References

Origins

1. Brian M. Fagan, *People of the Earth: An Introduction to World Prehistory* (Boston: Little, Brown and Company, 1986), 76.

2. Katharine Milton, "Diet and Primate Evolution," *Scientific American* 1993;269(2):86-93.

3. Fagan, *People of the Earth*, 77.

4. Adrienne Zihlman and Nancy Tanner, "Gathering and the Hominid Adaptation," in *Female Hierarchies*, ed. Lionel Tiger and Heather T. Fowler (Chicago: Beresford Book Service, 1975), 167.

5. Fagan, *People of the Earth*, 78.

6. Zihlman and Tanner, "Gathering and the Hominid Adaptation," in Tiger and Fowler, *Female Hierarchies*, 177.

7. Ronald L. Wallace, *Those Who Have Vanished: An Introduction to Prehistory* (Homewood: The Dorsey Press, 1983), 50.

8. Helene Roche, "The Beginnings of the Human Adventure," in *Prehistory: The World of Early Man*, ed. Jean Guilaine, trans. Stephen Bunson (Oxford: Facts on File, 1986), 33-41.

9. Fagan, *People of the Earth*, 91.

10. Milton, "Diet and Primate Evolution," 91.

11. Peter Andrews and Lawrence Martin, "Hominid dietary evolution," in *Foraging Strategies and Natural Diet of Monkeys, Apes, and Humans*, eds. A. Whiten and E. M. Widdowson (Oxford: Clarendon Press, 1992), 39-49.

12. Fagan, *People of the Earth*, 97.

13. Roche, "The Beginnings of the Human Adventure," in Guilaine and Bunson, *Prehistory: The World of Early Man*, 36.

14.   Fagan, *People of the Earth*, 98.

15.   Carol A. Bryant, et al, *The Cultural Feast: An Introduction to Food and Society* (New York: West Publishing Company, 1985), 26.

16.   Milton, "Diet and Primate Evolution," 93.

17.   Robert J. Blumenschine, "Hominid carnivory and foraging strategies, and the socio-economic function of early archeological sites," in *Foraging Strategies and Natural Diet of Monkeys, Apes, and Humans*, eds. A. Whiten and E. M. Widdowson (Oxford: Clarendon Press, 1992), 51-61.

18.   Robert J. Wenke, *Patterns in Prehistory: Humankind's First Three Million Years* (Oxford: Oxford University Press, 1984), 104.

19.   Marvin Harris, *Culture, People and Nature: An Introduction to General Anthropology*, 3rd ed. (New York: Harper and Row, 1980), 86.

20.   Fagan, *People of the Earth*, 129.

21.   Bryant, *The Cultural Feast: An Introduction to Food and Society*, 27-29.

22.   Fagan, *People of the Earth*, 126.

23.   Zihlman and Tanner, "Gathering and the Hominid Adaptation," in Tiger and Fowler, *Female Hierarchies*, 170-7.

24.   Colin Spencer, *The Heretic's Feast* (London: Fourth Estate, 1993), 16.

25.   A. W. Crompton and K. Hiiemae, "How mammalian teeth work," *Discovery* 1969;5(1):23-24.

26.   Kay Martin and Barbara Voorhies, *The Female of the Species* (New York: Columbia University Press, 1975).

27.   Fagan, *People of the Earth*, 146.

28.   Zihlman and Tanner, "Gathering and the Hominid Adaptation," in Tiger and Fowler, *Female Hierarchies*, 183.

29.   Stephen Boyden, *Western Civilization in Biological Perspective* (Oxford: Oxford University Press, 1988), 261.

30.   Spencer, *The Heretic's Feast*, 17.

31.   Karl Butzer, *Environment and Archaeology: An Ecological Approach to Prehistory* (Chicago: Aldine, 1971).

32.   Fagan, *People of the Earth*, 127.

33.   Milton, "Primate diet and gut morphology: implications for hominid evolution," in *Food and Evolution: Toward a Theory of Human Food Habits*. ed. Marvin Harris and Eric B. Ross (Philadelphia: Temple University Press, 1987), 93-116.

34.   Spencer, *The Heretic's Feast*, 17.

35.   S. B. Eaton and M. Konner, "Paleolithic nutrition: a consideration of its nature and current implications," *N Engl J Med* 1985;312:283-289.

36.   Spencer, *The Heretic's Feast*, 17.

37.   Jean Guilaine, "The First Farmers of the Old World," in *Prehistory: The World of Early Man*. ed. Jean Guilaine, trans. Stephen Bunson (Oxford: Facts on File, 1986), 81.

38.   Boyden, *Western Civilization in Biological Perspective*, 87.

39.   S. J. Ulijaszek, "Human dietary change," in *Foraging Strategies and Natural Diet of Monkeys, Apes, and Humans*, ed. A. Whiten and E. M. Widdowson (Oxford: Clarendon Press, 1992), pp 111-119.

40.   Boyden, *Western Civilization in Biological Perspective*, 120.

41.   Hugh Trowell and Denis Burkitt, "Emergence of Western diseases in sub-Saharal Africans," in *Western Diseases: their emergence and prevention*, eds. Hugh Trowell and Denis Burkitt (London: Edward Arnold Ltd, 1981), 15.

42.   Spencer, *The Heretic's Feast*, 28.

43.   Boyden, *Western Civilization in Biological Perspective*, 261.

44.   Trowell and Burkitt, "Emergence of Western diseases in sub-Saharal Africans," in Trowell and Burkitt, *Western Diseases: their emergence and prevention*, 19.

45.   Denis Burkitt and Hugh Trowell, *Refined Carbohydrate Foods and Disease: Some Implications of Dietary Fibre* (London: Academic Press, 1975), 140.

46.   Food and Agricultural Organization, *FAO Production Year-book* (Rome: FAO, 1992).

47.   Food and Agricultural Organization, *World Agricultural Statistics* (Rome: FAO, 1986).

48.   Alan Thein Durning and Holly B. Brough, "Reforming the Livestock Industry," in *State of the World, 1992*, ed. Lester Brown (New York: W. W. Norton and Company, 1992), 67.

49.   Food and Agricultural Organization, *The World Meat Economy in Figures* (Rome: FAO, 1984).

50.   Nikos Alexadratos, et al, *Agriculture from the perspective of population growth* (Rome: FAO, 1983).

51.   Durning and Brough, "Reforming the Livestock Industry," in Brown, *State of the World, 1992*

52.   Michael Klaper, *Vegan Nutrition: Pure and Simple* (Umatilla: Gentle World, Inc., 1987), 13.

53.   statistics from Agriculture Canada and the US Department of Agriculture

54.   Boyden, *Western Civilization in Biological Perspective*, 261.

55.   Milton, "Diet and Primate Evolution," 93.

Diet and Disease

1.   J. Litvak, et al, "The growing noncommunicable disease burden, a challenge for the countries of the Americas," *Bulletin of the Pan American Health Organization* 1988;21:156-171.

2.   World Health Organization, *Diet, nutrition, and the prevention of chronic diseases: Report of a WHO Study Group* (Geneva: World Health Organization, 1990), 54.

3.   Joint Nutrition Monitoring Evaluation Committee, *Nutrition Monitoring in the United States* (Hyattsville: US Department of Health and Human Services, 1986), 189.

4.   Stephen Boyden, *Western Civilization in Biological Perspective: Patterns in Biohistory* (Oxford: Clarendon Press, 1987), 240.

5.   Dudley Giehl, *Vegetarianism: A Way of Life* (New York: Harper and Row, 1979), 34.

6.   D. A. Snowdon, et al, "Meat consumption and fatal ischemic heart disease." *Preventive Medicine* 1984;13:490-500.

7.   V. Fonnebo, "Mortality in Norwegian Seventh-Day Adventists 1962-1986," *Journal of Clinical Epidemiology* 1992;45(2):157-67.

8.   Z. Chen, R. Peto, R. Collins, et al, "Serum cholesterol concentration and coronary heart disease in population with low cholesterol concentrations," *British Medical Journal* 1991;303:276-282.

9.   "Study boost for vegetarian diets", *Calgary Herald*, May 25, 1990, E10.

10.   A. Keys, *Seven Countries: A multivariate analysis of death and coronary heart disease* (Cambridge: Harvard University Press, 1980).

11.   D. A. Stallones, Ischemic heart disease and lipid in blood and diet," *Annual Review of Nutrition* 1983;3:155-185.

12.   J. Stamler, "Nutrition-related risk factors for the atherosclerotic disease—present status," *Prog. Biochem. Pharamcol* 1983;19:245-308.

13.   Health and Welfare Canada, *Nutrition Recommendations: Report of the Scientific Review Committee* (Ottawa: Government Publishing Centre, 1990), 40.

14.   Michael Klaper, *Vegan Nutrition: Pure and Simple* (Umatilla: Gentle World Inc., 1987), 5.

15.   F. M. Sacks, et al, "Plasma lipids and lipoproteins in vegetarians and controls," *New England Journal of Medicine* 1975;292: 1148-51.

16.   M. Sei, T. Miyoshi, "Changes in nutritional factors related to regional differences in the mortality of cardiovascular disease between 1966 and 1985 in Japan," *Japanese Journal of Hygiene* 1991;47(5):901-12.

17.   K. K. Carroll, P. M. Giovannetti, M. W. Huff, et al, "Hypocho-lesterolemic effect of substituting soybean protein for animal pro-tein in the diets of healthy young women," *Am J Clin Nutr* 1978;31:1312-1320.

18.   Health and Welfare Canada, *Nutrition Recommendations*, 37.

19.   L. H. Kushi, R. A. Lew, F. J. Stare, et al, "Diet and 20 year mortal-ity from coronary heart disease," *N Engl J Med* 1985;312:811-818.

20.   D. J. A. Jenkins, T. M. S. Wolever, A. V. Rao, et al, "Effect on blood lipids of very high intakes of fiber in diets low in saturated fat and cholesterol," *New Engl J Med* 1993;329:21-6.

21.   Dean Ornish, "Can you prevent-and reverse-CAD?," *Patient Care* 1991;25-41.

22.   D. Ornish, S. E. Brown, L. W. Scherwitz, et al, "Can lifestyle changes reverse coronary heart disease?: The Lifestyle Heart Trial," *Lancet* 1990;336:129-33.

23.   Joint Nutrition Monitoring Evaluation Committee, *Nutrition Monitoring in the United States*, 201.

24.   M. S. R. Hutt and D. P. Burkitt, *The Geography of Non-Infec-tious Disease* (Oxford: Oxford University Press, 1986), 28.

25.   D. Trichhopoulos, et al, "The effect of Westernization on urine estrogens, frequency of ovulation, and breast cancer risks: a study in ethnic Chinese women in the Orient and in the USA," *Cancer* 1984;53:187-92.

26.   M. Minowa, et al, "Dietary fiber intake in Japan," *Human Nutr. Appl Nutr.* 1983;37A:113-119.

27.   R. Doll and R. Peto, *The Causes of Cancer* (Oxford: Oxford University Press, 1981).

28.   T. Hirayama, "Mortality in Japanese with life-styles similar to Seventh-Day Adventists: strategy for risk reduction by lifestyle modification," *National Cancer Institute Monographs* 1985;69: 143-53.

29.   H. W. Lane, J. T. Carpenter, "Breast cancer: incidence, nutri-tional concerns, and treatment approaches," *J Am Diet Assoc*

1987;87:765-769.

30. W. C. Willet, M. J. Stampfer, et al, "Relation of meat, fat and fiber intake to the risk of colon cancer in a prospective study among women," *New Engl J Med* 1990;323:1664-72.

31. National Research Council. *Diet, Nutrition, and Cancer.* National Academy of Sciences, Washington, D.C. National Academy Press, 1982.

32. World Health Organization, *Diet, nutrition, and the prevention of chronic diseases,* 91.

33. D. P. Burkitt and H. C. Trowell, *Refined Carbohydrate Foods and Disease: Some Implications of Dietary Fibre* (London: Academic Press, 1975), 129.

34. G. Johansson, A. Holmen, L. Persson, et al, "The effect of a shift from a mixed diet to a lacto-vegetarian diet on human urinary and fecal mutagenic activity," *Carcinogenesis* 1992;13(2):153-7.

35. World Health Organization. *Diet, nutrition, and the prevention of chronic diseases,* 26.

36. Physicians Committee for Responsible Medicine. *Foods for Cancer Prevention* (fact sheet) (Washington: Physicians Committee for Responsible Medicine, 1992).

37. G. E. Fraser, et al, "A possible protective effect of nut consumption on risk of coronary heart disease: The Adventist Health Study," *Arch Intern Med* 1992;152(7):1416-24.

38. R. G. Zeigler, "Vegetables, fruits, and carotenoids and the risk of cancer," *Am J Clin Nutr* 1991;53:51S-9S.

39. M. Malter, G. Schriever, U. Eilber, "Natural killer cells, vitamins, and other blood components of vegetarian and omnivorous men," *Nutrition and Cancer* 1989;12(3):271-8.

40. G. K. Johansson, L. Ottova, J. A. Gustafsson, "Shift from a mixed diet to a lactovegetarian diet: influence on some cancer-associated intestinal bacteria enzyme activities," *Nutrition and Cancer* 1990;14(3-4):239-246.

41.   B. Jansson, "Geographic cancer risk and intracellular potassium/sodium ratios," *Cancer Detection & Prevention* 1986;9:171-94.

42.   "Red Meat Lovers Get Cancer Warning," *The Globe and Mail,* December 13, 1990, pg A1.

43.   Joint Nutrition Monitoring Evaluation Committee. *Nutrition Monitoring in the United States,* 189.

44.   World Health Organization. *Diet, nutrition, and the prevention of chronic diseases,* 74.

45.   Johanna T. Dwyer, "Health Aspects of a Vegetarian Diet," *Am J Clin Nutr* 1988;48:712-38.

46.   D. A. Snowdon, R. L. Phillips, "Does a vegetarian diet reduce the occurrence of diabetes?," *American Journal of Public Health* 1985;75:507-12.

47.   W. Bruns, "New knowledge of diet therapy of type 2 diabetes," *Zeitschrift Fur Die Gesemte Innere Medizin Und Ihre Grenzgebiete* 1990;45(10):290-4.

48.   A. N. Donaldson, "The relation of protein foods to hypertension." *Calif West Med* 1926;24:328-331.

49.   F. M. Sacks, et al, "Blood pressure in vegetarians," *Am J Epidemiol* 1974;100:390-398.

50.   I. L. Rouse, B. K. Armstrong, L. J. Beilin, "The relationship of blood pressure to diet and lifestyle in two religious populations," *J Hypertens* 1983;1:65-71.

51.   Joint Nutrition Monitoring Evaluation Committee. *Nutrition Monitoring in the United States,* 209.

52.   I. L. Rouse, L. J. Beilin, "Vegetarian and Other Complex Diets, Fiber Intake and Blood Pressure," in *Hypertension: Pathophysiology, Diagnosis and Management.* ed. JH Laragh, et al (New York: Raven Press, 1990), 241-55.

53.   World Health Organization. *Diet, nutrition, and the prevention of chronic diseases,* 59.

54.   L. B. Page, "Nutritional determinants of hypertension," *Curr Concepts Nutr* 1981;10:113-26.

55. Intersalt Cooperative Research Group, "Intersalt: an international study of electrolyte excretion and blood pressure. Results for 24 hour urinary sodium and potassium excretion," *British Medical Journal* 1988;297:319-328.

56. B. Armstrong, H. Clark, C. Martin, et al, "Urinary sodium and blood pressure in vegetarians," *Am J Clin Nutr* 1979;32:2472-2476.

57. B. M. Margetts, L. J. Beilin, R. Vandongen, et al, "A randomized controlled trial of the effect of dietary fibre on blood pressure," *Clin Sci* 1987;72:343- 350.

58. B. M. Margetts, L. J. Beilin, R. Vandongen, et al, "Vegetarian diet in mild hypertension: a randomized controlled trial," *Br Med J* 1986;293:1468-1471.

59. N. Gretz, E. Meisinger, M. Strauch, "Does a low protein diet really slow- down the rate of progression of chronic renal failure?," *Blood Purification* 1989;7(1):33-8.

60. M. J. Wiseman, et al, "Dietary composition and renal function in healthy subjects," *Nephron* 1987;46:37-42.

61. as quoted in Geihl, *Vegetarianism: A Way of Life*, 29-30.

62. Joint Nutrition Monitoring Evaluation Committee, *Nutrition Monitoring in the United States* (Hyattsville, Maryland: US Department of Health and Human Services, 1990), 82.

63. B. L. Riggs, L. J. Melton, "Involutional osteoporosis," *New Engl J Med* 1986:314;1676-1686.

64. S. R. Cummings, et al, "Epidemiology of osteoporosis and osteoporotic fractures," *Epidemiologic reviews* 1985;7:178-208.

65. Burkitt and Trowell, *Refined Carbohydrate Foods and Disease: Some Implications of Dietary Fibre*, 50.

66. World Health Organization. *Diet, nutrition, and the prevention of chronic diseases*, 67.

67. D. M. Hegsted, "Calcium and osteoporosis," *J Nutr* 1986;116: 2316-9.

68. Joint Nutrition Monitoring Evaluation Committee. *Nutrition Monitoring in the United States*, 252.

69.   L. Allen, "Protein induced hypercalcuria: a longer term study," *Amer J Clin Nutr* 1979;32:485.

70.   A. G. Marsh, T. V. Sanchez, O. Michelsen, et al, "Vegetarian lifestyle and bone mineral density," *Amer J Clin Nutr* 1988;48:837-41.

71.   F. Tylavsky, J. J. B. Anderson, "Dietary factors in bone health of elderly lactoovovegetarian and omnivorous women," *Amer J Clin Nutr* 1988;48:842-9.

72.   W. G. Robertson, et al, "Should recurrent calcium oxalate stone formers become vegetarians?," *British Journal of Urology* 1979;51:427-31.

73.   W. G. Robertson, et al, "The effect of high animal protein intake on the risk of calcium stone formation in the urinary tract," *Clinical Science* 1979;57:285-88.

74.   M. Marangella, et al, "Effect of animal and vegetable protein intake on oxalate excretion in idiopathic calcium stone formers," *British Journal of Urology* 1989;63(4):348-51.

75.   American Medical Association, *Family Medical Guide* (New York: Random House, 1982), 489.

76.   F. Pixley, J. Mann, "Dietary factors in the etiology of gall stones: a case control study," *Gut* 1988;29:1511-5.

77.   K. M. Maclure, et al, "Dietary predictors of symptom-associated gallstones in middle-aged women," *Amer J Clin Nutr* 1990; 52 (5):916-22.

78.   Hutt and Burkitt. *The Geography of Non-Infectious Disease*, 126.

79.   J. Kjeldsen-Kragh, et al, "Controlled trial of fasting and one-year vegetarian diet in rheumatoid arthritis," *Lancet* 1991; 338 (8772): 899-902.

80.   R. Frentzel-Beyme, J. Claude, U. Eilber, "Mortality among German vegetarians: first results after five years of follow-up," *Nutrition and Cancer* 1988;11:117-26.

Plants, Animals, and the Planet

1. K. E. Erikkson and K. H. Robert, "From the Big Bang to Sustainable Societies," *Reviews in Oncology* 4(2) 1991: 10.

2. Stephen Boyden, *Western Civilization in Biological Prespective* (Toronto: Oxford University Press, 1987), 7-10.

3. World Conservation Union, World Wide Fund for Nature, and United Nations Environment Programme, *Caring for the Earth* (Geneva: The World Conservation Union, World Wide Fund for Nature, and the United Nations Environment Programme, 1992), 10-20.

4. Jeremy Rifkin, *Beyond Beef* (New York: Dutton, 1992).

5. Food and Agriculture Organization of the United Nations, *The World Meat Economy in Figures* (Rome: Food and Agriculture Organization, 1984).

6. Paul Harrison, *The Third Revolution* (New York: I.B. Tauris & Co., 1992), 116-121.

7. T. Young and M. P. Burton, *Agricultural sustainability: definitions and implications for agricultural and trade policy* (Rome: Food and Agriculture Organization, 1992).

8. A. B. Daugherty, *Major Uses of Land in the US* (Washington: United States Deparment of Agriculture, 1991.

9. Harrison, *The Third Revolution*, 95.

10. L. Jacobs, "Amazing Graze: How the Livestock Industry Is Ruining the American West," *Desertification Control Bulletin* no 17. 13-17.

11. Rifkin, *Beyond Beef*, 145.

12. Donella Meadows, Dennis L. Meadows, and Jorgen Randers, *Beyond the Limits* (Post Mills: Chelsea Green Publishing Company, 1992), 60.

13. Harrison, *The Third Revolution*, 97.

14. S. B. Hecht, "The Sacred Cow in the Green Hell: Livestock

and Forest Conversion in the Brazilian Amazon," *Ecologist* 19(6) 1989: 220-234.

15.   Christopher Uhl and Geoffery Parker, "Our Steak in the Jungle," *BioScience* 36(10), 642.

16.   John Robbins, *Diet for A New America* (Santa Cruz: Stillpoint Publishing, 1986).

17.   Uhl, "Our Steak in the Jungle", 642.

18.   Meadows, *Beyond the Limits,* 56-57.

19.   S. Poster, *Water for Agriculture: Facing the Limits* (Washington: World Watch Institute, 1989).

20.   Alan T. Durning and Holly B. Brough, "Reforming the Livestock Industry" in *State of the World 1992,* ed. Lester Brown (New York: W.W. Norton and Company, 1992), 67.

21.   Lappe, Francis Moore, *Diet for a Small Planet* (New York: Ballantine Books, 1982), 76.

22.   William Graves, "When the well's dry, we know the worth of water," *National Geographic* (November 1993), 1.

23.   David Pimental and Marcia Pimentel, *Food, Energy and Society* (London: Edward Arnold, 1979), 59.

24.   Pimentel, *Food, Energy and Society,* 90.

25.   Pimentel, *Food, Energy and Society,* 95.

26.   Meadows, *Beyond the Limits,* 70-72.

27.   Judith Stone, "Bovine Madness" *Discover* (February, 1989), 38-40.

28.   Durning, "Reforming the Livestock Industry", 72.

29.   Rifkin, *Beyond Beef.*

30.   Stone, "Bovine Madness", 40.

31.   J. N. Pretty and G. R. Conway, *Agriculture as a Global Polluter* (London: International Institute for Sustainable Development, 1989).

32. Michael Klaper, *Vegan Nutrition* (Umatilla: Gentle World, 1987), 35.

33. G. Tamminga and J. Wijnando, "Animal Waste Problems in the Netherlands" in *Farming and the Countryside* ed. N. Hanley (Wallingford: CAB International, 1991).

34. Raymond C. Loehr, *Pollution Control for Agriculture* (Orlando: Academic Press, 1984).

35. Sue Armstrong, "Marooned in a Mountain of Manure," *New Scientist*, 26 November 1988.

36. Michael Parfit, "Troubled Waters Run Deep," *National Geographic* (November, 1993), 78.

37. Robbins, *Diet for A New America*.

38. Durning, "Reforming the Livestock Industry", 70.

39. Nikos Alexadratos, et al., *Agriculture from the perspective of population growth* (Rome: Food and Agriculture Organization of the United Nations, 1983).

40. George Schuyler, *Hunger in a Land of Plenty* (Cambridge: Schenkman Publishing Company, 1980).

41. David Barkin, Rosemary Batt, and Billie R. DeWalt, *Food Crops vs. Feed Crops* (London: Lynne Rienner Publishers, 1990), 35-40.

42. Durning, "Reforming the Livestock Industry", 75.

43. Orville Freeman, "Meeting the Food Needs of the Coming Decade," *The Futurist* (November-December, 1990), 15-20.

44. Harrison, *The Third Revolution*, 205.

45. Freeman, "Meeting the Food Needs of the Coming Decade", 18.

46. United Nations Department of International Economic and Social Affairs, *World Population Prospects* (New York: United Nations Department of International Economic and Social Affairs, 1988).

47. Freeman, "Meeting the Food Needs of The Coming Decade", 20.

48. Meadows, *Beyond the Limits*, 56-57.

49.   Lester Brown and John Young, "Feeding the World in the Nineties" in *State of The World 1990*, ed. Linda Starke (New York: W.W. Norton and Company, 1990).

50.   Freeman, "Meeting the Food Needs of The Coming Decade", 18-20.

51.   Pimentel, *Food, Energy and Society*, 142.

52.   Maarten Chrispeels and David Sadava, *Plants, Food, and People* (San Francisco: W. H. Freeman and Company, 1977), 75.

53.   Arnold Bender, *Meat and meat products in human nutrition in developing countries* (Rome: Food and Agriculture Organization of the United Nations, 1992).

54.   Lester Brown and Erik Eckholm, *By Bread Alone* (New York: Praeger Publishers, 1974).

55.   Pimentel, *Food, Energy and Society*, 142.

Animal Farming

1.   Stephen Boyden, *Western Civilization in Biological Perspective* (New York: Oxford University Press, 1987), 92.

2.   Michael W. Fox, *Farm Animals* (Baltimore: University Park Press, 1984), 1.

3.   David C. Coats, *Old McDonald's Factory Farm* (New York: The Continuum Publishing Company, 1989), 17.

4.   Ruth Harrison, *Animal Machines* (London: Vincent Stuart, 1964).

5.   Marian Dawkins, *Animal Suffering: The Science of Animal Welfare* (London: Chapman and Hall, 1980).

6.   Jim Mason and Peter Singer, *Animal Factories* (New York: Harmony Books, 1990), 5-7.

7.   Alan T. Durning and Holly B. Brough, "Reforming the Livestock Industry" in *State of the World 1992*, ed. Lester Brown (New York: W.W. Norton and Company, 1992), 68.

8.   Mark Gold, *Assault and Battery* (London: Pluto Press, 1983).

9.   Coats, *Old McDonald's Factory Farm*, 84.

10.   Fox, *Farm Animals*, 7-9.

11.   Fox, *Farm Animals*, 31.

12.   Coats, *Old McDonald's Factory Farm*, 92.

13.   Fox, *Farm Animals*, 19.

14.   R. Brambell, *Report of the Technical Committee to Enquire into the Welfare of Animals Kept under intensive livestock husbandry systems* (London: Her Majesty's Stationary Office, 1965).

15.   Ross H. Hall, *Food for Nought* (New York: Vintage Books, 1974), 107.

16.   Fox, *Farm Animals*, 138.

17.   Hall, *Food for Nought*, 101.

18.   Mason, *Animal Factories*, 28.

19.   Orville Schell, *Modern Meat* (New York: Random House, 1984), 79.

20.   Gold, *Assault and Battery*.

21.   Fox, *Farm Animals*, 115.

22.   Coats, *Old McDonald's Factory Farm*, 50-56.

23.   Coats, *Old McDonald's Factory Farm*, 61.

24.   Mason, *Animal Factories*, 9-10

25.   Coats, *Old McDonald's Factory Farm*, 39.

26.   Schell, *Modern Meat*, 45.

27.   Fox, *Farm Animals*, 72.

28.   Mason, *Animal Factories*, 24.

29.   Mason, *Animal Factories*, 7.

30.   Fox, *Farm Animals*, 193.

31.   David W. Sainsbury, "The Influence of Environmental Factors

on the Health of Livestock," *Proceedings of the First International Livestock Environment Symposium.* St. Joseph: American Society of Agricultural Engineers, 1974.

32.   Mason, *Animal Factories,* 50.

33.   Mason, *Animal Factories,* 54.

34.   Richard Lacey, *Unfit for Human Consumption* (Toronto: Souvenir Press, 1991), 31.

35.   Hall, *Food for Nought* (New York: Vintage Books, 1974), 88.

36.   Schell, *Modern Meat,* 6-20.

37.   J. Scharffenberg, *Problems with Meat* (Santa Barbara: Woodbridge Press, 1982).

38.   Schell, *Modern Meat,* 41.

39.   Lacey, *Unfit for Human Consumption,* 53.

40.   Schell, *Modern Meat,* 327.

41.   Mason, *Animal Factories,* 105.

42.   Daisie Radner and Michael Radner, *Animal Consciousness* (New York: Prometheus Books, 1989), 19-20.

43.   Radner, *Animal Consciousness,* 25-37.

44.   Tom Regan, *All that dwell therein* (Berkeley: University of California Press, 1982), 5.

45.   Colin Spencer, *The Heretic's Feast* (London: Fourth Estate, 1993), 189.

46.   Fox, *Farm Animals,* 228.

47.   Jon Franklin, *Molecules of the Mind* (New York: Dell Publishing Co., 1986), 131-135.

48.   Franklin, *Molecules of the Mind,* 214-215.

49.   Donald Griffin, *The Question of Animal Awareness* (New York: Rockefeller University Press, 1976), 104.

50.   Donald Griffin, *The Question of Animal Awareness,* 69.

51.   Richard Watson, "Self-Consciousnes and the Rights of Nonhu-

man Animals and Nature," *Environmental Ethics* 1 (Summer 1979), 99-129.

52.   Peter Singer, *Animal Liberation* (New York: Random House, 1975).

53.   Regan, *All that dwell therein,* 1-39.

54.   Spencer, *The Heretic's Feast,* 209.

Philosopher, Shramans, and Reformers

1.   D. A. Dombrowski, *The Philosophy of Vegetarianism* (Boston: The University of Massachusetts Press, 1984).

2.   Daphne A. Roe, "History of Promotion of Vegetable Cereal Diets," *J Nutr* 116:1355-1363, 1986.

3.   Colin Spencer, *The Heretic's Feast* (London: Fourth Estate, 1993), 96.

4.   *The New Jerusalem Bible: Reader's Edition* (London: Doubleday, 1990).

5.   Janet Barkas, *The Vegetable Passion* (London: Routledge & Kegan Paul, 1975), 46.

6.   Dudley Geihl, *Vegetarianism: A Way of Life* (New York, Harper and Row, 1979), 169.

7.   Spencer, *The Heretic's Feast,* 122-3.

8.   Geihl, *Vegetarianism: A Way of Life,* 163.

9.   Spencer, *The Heretic's Feast,* 140.

10.   Geihl, *Vegetarianism: A Way of Life,* 163.

11.   Spencer, *The Heretic's Feast,* 110.

12.   Roe, "History of Promotion of Vegetable Cereal Diets," pp 1360.

13.   Barkas, *The Vegetable Passion,* 75.

14.   William E. A Axon, *Shelley's Vegetarianism* (New York: Haskell House, 1890).

15. D. A. Dombrowski, *The Philosophy of Vegetarianism*, 25.

16. Barkas, *The Vegetable Passion*, 154-159.

17. Spencer, *The Heretic's Feast*, 279-281.

18. *Little Brown Book of Anecdotes*, ed. Clifton Fadiman (Toronto: Little Brown and Company, 1985), 500-501.

19. Albert Schweitzer, *Reverence for Life*.

20. Geihl, *Vegetarianism: A Way of Life*, 198.

21. Clare Rosenfield, *Gurudev Chitrabhanu: A Man with a Vision* (New York: Jain Meditation International Center, 1981), 286.

22. *The Bhagavad Gita,* trans. Barbara Stoler Miller (New York: Bantam Books, 1986), 137-138.

23. *The Bhagavad Gita,* trans. Shri Purohit Swami (London: Faber and Faber, 1935), 71-72.

24. Thomas Alexander Wise, *Commentary on the Hindu System of Medicine* (Amsterdam: Oriental Press), xi-xii.

25. Chandran D. S. Devanesen, *The Making of the Mahatma* (Bombay: Orient Longmans, 1969), 4-7.

26. Roshi Philip Kapleau, *A Buddhist Case for Vegetarianism* (London: Rider, 1983).

27. *Sources of Indian Tradition, Volume One.* ed. and rev. Ainslie T. Embree. (New York: Columbia University Press, 1993), 245.

28. *Sources of Indian Tradition, Volume One,* 144-6.

29. Spencer, *The Heretic's Feast*, 349-350.

30. F. J. Simoons, *Food in China: A Cultural and Historical Inquiry* (Boston: CRC Press), 32.

31. Simoons, *Food in China: A Cultural and Historial Inquiry*, 34.

32. Thelma Barer-Stein, *You Eat What You Are: A Study of Canadian Ethnic Food Traditions* (Toronto: McClelland and Stewart, 1979), 107.

33. Margaret Leeming, *A History of Food: From Manna to Microwave* (London: BBC Book, 1991), 37.

34. Spencer, *The Heretic's Feast*, 350.

35. Barer-Stein, *You Eat What You Are*, 338.

36. Leeming, *A History of Food*, 36.

37. "More Canadians turn vegetarian". *The Calgary Herald.* November 27, 1992, pp C5.

38. Marie Nightengale. "Vegetarians gain new respect". *The Halifax Chronicle Herald.* July 3, 1991, pp B3.

Plant-Food Nutrition

1. Claude Villee, *Biology* (Toronto: Saunders College Publishing, 1985).

2. Minister of National Health and Welfare, *Action Towards Health Eating* (Ottawa: Minister of Supply and Services, 1990), 22.

3. Nathanial Altman, "Revising the Basic Four", *Vegetarian Times* (September/October 1977).

4. J. C. King and S. H. Cohenour, "Evaluation and Modification of the basic four food group guide," *Journal of Nutrition Education* (10) 1978: 27-29.

5. U.S. Department of Health and Human Services. *The Surgeon General's Report on Nutrition and Health* (Washington: U.S. Department Health and Human Services, 1988).

6. R. R. Butrum, C. K. Clifford, and E. Lanze, "NCI dietary guidelines: rationale", *American Journal of Clinical Nutrition* (48) 1988: 888-95.

7. Health and Welfare Canada, Canada's Food Guide to Healthy Eating (Ottawa: Minister of Supply and Services, 1992).

8. Andrew Kupfer, "Where's the Beef?" *Fortune* 29 July 1991, 163-164.

9. Physicians Committee for Responsible Medicine, *The New Four Food Groups* (Washington: Physicians Committee for Responsible Medicine, 1991).

10.   Physicians Committee for Responsible Medicine, *The New Four Food Groups*.

11.   Ian. L. Rouse and Lawrence J. Beilin, "Vegetarian and Other Complex Diets, Fiber Intake and Blood Pressure," *Hypertension: Pathophysiology, Diagnosis and Management*, ed. J.H. Laragn et al (New York: Raven Press Ltd., 1990).

12.   J. F. Freeland-Graves, "Mineral adequacy of vegetarian diets," American Journal of Clinical Nutrition (48) 1988: 859-62.

13.   J. R. Marier, "Magnesium content of the food supply in the modern-day world," *Magnesium* (5) 1986: 1-8.

14.   American Dietetic Association, "Position of the American Dietetic Association: Vegetarian Diets," *ADA Reports* (88) 1990: 351-355.

15.   M. B. Zemel, "Calcium Utilization: effect of varying level and source of dietary protein," *American Journal of Clinical Nutrition* (48) 1988: 880-883.

16.   Health and Welfare Canada, *Recommended Nutrient Intakes for Canadians*, (Minister of Supply and Services, 1983), 36.

17.   Michael Klaper, *Vegan Nutrition* (Umatilla: Gentle World Inc, 1988), 45.

18.   J. Kelsay, C. W. Frazier, et al, "Impact of variation in carbohydrate intake on mineral utilization by vegetarians" American Journal of Clinical Nutrition (48) 1988: 875-879.

19.   American Dietetic Association, *ADA Reports*, 351-355.

20.   V. Herbert, "Vitamin B-12: plant sources, requirements, and assay," American Journal of Clinical Nutrition, (48) 1988: 852-8.

21.   P. Millet, et al, "Nutient Intake and vitamin status of healthy French vegetarians and non-vegetarians," *American Journal of Clinical Nutrition* (50) 1989: 718-721.

Bibliography

Books

Alexadratos, Nikos, et al. *Agriculture from the perspective of population growth.* Rome: FAO, 1983.

American Medical Association. *Family Medical Guide.* New York: Random House, 1982.

Andrews, Peter and Lawrence Martin. "Hominid dietary evolution." In *Foraging Strategies and Natural Diet of Monkeys, Apes, and Humans,* edited by A. Whiten and E.M. Widdowson, 39-49. Oxford: Clarendon Press, 1992.

Axon, William E. A. *Shelley's Vegetarianism.* New York: Haskell House, 1890.

Barer-Stein, Thelma. *You Eat What You Are: A Study of Canadian Ethnic Food Traditions.* Toronto: McClelland and Stewart, 1979.

Barkas, Janet. *The Vegetable Passion.* London: Routledge & Kegan Paul, 1975.

Barkin, David, Batt, Rosemary, and Billie R. DeWalt. *Food Crops vs. Feed Crops.* London: Lynne Rienner Publishers, 1990.

Bender, Arnold. *Meat and meat products in human nutrition in developing countries.* Rome: F.A.O., 1992.

Blumenschine, Robert J. "Hominid carnivory and foraging strategies, and the socio-economic function of early archeological sites." In *Foraging Strategies and Natural Diet of Monkeys, Apes, and Humans,* edited by A Whiten and E.M. Widdowson, 51-61. Oxford: Clarendon Press, 1992.

Boyden, Stephen. *Western Civilization in Biological Perspective.* Oxford: Oxford University Press, 1988.

Brambell, R. *Report of the Technical Committee to Enquire into the Welfare of Animals Kept under intensive livestock husbandry systems.* London: Her Majesty's Stationary Office, 1965.

Brown, Lester and Erik Eckholm. *By Bread Alone.* New York: Praeger Publishers, 1974.

Brown, Lester and John Young. "Feeding the World in the Nineties." In *State of The World 1990* edited by Linda Starke, New York: W.W. Norton and Company, 1990.

Bryant, Carol A, et al. *The Cultural Feast: An Introduction to Food and Society* New York: West Publishing Company, 1985.

Burkitt, Denis and Hugh Trowell, *Refined Carbohydrate Foods and Disease: Some Implications of Dietary Fibre* (London: Academic Press, 1975.

Butzer, Karl. *Environment and Archaeology: An Ecological Approach to Prehistory* Chicago: Aldine, 1971.

Caring for the Earth. The World Conservation Union, World Wide Fund for Nature, and the United Nations Environment Programme. Geneva, 1992.

Chrispeels, M. J. and David Sadava. *Plants, Food, and People.* San Francisco: W. H. Freeman and Company, 1977.

Coats, David C. *Old McDonald's Factory Farm.* New York: The Continuum Publishing Company, 1989. pg 17.

Conniff R. "California: Desert in Disguise." *National Geographic.* November, 1993.

Daugherty, A.B. *Major Uses of Land in the US.* Washington: United States Deparment of Agriculture, 1991.

Dawkins, M. *Animal Suffering: The Science of Animal Welfare.* London: Chapman and Hall, 1980.

Devanesen, Chandran D. S. *The Making of the Mahatma.* Bombay: Orient Longmans,   1969.

Doll R., and R. Peto. *The Causes of Cancer.* Oxford: Oxford University Press, 1981.

Dombrowski, D. A. *The Philosophy of Vegetarianism.* Boston: The University of Massachusetts Press, 1984.

Durning, Alan Thein and Holly B. Brough. "Reforming the Livestock Industry." In *State of the World, 1992,* edited by Lester Brown, 60-75. New York: W. W. Norton and Company, 1992.

Fagan, Brian M. *People of the Earth: An Introduction to World Prehistory.* Boston: Little, Brown and Company, 1986.

Food and Agricultural Organization, *The World Meat Economy in Figures.* Rome: FAO, 1984.

Food and Agricultural Organization, *World Agricultural Statistics.* Rome: FAO, 1986.

Food and Agricultural Organization, *FAO Production Yearbook.* Rome: FAO, 1992.

Fox, Michael W. *Farm Animals.* Baltimore: University Park Press, 1984, pg 1.

Franklin, Jon. Molecules of the Mind. New York: Dell Publishing Co., 1986.

Giehl, Dudley. *Vegetarianism: A Way of Life.* New York: Harper and Row, 1979.

Gold, Mark. *Assault and Battery.* London: Pluto Press, 1983.

Griffin, Donald. *The Question of Animal Awareness.* New York: Rockefeller University Press, 1976.

Guilaine, Jean. "The First Farmers of the Old World." In *Prehistory: The World of Early Man,* edited by Jean Guilaine, translated by Stephen Bunson, 71-82. Oxford: Facts on File, 1986.

Hall, Ross H. Food for Nought. New York: Vintage Books, 1974.

Harris, Marvin. *Culture, People and Nature: An Introduction to General Anthropology.* 3rd ed. New York: Harper and Row, 1980.

Harrison, Paul. *The Third Revolution.* New York: I.B. Tauris & Co., 1992.

Harrison, Ruth. *Animal Machines.* London: Vincent Stuart, 1964.

Health and Welfare Canada. *Action Towards Health Eating.* Ottawa: Health and Welfare Canada, 1990.

Health and Welfare Canada. *Canada's Food Guide to Healthy Eating.* Ottawa: Minister of Supply and Services, 1992.

Health and Welfare Canada. *Nutrition Recommendations: Report of the Scientific Review Committee.* Ottawa: Government Publishing Centre, 1990..

Health and Welfare Canada. *Recommended Nutrient Intakes for Canadians.* Minister of National Health and Welfare, 1983.

Hutt, M. S. R. and D. P. Burkitt. *The Geography of Non-Infectious Disease.* Oxford: Oxford University Press, 1986.

Joint Nutrition Monitoring Evaluation Committee. *Nutrition Monitoring in the United States.* Hyattsville: US Department of Health and Human Services, 1986.

Joint Nutrition Monitoring Evaluation Committee. *Nutrition Monitoring in the United States.* Hyattsville, Maryland: US Department of Health and Human Services, 1990

Kapleau, Roshi Philip. *A Buddhist Case for Vegetarianism.* London: Rider, 1983.

Keys A. *Seven Countries: A multivariate analysis of death and coronary heart disease.* Cambridge: Harvard University Press, 1980.

Klaper, Michael. *Vegan Nutrition: Pure and Simple.* Umatilla: Gentle World, Inc., 1987.

Lacey, Richard. *Unfit for Human Consumption.* Toronto: Souvenir Press, 1991.

Lappe, Francis Moore. *Diet for a Small Planet.* New York: Ballantine Books, 1982.

Leeming, Margaret. *A History of Food: From Manna to Microwave.* London: BBC Book, 1991.

Little Brown Book of Anecdotes, edited by Clifton Fadiman. Toronto: Little Brown and Company, 1985, 500-501.

Loehr, Raymond C. *Pollution Control for Agriculture.* Orlando: Academic Press, 1984.

Martin, Kay and Barbara Voorhies. *The Female of the Species.* New York: Columbia University Press, 1975.

Mason, Jim and Peter Singer. *Animal Factories.* New York: Harmony Books, 1990.

Meadows, Donella, Dennis L. Meadows, and Jorgen Randers. *Beyond the Limits.* Post Mills: Chelsea Green Publishing Company, 1992.

Milton, Katherine. "Primate diet and gut morphology: implications for hominid evolution." In *Food and Evolution: Toward a Theory of Human Food Habits,* edited by Marvin Harris and Eric B. Ross, 93-116. Philadelphia: Temple University Press, 1987.

National Research Council. *Diet, Nutrition, and Cancer.* Washington, D.C: National Academy Press, 1982.

Physicians Committee for Responsible Medicine. *The New Four Food Groups.* Washington: Physicians Committee for Responsible Medicine, 1991.

Physicians Committee for Responsible Medicine. *Foods for Cancer Prevention* (fact sheet). Washington: Physicians Committee for Responsible Medicine, 1992.

Pimentel, David and Marcia Pimentel. *Food, Energy and Society.* London: Edward Arnold, 1979.

Poster S. *Water for Agriculture: Facing the Limits.* Washington: World Watch Institute, 1989.

Pretty, J. N. and G. R. Conway. *Agriculture as a Global Polluter.* London: International Institute for Sustainable Development, 1989.

Radner, Daisie and Michael Radner. *Animal Consciousness.* New York: Prometheus Books, 1989.

Regan, Tom. *All that dwell therein.* Berkeley: University of California Press, 1982.

Rifkin, Jeremy. *Beyond Beef.* New York: Dutton, 1992.

Robbins, John. *Diet for A New America.* Santa Cruz: Stillpoint Publishing, 1986.

Roche, Helene. "The Beginnings of the Human Adventure." In *Prehistory: The World of Early Man,* edited by Jean Guilaine, translated by Stephen Bunson, 33-41. Oxford: Facts on File, 1986.

Rosenfield, Clare. *Gurudev Chitrabhanu: A Man with a Vision* (New York: Jain Meditation International Center, 1981.

Rouse I. L., Beilin L. J. "Vegetarian and Other Complex Diets, Fiber Intake and Blood Pressure." In *Hypertension: Pathophysiology, Diagnosis and Management.* edited by J. H. Laragh, et al, 241-55. New York: Raven Press, 1990.

Sainsbury, David W. "The Influence of Environmental Factors on the Health of Livestock," *Proceedings of the First International Livestock Environment Symposium.* St. Joseph: American Society of Agricultural Engineers, 1974.

Schell, Orville. *Modern Meat.* New York: Random House, 1984, pg 79.

Scharffenberg, J. *Problems with Meat.* Santa Barbara: Woodbridge Press, 1982.

Schuyler, George. *Hunger in a Land of Plenty.* Cambridge: Schenkman Publishing Company, 1980.

Schweitzer, Albert. *Reverence for Life.*

Simoons, F. J., *Food in China: A Cultural and Historial Inquiry.* Boston: CRC Press.

Singer, Peter. *Animal Liberation.* New York: Random House, 1975.

Sources of Indian Tradition, Volume One. edited and revised by Ainslie T. Embree. New York: Columbia University Press, 1993.

Spencer, Colin. *The Heretic's Feast.* London: Fourth Estate, 1993.

Surgeon General of the United States. *The Surgeon General's Report on Nutrition and Health.* Washington: U.S. Department Health and Human Services, 1988.

Tamminga, G. and J. Wijnando. "Animal Waste Problems in the Netherlands." In *Farming and the Countryside* edited by N. Hanley. Wallingford: CAB International, 1991.

The Bhagavad Gita, translated by Barbara Stoler Miller. New York: Bantam Books, 1986.

The Bhagavad Gita, translated by Shri Purohit Swami. London: Faber and Faber, 1935.

The New Jerusalem Bible: Reader's Edition. London: Doubleday, 1990.

Trowell, Hugh and Denis Burkitt. "Emergence of Western diseases in sub-Saharal Africans." In *Western Diseases: their emergence and prevention,* edited by Hugh Trowell and Denis Burkitt, 2-30. London: Edward Arnold Ltd, 1981.

Ulijaszek, S. J. "Human dietary change." In *Foraging Strategies and Natural Diet of Monkeys, Apes, and Humans,* edited by A. Whiten and E.M. Widdowson, 111-119. Oxford: Clarendon Press, 1992.

United Nations Department of International Economic and Social Affairs. *World Population Prospects,* 1988.

Villee, Claude. *Biology.* Toronto: Saunders College Publishing, 1985.

Wallace, Ronald L. *Those Who Have Vanished: An Introduction to Prehistory.* Homewood: The Dorsey Press, 1983.

Wenke, Robert J. *Patterns in Prehistory: Humankind's First Three Million Years* Oxford: Oxford University Press, 1984.

Wise, Thomas Alexander. *Commentary on the Hindu System of Medicine.* Amsterdam: Oriental Press, 1926.

World Health Organization. *Diet, nutrition, and the prevention of chronic diseases: Report of a WHO Study Group.* Geneva: World Health Organization, 1990.

Young, T. and M. P. Burton. *Agricultural sustainability: definitions and implications for agricultural and trade policy.* Rome: F.A.O., 1992.

Zihlman, Adrienne and Nancy Tanner. "Gathering and the Hominid Adaptation." In *Female Hierarchies,* edited by Lionel Tiger and Heather T. Fowler, 161-177. Chicago: Beresford Book Service, 1975.

Journal Articles

Allen L. "Protein induced hypercalcuria: a longer term study." *Amer J Clin Nutr* 1979;32:485.

Altman N. Revising the Basic Four. *Vegetarian Times* 1977 (September/October).

American Dietetic Associaton. "Position of the American Dietetic Association: Vegetarian Diets." *ADA Reports* 1988:3:351-355.

Armstrong B, Clark H, Martin C, et al. "Urinary sodium and blood pressure in vegetarians." *Amer J Clin Nutr* 1979;32:2472-2476.

Armstrong S. "Marooned in a Mountain of Manure." *New Scientist.* Nov. 26, 1988.

Bruns W. "New knowledge of diet therapy of type 2 diabetes." *Zeitschrift Fur Die Gesemte Innere Medizin Und Ihre Grenzgebiete* 1990;45(10):290-4.

Butrum RR, Clifford CK, Lanze E. "NCI dietary guidelines: rationale." *Am J Clin Nutr* 1988;48:888-95.

Carroll KK, Giovannetti PM, Huff MW, et al. "Hypocholesterolemic effect of substituting soybean protein for animal protein in the diets of healthy young women." *Amer J Clin Nutr* 1978; 31: 1312-1320.

Chen Z, Peto R, Collins R, et al. "Serum cholesterol concentration and coronary heart disease in population with low cholesterol concentrations." *British Medical Journal* 1991;303:276-282.

Crompton, A. W. and K. Hiiemae. "How mammalian teeth work." *Discovery* 1969;5(1):23-24.

Cummings SR. et al. "Epidemiology of osteoporosis and osteoporotic fractures." *Epidemiologic reviews* 1985;7:178-208.

Donaldson AN. "The relation of protein foods to hypertension." *Calif West Med* 1926;24:328-331.

Dwyer JT. "Health Aspects of a Vegetarian Diet," *Am J Clin Nutr* 1988;48:712-38.

Eaton SB, Konner M. "Paleolithic nutrition: a consideration of its nature and current implications." *N Engl J Med* 1985;312:283-289.

Erikkson KE, Robert KH. "From the Big Bang to Sustainable Societies." *Reviews in Oncology* 1991;4(2):10.

Fonnebo, V. "Mortality in Norwegian Seventh-Day Adventists 1962-1986." *Journal of Clinical Epidemiology* 1992;45(2):157-67.

Freeman, Orville. "Meeting the Food Needs of The Coming Decade." *The Futurist* 1990 (November-December) 15-20.

Fraser GE, et al. "A possible protective effect of nut consumption on risk of coronary heart disease: The Adventist Health Study." *Arch Intern Med* 1992;152(7):1416-24.

Freeland-Graves JF. "Mineral adequacy of vegetarian diets." *Am J Clin Nutr* 1988;48:859-62.

Frentzel-Beyme R, Claude J, Eilber U. "Mortality among German vegetarians: first results after five years of follow-up." *Nutrition and Cancer* 1988;11:117-26.

Gretz N, Meisinger E, Strauch M. "Does a low protein diet really slow-down the rate of progression of chronic renal failure?." *Blood Purification* 1989;7(1):33-8.

Hecht SB. "The Sacred Cow in the green Hell: livestock and forest conversion in the Brazilian Amazon." *Ecologist.* 1989;19(6): 220-234.

Hegsted DM. "Calcium and osteoporosis" *J Nutr* 1986;116:2316-9.

Herbert V. "Vitamin B-12: plant sources, requirements, and assay." *Am J Clin Nutr* 1988;48:852-8.

Hirayama T. "Mortality in Japanese with life-styles similar to Seventh-Day Adventists: strategy for risk reduction by lifestyle modification." *National Cancer Institute Monographs* 1985;69: 143-53.

Intersalt Cooperative Research Group. "Intersalt: an international study of electrolyte excretion and blood pressure. Results for 24 hour urinary sodium and potassium excretion." *British Medical Journal* 1988;297:319-328.

Jacobs L. "Amazing Graze: how the livestock industry is ruining the American West." *Desertification Control Bulletin* no 17:p 13-17.

Jansson B. "Geographic cancer risk and intracellular potassium/ sodium ratios." *Cancer Detection & Prevention* 1986;9:171-94.

Jenkins DJA, Wolever TMS, Rao AV, et al. "Effect on blood lipids of very high intakes of fiber in diets low in saturated fat and cholesterol." *New Engl J Med* 1993;329:21-6.

Johansson GK, Ottova L, Gustafsson JA. "Shift from a mixed diet to a lactovegetarian diet: influence on some cancer-associated intestinal bacteria enzyme activities." *Nutrition and Cancer* 1990;14(3-4):239-246.

Johansson G, Holmen A, Persson L, et al. "The effect of a shift from a mixed diet to a lacto-vegetarian diet on human urinary and fecal mutagenic activity." *Carcinogenesis* 1992;13(2):153-7.

Kelsay J, Frazier CW, Prather ES, et al. "Impact of variation in carbohydrate intake on mineral utilization by vegetarians." *Am J Clin Nutr* 1988;48:875-879.

King JC, Cohenour SH, et al. "Evaluation nd Modification of the basic four food group guide." *Journal of Nutrition Education* 1978;10;27-29.

Kjeldsen-Kragh J, et al. "Controlled trial of fasting and one-year vegetarian diet in rheumatoid arthritis." *Lancet* 1991; 338 (8772): 899-902.

Kupfer, Andrew. "Where's the Beef?" *Fortune* 29 July 1991, 163-164.

Kushi LH, Lew RA, Stare FJ, et al. "Diet and 20 year mortality from coronary heart disease." *N Engl J Med* 1985;312:811-818.

Lane HW, Carpenter JT. "Breast cancer: incidence, nutritional concerns, and treatment approaches." *J Am Diet Assoc* 1987;87: 765-769.

Litvak J, et al. "The growing noncommunicable disease burden, a challenge for the countries of the Americas." *Bulletin of the Pan American Health Organization* 1988;21:156-171.

Maclure KM, et al. "Dietary predictors of symptom-associated gallstones in middle-aged women." *Amer J Clin Nutr* 1990;52(5): 916-22.

Malter M, Schriever G, Eilber U. "Natural killer cells, vitamins, and other blood components of vegetarian and omnivorous men." *Nutrition and Cancer* 1989;12(3):271-8.

Marangella M, et al. "Effect of animal and vegetable protein intake on oxalate excretion in idiopathic calcium stone formers." *British Journal of Urology* 1989;63(4):348-51.

Margetts BM, Beilin LJ, Vandongen R, et al, "Vegetarian diet in mild hypertension: a randomized controlled trial." *Br Med J* 1986; 293:1468-1471.

Margetts BM, Beilin LJ, Vandongen R, et al. "A randomized controlled trial of the effect of dietary fibre on blood pressure." *Clin Sci* 1987;72:343-350.

Marier JR. "Magnesium content of the food supply in the modern-day world." *Magnesium* 1986;5:1-8.

Marsh AG, Sanchez TV, Michelsen O, et al. "Vegetarian lifestyle and bone mineral density." *Amer J Clin Nutr* 1988;48:837-41.

Millet P, et al. "Nutient Intake and vitamin status of healthy French vegetarians and non-vegetarians." *Am J Clin Nutr* 1989;50:718-721.

Milton K. "Diet and Primate Evolution." *Scientific American* 1993;269(2):86-93.

Minowa M, et al. "Dietary fiber intake in Japan." *Human Nutr. Appl Nutr.* 1983;37A:113-119.

Ornish D. "Can you prevent-and reverse-CAD?." *Patient Care* 1991;25-41.

Ornish D, Brown SE, Scherwitz LW, et al. "Can lifestyle changes reverse coronary heart disease?: The Lifestyle Heart Trial." *Lancet* 1990;336:129-33.

Page LB. "Nutritional determinants of hypertension." *Curr Concepts Nutr* 1981;10:113-26.

Parfit M. "Troubled Waters Run Deep." *National Geographic.* 1993 (November) 78.

Pixley F, Mann J. "Dietary factors in the etiology of gall stones: a case control study." *Gut* 1988;29:1511-5.

Riggs BL, Melton LJ. "Involutional osteoporosis." *New Engl J Med* 1986:314;1676-1686.

Robertson WG, et al. "Should recurrent calcium oxalate stone formers become vegetarians?." *British Journal of Urology* 1979;51:427-31.

Robertson WG, et al. "The effect of high animal protein intake on the risk of calcium stone formation in the urinary tract." *Clinical Science* 1979;57:285-88.

Roe, Daphne A. "History of Promotion of Vegetable Cereal Diets." *J Nutr.* 116:1355-1363, 1986.

Rouse IL, Armstrong BK, Beilin LJ. "The relationship of blood pressure to diet and lifestyle in two religious populations." *J Hypertens* 1983;1:65-71.

Sacks FM, et al. "Blood pressure in vegetarians" *Am J Epidemiol* 1974;100:390-398.

Sacks FM, et al. "Plasma lipids and lipoproteins in vegetarians and controls." *New England Journal of Medicine* 1975;292:1148-51.

Sei M, Miyoshi T. "Changes in nutritional factors related to regional differences in the mortality of cardiovascular disease between 1966 and 1985 in Japan." *Japanese Journal of Hygiene* 1991; 47(5):901-12.

Snowdon DA, et al. "Meat consumption and fatal ischemic heart disease." *Preventive Medicine* 1984;13:490-500.

Snowdon DA, Phillips RL. "Does a vegetarian diet reduce the occurrence of diabetes?." *American Journal of Public Health* 1985;75:507-12.

Stallones DA. "Ischemic heart disease and lipid in blood and diet." *Annual Review of Nutrition* 1983;3:155-185.

Stamler J. "Nutrition-related risk factors for the atherosclerotic disease—present status." *Prog. Biochem. Pharamcol* 1983;19:245-308.

Stone J. "Bovine Madness." *Discover* 1989 (February) 38-40.

Trichhopoulos D, et al. "The effect of Westernization on urine estrogens, frequency of ovulation, and breast cancer risks: a study in ethnic Chinese women in the Orient and in the USA." *Cancer* 1984;53:187-92.

Tylavsky F, Anderson JJB. "Dietary factors in bone health of elderly lactoovovegetarian and omnivorous women." *Amer J Clin Nutr* 1988;48:842-9.

Uhl C, Parker G. "Our Steak in the Jungle." *BioScience* 1991;36 (10):642.

Watson, Richard. Self-Consciousnes and the Rights of Nonhuman Animals and Nature. *Environmental Ethics.* Vol(1): Summer 1979, pg 99-129.

Willet WC, Stampfer MJ, et al. "Relation of meat, fat and fiber intake to the risk of colon cancer in a prospective study among women." *New Engl J Med* 1990;323:1664-72.

Wiseman MJ, et al. "Dietary composition and renal function in healthy subjects." *Nephron* 1987;46:37-42.

Zeigler RG. "Vegetables, fruits, and carotenoids and the risk of cancer." *Amer J Clin Nutr* 1991;53:51S-9S.

Zemel MB. "Calcium Utilization: effect of varying level and source of dietary protein." *Am J Clin Nutr* 1988;48:880-883.

Newspaper Articles

"More Canadians turn vegetarian". *The Calgary Herald.* 27 November 1992, C5.

Nightengale, Marie. "Vegetarians gain new respect". *The Halifax Chronicle Herald.* 3 July 1991, B3.

"Red Meat Lovers Get Cancer Warning." *The Globe and Mail.* 13 December 1990, A1.

"Study boost for vegetarian diets". *Calgary Herald.* 25 May 1990, E10.

A REASON
FOR JOY

THOMAS PAUL THIGPEN

NAVPRESS ⊙®

A MINISTRY OF THE NAVIGATORS
P.O. BOX 6000, COLORADO SPRINGS, COLORADO 80934

The Navigators is an international Christian
organization. Jesus Christ gave His followers the
Great Commission to go and make disciples
(Matthew 28:19). The aim of The Navigators is
to help fulfill that commission by multiplying
laborers for Christ in every nation.

NavPress is the publishing ministry of The Navigators. NavPress publications are tools to help
Christians grow. Although publications alone
cannot make disciples or change lives, they can
help believers learn biblical discipleship, and
apply what they learn to their lives and
ministries.

Cover photo: David Muench

Printed in the United States of America

In memory of my father—
a good and faithful servant of God who has now
entered into the Joy of his Master

CONTENTS

AUTHOR

Thomas Paul Thigpen is a man with diverse interests and experience. In recent years, he has worked as an author and editor for various Christian periodicals. He has written four children's books, all published by David C. Cook: *Stories in the Sky*; *Angels in the Air*; *Guest of the Animals*; and *Come Sing God's Song*.

Paul has ministered as a youth evangelist and counselor, a leader in collegiate ministry, and a speaker in seminars and churches. He received a B.A. in Religious Studies from Yale University, and is now working toward an M.A. and a Ph.D. in Historical Theology from Emory University.

Paul and his wife, Leisa, live with their daughter, Lydia, in Atlanta, Georgia.

O Lord . . . I write this book for love of Your love.
AUGUSTINE

☐

Others before me have gone much further into these holy mysteries than I have gone, but if my fire is not yet large it is yet real, and there may be those who can light their candle at its flame.
A. W. TOZER

☐

Perhaps this is the reason why only a few arrive at spiritual joy: For since they do not seek God, they cannot rejoice and be glad.
MARTIN LUTHER

AN ANCIENT PROPOSAL

Some books, in order to tell about one thing, must turn their primary attention to something else. This book is of that sort. Its subject is joy. But to speak accurately of joy, we must focus instead on seeing, knowing, and loving the Lord.

A good book should make a single, central claim about the subject it examines. All that it says, on every page, should point to the one reality it hopes to present. That being the case, I've desired to sharpen every line of this essay into an arrow directing our attention to what I'm convinced is the true relationship between joy and our walk with God. The relationship, as I understand it, is simply this: *To discover joy, we must abandon the search for it, and go looking instead for the One who is Himself joy to see, to know, and to love.*

My proposal isn't novel or original; if it were, I'd be hesitant to make it. The understanding of joy I attempt to present here, along with the response it requires from us, is rather an ancient one I've encountered in years of studying the Scriptures and the history of theology. But every age has its own peculiar blindness. Somehow our generation in the Church (in the West, at least) seems frequently to forget that the pursuit of happiness, if it's not undertaken as the pursuit of God, is a futile and idolatrous journey.

Though that insight is forgotten, it's certainly not hidden. The joy in the Lord that we seek in fact speaks to us all through the Scripture—sometimes barely whispering, as in Lamentations; sometimes shouting, as in so many of the Psalms. It also appears in bright spots across two thousand years of Church history. We hear it there in some of the best minds and purest hearts of every age and ecclesiastical tradition.

Joy rings through Augustine's *Confessions* and dances through the life of Francis of Assisi. It shines in the brilliant light reflected through the minds of Thomas Aquinas, Jonathan Edwards, and Karl Barth. From the desert retreat of Anthony in ancient Egypt to the lecture rooms of C. S. Lewis in modern England, we can hear the refrain of a jubilant chorus that challenges us to "enter into the joy of your master" (Matthew 25:21, NASB)—which necessarily requires that we first become servants.

The Scriptures and the history of the Church have thus taught me much of what is in this book, and that's how it should be. Even so, in writing it I'm not quite like the old Egyptian monk who was refused instruction by a revered teacher because, as the teacher observed, "his business is getting credit by retailing what others have said to him." Happily, Scripture and historical study were not the only places I encountered this reality. What I found there was a confirmation and an explanation of my own experiences of joy, however meager those experiences may be when compared to the fullness God intends for us. So a personal testimony about my encounters with Joy Himself provides an important part of the following discussion.

But only a part. For I've admittedly tasted no more than the splashing spray of that ocean of Living Water for which

I, and all the world, am feverish with thirst. I'm only a parched traveler pointing out a few oases for the sake of my comrades on the journey.

A few words about this book's structure: The first three Gospels tell the "good news of great joy" by plunging right into the action of Jesus' life on earth. But John, who wrote his Gospel last and had the most time to ponder the events in his walk with Christ, chose to begin his account with a cosmic perspective. He located his history and theology within the framework of eternity: "In the beginning was the Word...."

Because we so readily think about joy in terms of scattered and perhaps unrelated experiences of pleasure—in short, we think not about *Joy*, but rather about *joys*—it seemed to me important to imitate John's approach by finding the overarching framework that holds the discussion together. So the first chapter takes a long step backward from daily life to view Joy from the perspective of its ultimate source: the nature of God.

Following that is a close-up view of my own experience, and then a more focused analysis of the terms in our discussion. The remainder of the book is an attempt to relate this understanding of joy specifically to other aspects of our walk with God. Judging from the wide-ranging table of contents alone, you might conclude that we've set out to explain the whole of Christian life; but each chapter's focus actually remains on joy. That means, for example, that the chapter on anger is not an exhaustive treatment of the subject, but rather some thoughts on the much narrower topic of how anger and joy are related.

At the beginning of each chapter are several quotes from Scripture and other sources. Please resist the temptation to skim or ignore them; they articulate most clearly the biblical basis of each chapter and the heart of the discussions that follow them. A few moments of meditation on them both before and after you read the corresponding chapter will immeasurably enrich your study.

Finally, the essay's structure has been influenced by my love for the Psalms. That most joyful (and, paradoxically, most mournful) of biblical books echoes with jubilation because the writers are so deeply aware that God, the source of joy, is near: "In Thy presence is fulness of joy; in Thy right hand there are pleasures forever" (Psalm 16:11, NASB).

Such an awareness explains one of the most striking features of the psalmists' poetry: their tendency to move easily back and forth between speaking to us about God and speaking to God Himself. It's as if they recognize that the Lord's constant nearness assures that any conversation has at least three parties.

It seems to me, as it apparently did to them, only silly to write *about* a God who's reading over my shoulder, without at the same time writing *to Him*. Thus, this book will reflect a similar style. The words in italics interspersed throughout the text are prayers recognizing God's participation in our conversation.

I'm grateful to many folks for their help in writing this book: First, to the faculty of the historical theology department at Emory University in Atlanta, who have introduced me to many of the Christian thinkers you'll meet in these pages. Second, I'm grateful for the kindness of the staff of NavPress, folks like Kathy Yanni, Traci Mullins, Jon Stine, Debby Weaver, and others, whose patience and wisdom have been so helpful in the process. Thanks also to Don Simpson for first approaching me about the work; his enthusiasm convinced me that others would also be interested. And finally, of course, I give loving thanks to my wife and daughter. My joy in them has been multiplied by their heroic endurance these past few months.

I fully expected as I began this work that the enemy would not let me write about joy without making at least a few minor attempts to steal mine. Just now, my daughter has strep throat and poison ivy sores. My wife and I have toothaches. Some of the books I need are missing from the library and out of print. Our brand-new car has mechanical problems, our piano stands gutted and waiting for a second try at radical surgery, and my favorite fish in our aquarium just died. These are all petty irritations and losses, of course, and I'm grateful to be spared any major problems for the time being. But when it comes to losing our joy, the size of the problem is not always relevant. It's often "the little foxes that ruin the vineyards" (Song of Songs 2:15).

If you have your share of foxes, too—whatever their size—come with me now for a closer look at the great gladness God has promised us. "My soul will boast in the LORD; let the afflicted hear and rejoice. Glorify the LORD with me; let us exalt his name together" (Psalm 34:2-3).

PART I

THE
FOUNT OF
JOY

"This is my Son, whom I love; with him I am well pleased. "
MATTHEW 3:17

□

"Father, I want those you have given me to be with me where I am, and to see my glory, the glory you have given me because you loved me before the creation of the world. "
JOHN 17:24

□

I was there when he set the heavens in place, when he marked out the horizon on the face of the deep . . . . I was the craftsman at his side. I was filled with delight day after day, rejoicing always in his presence, rejoicing in his whole world and delighting in mankind.
PROVERBS 8:27,30-31

□

Joy to the world! The Lord is come . . . . Let men their songs employ; while fields and floods, rocks, hills, and plains repeat the sounding joy . . . . He comes to make His blessings flow far as the curse is found.
ISAAC WATTS

□

We are all strings in the concert of His joy.
JAKOB BOEHME

CHAPTER 1

IN THE BEGINNING WAS JOY

In the beginning was Joy.
And the Joy was with God, and the Joy flowed within God.

For the Father eternally beheld the Son, and loved Him; and the Son beheld the Father, and loved Him; and the Father and Son beheld and loved the Spirit, and were Themselves beheld as the Spirit's beloved. Springing from that eternal love was a mutual delight in the beauty of perfect holiness. So the love that holds all things together by its limitless power was the fount of Joy, the mouth of a mighty river that flows singing in superabundance from the heart of God.

God had no need of a universe; His Joy was complete without it. But in the infinite overflow of His love, He willed that all things might come into being, that His Joy might fill all things. So God loved the universe into existence.

And God saw that it was good, very good. And He delighted in His work.

He filled the cosmos with light, and life, and glory. He fashioned other wills to be loved by Him and to love Him in return. All things were attracted to the beauty of holiness shining from their Creator; all things turned their faces unceasingly toward the Father, the Son, and the Spirit; all things beheld God, and loved Him, and delighted themselves in His holiness. Thus "the morning stars sang together, and all the sons of God shouted for joy" (Job 38:7, NASB).

This music of the cosmos was a willing symphony, so that all things might freely play a part in the grand harmony of the Trinity, and none be left silent. Each had a voice to raise in that glad chorus; each creature could make itself a gift of gratitude to God, an echo of His glory, a vessel of His Joy.

But one face chose to turn away, and to look instead toward himself. He raised and distorted his voice, and lured others away from the rejoicing throng; he became the Adversary. So the harmony was diminished. Yet the song was not silenced; Joy found other channels in which to flow.

For God plowed up the soil of a planet as it sang around its sun, and His wisdom shaped its dust into His own image and likeness. His love breathed life into the form, so that a living soul opened his eyes to behold the divine Countenance. The creature delighted in the vision of his Creator, and Joy flowed through him into the furrows of the planet dug by the hand of God.

But the defiant one, the Adversary, was near—now a warped and abandoned instrument. All around him the music of the cosmos demanded sympathetic vibrations from the broken strings of his heart, but the strings could only respond by trembling in horror. He hated the music. In its beauty he heard only noise; in its harmony he found only a unison note of judgment, a universal assent that he had turned his back on the One who was life Himself.

Devoid of heaven's music, he was devoid of heaven's

Joy. The bright river flowed all around him, but no longer through him; he had become a thirsty pit, a searing desert, a withered anti-oasis swallowed up by a universe of blossoming song. So he slithered to the planet of God's furrows, plotting a drought that would extend the borders of his own desolation.

And he succeeded. He caught the attention of the divine image, and lured the creatures' gaze away from the Face of God. When they turned their backs on His love, the floodgates of Joy were closed, the furrows filled in. And the swirling dust of the drought filled their eyes and ears, blinding them to the sight of heaven, deafening them to its music. So the planet succumbed to thirst, darkness, and silence.

The creatures on the desert planet never forgot that Joy had once flowed. Their very thirst was evidence that they had been created to drink. Above them they saw the handiwork of God, and His footprints below were left in the dust that had once been a garden. Sometimes they lifted their faces, straining their vision to the borders of their blindness for a glimpse of the Fount of Joy. And though His countenance was hidden, they heard His voice, and a faint, passing note from the cosmic melody.

But in the fullness of time, the Fount became flesh, and dwelt among us, full of light and song. We beheld His Face, and heard Him sing. And wherever He placed His foot, the desert bloomed. Dying an emptied vessel, and buried in the wilderness, He rose again a gushing Spring, bursting open the deepest caverns of the desert with the surging torrents of His love. By Him the floodgates were opened, the furrows dug again, until the hills themselves burst into music, and the trees of the field clapped their hands (Isaiah 55:12).

So once again the living river flows singing in superabundance from the heart of God to the world. But the earth is not yet filled with the glory of God as the waters cover the sea. Our gardens are still surrounded by deserts, because Joy lies dammed in valleys that must be lifted up, or frozen on mountaintops that must be brought low.

Meanwhile, all creation groans in hope, longing to exchange earth's sighing for a song. And we, the beloved children of God on our journey home through the wilderness, must turn our faces toward His face, drink deeply of His Joy, and sing.

As the deer pants for streams of water,
so my soul pants for you, O God.
My soul thirsts for God, for the living God.
When can I go and meet with God?
PSALM 42:1-2

□

When the LORD brought back the captives to Zion,
we were like men who dreamed.
Our mouths were filled with laughter,
our tongues with songs of joy.
PSALM 126:1-2

□

That we might all be mad for love of Him who for love of
us was called mad!
TERESA OF AVILA

□

This joy is a fruit that proceeds from faith after much wrestling; and
doth not presently flow from faith, not so soon as ever a Christian begins
to believe, but after a time; and then the heart is joyous; but never filled
with joy before believing. Afterwards, and when a man hath had the
sweet dew of the promises dripping upon him, but many a day after, let
him look for this joy.
THOMAS HOOKER

□

My assumption is that the story of any one of us is in some measure the
story of us all.
FREDERICK BUECHNER

CHAPTER 2

"MY SOUL THIRSTS FOR YOU..."

I was born on that desert planet, where rebellion has dried up the streams of heaven; and I was born thirsty.

As a child I knew what most children probably know, but are trained to forget: We were created to drink from the river of Joy. I'm not talking here about how children have a knack for taking pleasure in simple things, though that's certainly an admirable trait, whether in children or adults. I mean instead that they seem to be naturally aware that alongside this visible universe is an invisible one; that the invisible one holds our destiny; and that the Final Reality behind both is a Person.

Of course, I've never heard a child put it quite that way. But if you watch little ones at play for very long, you know that they tend to accept this model of the universe without question. They talk seriously about things that can't be seen, powers that can't be understood, relationships between visible and invisible realities that can be predicted but not controlled. They assume that personalities lurk behind or within animals, objects, even places. And they insist that ultimately all things fall into one of two categories—good or evil—either by corruption or by allegiance. For them, Someone has made rules and has decided that life must be, above all, "fair," with good the victor in the end.

In short, even if we had never told children a single fairy tale, they would probably have created their own— may indeed *have* themselves created some of the ones we all know. For in their view, the fairy tale comes closest in many ways to reflecting the genuine shape of Things as They Are. They have no doubt that beings without physical bodies exist, and are involved in our lives; that sickness might be healed by a power greater than medicine; that staffs can turn into snakes and back into staffs again. Miracles are for them so natural that they're hardly miraculous. And above all, they know somehow that they were made to live "happily ever after."

Of course, the child raised in a Christian family that takes the biblical view of reality seriously will usually discover that the imagined wonders of fairy tales are misty and pale next to the solid and brilliant events of sacred history. The Bible is brimming with affirmations of the reality of angels and demons, incalculable powers, astounding miracles. In fact, I've never read a fairy tale as thrilling as the story of the Exodus, as intriguing as the story of Joseph, or as beautiful as the story of David. The fears and hopes of all the folk tales of the ages find their true meaning in the story of the Incarnation. And the book of Revelation is the prophecy that shows every "happily ever after" to be only a faint echo of the glorious biblical promise.

When I say, then, that most children probably know we are created to drink from the river of Joy, I'm saying that they know the basics of a broader reality that many of the ancient pagans also knew—but most modern pagans deny. Children know that this world is not the only world, and that the other World is home.

They know, that is, until their minds and hearts are sacrificed to the Moloch of modern rationalism. This world tells them that it alone exists. It insists that their thirst for another world is an illusion—or worse yet, that the thirst is real but that this world itself is the drink they're looking for.

By the time I became a teenager, I too had come to believe that lie of this world. For me, the visible Machine surrounding us was the sum total of reality—no God, no spirits, no heaven, no life after death. At least, that's what my modern-educated mind insisted. But on rare occasions, usually unexpectedly, my heart rebelled.

How do I describe that rebellion? It always took place when I was alone. Once it was on a summer afternoon at the height of a sudden thunderstorm. Again, it happened on a spring morning when my ear caught the low moan of a mourning dove. It came several times at the beach as I listened to the deafening lullaby of the waves, and again when I once looked up to see the icy vastness of a clear sky on a winter night.

Each time, the sensation was the same. Beyond whatever sight or sound met me in the physical world, it was as if I heard what could only be called a single note played on a trumpet from a distant country. In such a moment I would fall motionless, arrested by the surpassing sweetness of that sound. And I ached so deeply to hear the entire melody that my eyes would moisten with homesickness for a Land I'd never seen.

The feeling was an intense and confusing combination of refreshment and longing, sweetness and pain. Like a sword dipped in honey, it would pierce me through, then vanish. Overwhelmed by simultaneous pleasure and grief, I felt as if I'd discovered a best friend and then lost him again forever, in only an instant.

My Lord, if only I'd realized then that You were that Friend;

that Your Song had soared over my noisy barricades and run me through. But those moments seemed a mockery, because I'd abandoned all hope of any Voice within the thunder, or any Face behind the clouds. I was a fool.

Moments like those awakened my heart's thirst. They were fleeting witnesses to that other World, the taste of a crystal spray from the rushing waters of a mighty invisible River. But for years I convinced myself each time when the taste vanished that it was only an illusion.

Oddly enough, when I finally came to the place of faith in my senior year of high school, I at first made no conscious connection between God and my brief experiences with Joy (for I know now that's what it was). My confession of Christ as Savior and Lord was an intellectual assent to the truth of the gospel, and an act of willing submission to Someone who had slowly convinced me "that he exists and that he rewards those who earnestly seek him" (Hebrews 11:6). But only two months later did I begin to discover one of the most precious of those rewards.

I was alone, reading the Scripture and praying for God's will to be done in my life. As I prayed and meditated on the thrilling descent of the Holy Spirit at Pentecost, somehow I realized for the first time the significance of the name "Immanuel"—which means, of course, "God with us" (Matthew 1:23). In an instant, so many thoughts and insights flooded together at once that I may never be able to distinguish them all. I can only say now that in that moment, the nearness of God became a lasting reality in my consciousness. I was standing in His presence; I could never *escape* His presence; and I began to laugh.

Blessed Holy Spirit, how You made me laugh! You baptized me in gladness and awakened me to praise. You drowned my grief, burst my fetters, washed me clean.

Precious Son of God, You assured me that night that You had purchased me with Your blood, and so You would never leave me nor forsake me. You turned my mourning into dancing, put off my sackcloth, clothed me with radiance (Psalm 30:11).

Gracious Father, I knew in that moment You were the One I had sought beyond the world's edge. Yours was the Voice calling from eternity; Yours was the Face from whose love flowed all Joy. And You were no longer distant. You were standing beside me, and dwelling within me.

That night, my Lord, I fell utterly in love with You. You became my delight. I realized then that You, and You alone, are the only Destination worth the journey. And by a grace I could never merit, You have set my feet on the road home. Till I arrive, my God, my soul pants for You. . . .

For a solid week afterward, I laughed. I was like a madman—mad for love, beside myself as if, like the apostles at Pentecost, "drunk with new wine" (Acts 2:1-15). Wherever I looked, I saw His face looking back: in Scripture, in other Christians, in the sunset. And each time I saw Him, I fell in love with Him once more. That love washed me again and again with delight in the knowledge that He was my Father, that He had a place prepared for me. The joy of His presence filled me with sweetness, and the joy of His promise filled me with longing.

Those overwhelming waters of joy finally subsided, but I think it's safe to say that since then, they've always flowed inside me to one degree or another. Sometimes they move slowly, quietly, strongly, in subterranean caverns, where I can sense them only if I pay close attention. At other times they spring up to the surface unexpectedly, refreshing and clear. At still other times they rush along once more in a conquering deluge, sweeping aside the debris of my heart and scrubbing it clean.

Such has been my own experience. But the form that joy in the Lord takes seems to vary from believer to believer.

My story sounds much like what others have told me of theirs. Yet still others have described their delight in God as something less sudden or dramatic. To a great extent, I suspect, the living water probably takes the shape of the vessel it fills. Each temperament provides its own lovely form for containing and pouring forth the beauty of His joy.

Nevertheless, whatever the shape of our vessel, of one thing we can be sure: God wants to fill us. Jesus has promised us joy (John 15:11). Though we can't always be laughing, the divine river should be running through us, even if it's underground. And whether it rushes along in a torrent or flows by in a trickle, it will be cutting in all of us a deep ravine, changing forever the landscape of our souls.

Meanwhile, we have a journey to make, and the land we're passing through is dry. So we must look more closely at what we mean when we speak of joy in order to learn how we can open ourselves to the living water. Only then can we, as the psalmist said, make the roadside a garden as we go:

> "Blessed are those whose strength is in you, who have set their hearts on pilgrimage. As they pass through the Valley of [Weeping], they make it a place of springs." (Psalm 84:5-6)

I denied myself nothing my eyes desired;
I refused my heart no pleasure.
My heart took delight in all my work,
and this was the reward for all my labor.
Yet when I surveyed all that my hands had done
and what I had toiled to achieve,
everything was meaningless, a chasing after the wind;
nothing was gained under the sun.
ECCLESIASTES 2:10-11

□

"My people have committed two sins:
They have forsaken me,
the spring of living water,
and have dug their own cisterns,
broken cisterns that cannot hold water."
JEREMIAH 2:13

□

You have made us for Yourself, and our heart is restless
until it rests in You.
AUGUSTINE

□

We must acknowledge that God is happiness itself.
BOETHIUS

CHAPTER 3

BROKEN CISTERNS

The pursuit of happiness is the unhappiest of pursuits.

Its way is plagued with conflicting road signs, dangerous detours, dead ends. Like rats in a maze, we who pursue happiness try first one opening and then another, yet we never seem to find our way to the goal. And if we finally tire of the search, we can only cry out with the biblical writer who himself tried every possible path: "Vanity of vanities; all is vanity" (Ecclesiastes 1:2, KJV).

Nevertheless, the pursuit of happiness is also the most human of all pursuits. Wise men and women in every age have agreed that the quest for contentment is at the very core of our nature. And no wonder: We're creatures who can imagine things as they could be, comparing them with things as they are. Yet the possibility always seems better than the reality.

To make matters worse, we violently disagree about how to arrive at the destination we all seek. Some look for happiness in external pleasures, others look within themselves. Some seek it in people, others in places or things. Still others experience a few fleeting unexpected feelings of contentment and conclude that such brief moments are all we can have of happiness.

The problem is aggravated by our confusion about exactly what it is we mean when we speak of "happiness" or "joy." So, to examine the dilemma more carefully and to seek its resolution in the light of the gospel, we must attempt to give at least a working definition for our terms. That task requires first a realistic look at the nature of the human will, because—as we'll soon see—the daily choices we make determine to a great extent just how happy or joyful we will be.

The direction of the will

When biblical writers speak of the will, they usually call it the "heart." To describe the choices of the heart, they often use the imagery of *direction*, saying that the heart is turned, inclined, or drawn *toward* something or someone it loves (Genesis 34:3, Deuteronomy 17:17, 1 Kings 11:4). They also say that the heart can be led by the "eyes"—that is, the will moves in the direction of what it perceives as good and desirable, as if attracted to it (Job 31:7, Psalm 141:4).

Consequently, to love God is depicted as turning the heart toward Him, while to sin is pictured as turning the heart away from Him (Deuteronomy 29:18; 30:17; 1 Kings 8:48; 11:4,9; Jeremiah 17:5; Hebrews 3:12). The "upright in heart" are thus those with the proper posture toward God (Psalms 32:11, 36:10, 64:10).

Throughout the history of Christian theology, the Church's understanding of the nature of the human will has been deeply influenced by this biblical description. Within the ancient, and what I would call "classical," tradition of Western Christian thought, we continually find common ground in this regard among deep thinkers as diverse and as far apart as Augustine in the fifth century, Anselm of Canterbury in the eleventh, Thomas Aquinas in the thirteenth, John Calvin in the sixteenth, and Jonathan Edwards in the eighteenth.

According to this traditional understanding of what the Bible has described, to love is to "incline" the will in a particular direction, to move the will in desire toward something we perceive as good. Our attraction to what is good (or at least what *we* perceive as good) causes our wills to "reach toward" it in love. Our desire is to possess that good, to unite it somehow with ourselves.

In this classical view, then, God made the human will to be turned above all toward Himself, to be attracted to Him, to move in His direction—in short, to love Him. His perfect goodness should attract us by its moral beauty, so that we pray as David prayed: "One thing I ask of the LORD, this is what I seek: that I may dwell in the house of the LORD all the days of my life, to gaze upon the beauty of the LORD . . . " (Psalm 27:4). But when we sin, we turn our will away from God and move further from Him.

This ancient and biblically founded approach to understanding the human will has been a common and fruitful one throughout the history of the Church. It's been fruitful in my own life as well, because it reflects so accurately my own experience. When I act in love toward God, I, too, sense that my heart is turned toward Him and that my will reaches out toward the beauty of His great goodness. On the other hand, when I act sinfully, I sense that my heart is turned away from God, turning instead toward something else, reaching out for it because, for the moment, I love it more than I love Him.

To view the human will in this way provides a useful context for thinking about human happiness and human joy. It allows us to suggest some definitions for both based on the biblical imagery of the will's motion and direction.

The meaning of happiness

With this "directional" picture of the heart or will in mind, I think our best clue to the meaning of the term "happiness" is found in the root of one of its close synonyms: *contentment*. This word has the same root as the English word "contain." To be content is actually to *contain* or possess something that your mind has perceived as good and your will has reached out for. In my definition, then, to be happy—that is, happy at least for a time—is to be content in the sense of *being satisfied because we have obtained something good that we've desired*. As Aquinas described it, happiness "brings desire to rest."

In this sense, happiness is not so much a feeling as it is a condition or a state of being. It's a calming of the heart's activity resulting from our acquisition of what we've sought. This means that we can speak of happiness (though not in an ultimate sense) with regard to the fulfillment of particular desires.

The Bible refers to happiness in this sense, for example, when it talks about the formerly barren woman who is happy because she now has the children she desired (Psalm 113:9). A wife is happy in having a husband (Deuteronomy 24:5); a court official is happy to have the king's wisdom (2 Chronicles 9:7); a shepherd is happy to find a lost sheep (Matthew 18:13).

Perhaps the best biblical portrait of the condition I'd call happiness is in David's brief but beautiful psalm about the contentment of humility. There he sings, "I have stilled and quieted my soul; like a weaned child with its mother, like a weaned child is my soul within me" (Psalm 131:2). Anyone who has ever watched an infant grow beyond the nursing stage can recognize here the peaceful picture of a child who has ceased struggling to nurse because it already has the nourishment it desires.

Given this understanding of happiness, we can see why our pursuit of it is so difficult: Such a state is at best temporary and fragile, dependent on circumstances. Our English word "happy" has in fact the same root as our word "happenstance." The conditions for this kind of contentment are not always under our control; we can't always have what we want.

Yet the pursuit of happiness is more elusive still. Even if we acquire the thing we want, we may lose it again. And even if we don't lose it, the sense of satisfaction may fade as we find ourselves attracted to something else. Worse yet, we may discover that our perceptions were wrong, and what we thought was good was actually evil. So happiness of this sort is inherently fickle.

Is there, then, no genuine and enduring happiness? Yes, there is. But if we would speak of such an ultimate Happiness, we must look for the corresponding ultimate Good that the heart might seek, a Good that would make all other goods pale by comparison, and which could never be lost.

You alone, Lord, are that Good. You are Goodness itself, the One from whom comes "every good and perfect gift." You have made us for Yourself, and Your perfect will is that we would turn our wills toward You, to seek You above all else as our great Good, finding our happiness in possessing You. The pursuit of happiness is universal, Lord, because You have created all people for Happiness. You have "set eternity in the hearts of men" (Ecclesiastes 3:11), and when they seek eternity, whether they know it or not, they seek You.

A futile quest in this life
An old Arabic legend claims that when Adam and Eve were driven out of the Garden of Eden, the angel who held the flaming sword said to them, "Henceforth your hearts must

be your paradise." The terrible truth, of course, was that their rebellion had begun in their hearts, and without new hearts they could never again enjoy contentment. So our race has for ages wandered the earth in misery, with the faint memory that the happiness of walking in the Garden with God was once a reality, but now is lost.

Yet Jesus came to make it possible for us to be reconciled to God, that we might again walk with Him, and possess Him as our Father. In giving us new hearts, as God promised through Ezekiel (11:19), He has flung open again the gates to paradise. But we can't yet walk in.

When we're made part of Christ's household, God belongs to us, and we belong to God (Hebrews 3:6). Jesus has gone to prepare a place for us in our Father's house (John 14:2-3). But we aren't home yet; and so the ultimate Happiness that comes from possessing the ultimate Good is not yet ours.

As Aquinas described it, the complete happiness of heaven will result from our being continually united to God in love there. Meanwhile, in the present life, the extent of our happiness must depend on how continually we're united to Him in love now. Because our love is imperfect, our happiness will be imperfect. So even the Christian who isn't looking for happiness in the wrong places can't expect happiness as a constant reality. That only comes in the next life.[1]

By its very nature, then, the pursuit of happiness in this world is a futile quest. Even in our search to know and love God, we can only know and love Him in part; and we simply won't be content until we have all of Him—or, we should say, until He has all of us—in heaven.

The prophecy of Jeremiah to an unfaithful people, when God tells them they've been searching for happiness in the wrong way, thus speaks vividly to us as well. The imagery is pointed: "My people have committed two sins," the Lord thundered. "They have forsaken me, the spring of living water, and have dug their own cisterns, broken cisterns that cannot hold water" (Jeremiah 2:13).

I believe that we all tend to be like the people of Jerusalem who heard this divine rebuke. We go looking for things to make us happy and think that if we can only acquire them, we can somehow hoard them. But even if we do chance to catch a little "rain," all our cisterns are broken, and before long, the things we desired have drained away. We may have small happinesses for a season, because we may possess a few good things for a season. But none of us will ever be fully satisfied until the day when, as John of the Cross so beautifully said it, we forever "plunge ourselves into God."[2]

Yet in the meantime, God has also promised that He Himself is "a spring of living water." Though we can't hold on to happiness in this life, we can be refreshed by the presence of God. And to speak of that refreshment is to return to our primary subject of concern: the meaning of Joy.

NOTES:
1. Thomas Aquinas, *Treatise on Happiness*, translated by John A. Oesterle (Englewood Cliffs, N.J.: Prentice-Hall, 1964), page 30.
2. John of the Cross, *The Collected Works of St. John of the Cross*, translated by Kieran Kavanaugh and Otilio Rodriguez (Washington, D.C.: ICS Publications, 1979), page 680.

O God, you are my God,
earnestly I seek you;
my soul thirsts for you,
my body longs for you,
in a dry and weary land
where there is no water.
I have seen you in the sanctuary
and beheld your power and your glory.
PSALM 63:1-2

☐

Then I will go to the altar of God,
to God, my joy and my delight.
PSALM 43:4

☐

The very sight of God causes delight. Hence he who sees
God cannot be without delight.
THOMAS AQUINAS

☐

Like the bee that sucks honey from all the wildflowers and will not use
them for anything else, the soul easily extracts the sweetness of love from
all the things that happen to her, that is, she loves God in them. Thus
everything leads her to love always the delight of loving God.
JOHN OF THE CROSS

☐

Man's chief end is to glorify God, and to enjoy Him forever.
THE WESTMINSTER SHORTER CATECHISM

CHAPTER 4

THE SPRING OF LIVING WATER

The murderous salt of the Dead Sea basin in Israel gives that body of water its name. So as I dried off in the sun from my first dip there some years ago, I thought of the story of Lot's wife, who had been turned into a pillar of salt somewhere in the vicinity (Genesis 19:26). My own skin and hair were so thickly caked with crystals that I had to wonder whether the resulting tingling sensation was anything like what she felt when her transformation had just begun.

It was July, so the heat intensified the effects of the salt. The water in my canteen had given out hours before, and my throat was possibly as parched as it's ever been. But this time the situation was infinitely worse, because I felt as if my whole body were crying out for a drink. From head to toe, my skin itself was thirsty.

You can imagine my great delight, then, when a friend brought me through the burning sand and stones to a nearby oasis called En Gedi. Shady and green, this little garden surrounded a small waterfall of fresh, cold streams pouring from a cave in its heart. The resulting pool made that patch of desert blossom and bear the sweetest of fruits.

When I came to the edge of the water, I plunged into the falls. My whole body seemed to drink and find refreshment. For the moment, I was in paradise. No wonder David made this very oasis his retreat when Saul was pursuing him (1 Samuel 23:29).

The delight I felt at the oasis that day is the perfect physical image for what we call joy. In fact, life-giving water is perhaps the most common biblical metaphor for this experience: "The desert and the parched land will be glad," Isaiah prophesied. "The wilderness will rejoice and blossom . . . . It will rejoice greatly and shout for joy . . . . Water will gush forth in the wilderness and streams in the desert. The burning sand will become a pool, the thirsty ground bubbling springs" (Isaiah 35:1-2,6-7).

We all know that kind of refreshing delight, what the Puritan theologian Jonathan Edwards called a "sweetness" that can fill us at times with pleasure. The joy may be brief or sustained, subtle or overwhelming. Its immediate source may be a thought, a sight, a sound, a touch. Whatever kind it is, we all agree that joy is desirable, a great good.

But how does this joy differ from happiness? Some would say it's simply a matter of intensity; others would claim it depends on the source. I think, however, that the two experiences are in different categories altogether, though they certainly can come to us at the same time, and are often related. The briefest definition I could offer is this: *Joy is the sense of delight that arises within us in the presence of someone or something we love.*

We should note here that while happiness, according to our earlier definition, is a condition or state of being, joy is a "sense." Edwards called it, in the language of his day, an "affection"; today we might use the word "feeling," though with a deeper significance than is usually attached to that term. Because "sense" can refer to a broader and more generalized feeling, awareness, or realization, it seems to me the best choice of words for now.

To put it another way, joy is a *response* rather than a state of being. It depends, not on our *acquisition* of something, but rather on our *encounter* with something. Happiness possesses, joy appreciates; happiness grasps, joy beholds. As theologian Karl Barth once observed, "Joy is really the simplest form of gratitude."[1]

This understanding of joy is found throughout the Bible. Joy is the appreciative response, for example, of a father to the goodness of wisdom he finds in his son (Proverbs 15:20). It's the exultation of a righteous person over the righteous reign of justice in the land (Proverbs 21:15). It's the delight taken by a citizen of Jerusalem in the sight of his native city's beauty (Psalm 48:1-2). In each of these cases, joy is the sense of delight arising in these people in the presence of someone or something they love.

A personal example

Perhaps a simple personal experience might serve best as a model for what we mean by joy and how it differs from happiness. When my wife and I had been married a few years, we both desired to have a child. That desire turned our hearts in a particular direction so that we acted to prepare for conception. Our wills, to use the ancient image we've described, "reached out" for the child we desired.

When our daughter, Lydia, was born, our desire was fulfilled, and so to that extent we were happy. We now possessed what we'd wanted, and our wills ceased striving in that direction. Our desire, as Aquinas put it, was "at rest."

By now the wish for another child has awakened in both of us, so to that extent, we're no longer happy. Our wills are turning once again in the direction of another pregnancy. And though it's natural and good for a couple to want children, we can be sure that this kind of happiness is necessarily limited. After we have two, we may want still another; but having three, we may not be content with the kind of relationship we have with them. Meanwhile, we know that someday either we will lose them, or they will lose us. So the state of happiness with regard to our children is necessarily fragile in this life.

On the other hand, the birth of my daughter was also a time of *joy*. In that precious moment when I witnessed the event, I was overwhelmed with a sense of delight, with an inner sweetness that came from enjoying the rare beauty of the sight before me: A new life had come into the world. I was, of course, also happy, for I now had the object of my desire. But the *joy* I felt at the moment was my heart's response to the beauty of the scene, to the glory and goodness of it all.

The difference as we've defined it is perhaps best illustrated in the fact that the doctor who delivered Lydia could share my joy, but not my happiness. Because she was my child, I could be happy at the birth in a way he could not; it was no satisfaction of a desire for him. But the beauty of the moment was not my possession. The doctor could appreciate that beauty as well, so he shared my joy.

Since that evening, Lydia has continued to be an occasion for delight. Whether or not I'm content—that is, happy—with our relationship at any given moment, a certain beauty often shines through her countenance, her words, or her actions. I love the goodness I see in her, and I rejoice at the sight. The same could be said of the beauty in my wife or my friends, in a majestic hymn or a perfect rose.

Sweetness and pain

This view of joy explains why the experience is at once sweet and painful (though the pain is sometimes lost in the immensity of the sweetness). The goodness we see, love, and delight in is not ours to possess, at least not yet. Still we long to be joined with it somehow. This longing for union with what we love finds its clearest earthly expression in the consummation of the marriage vow. But such a union is only a portrait of something much greater.

That great and ultimate Joy is what the Bible calls "the wedding supper of the Lamb," when we will appear in purity as the Bride of Christ, whom He has sought in love (Revelation 19:9). Toward that end, God draws us to Himself. He is the Bridegroom who woos us whenever we're attracted to goodness or when we find joy in some beauty.

Because beauty is the source of joy, our ultimate Joy must arise from our delight in the beauty of God, in the attractiveness of His goodness and holiness. That is the heart of joy. As Edwards reminded us, "All the beauty to be found throughout the whole creation, is but the reflection of the diffused beams of that Being who hath an infinite fulness of brightness and glory."[2]

You, my Lord, are the Bridegroom of whom it was sung, "We rejoice and delight in you; we will praise your love more than wine" (Song of Songs 1:4). For You are altogether beautiful with the beauty of perfect holiness, and I delight in You. You are the bright Morning Star, the Dayspring from on high, the Lily of the valley, the Fairest of ten thousand (Revelation 22:16; Luke 1:78; Song of Songs 2:1, 5:10).

All beauty flows from You and leads back to You, if we will only love enough to trace it back to You. I see Your beauty in the sunset, because it is Your garment; I see Your beauty in my wife, because she is Your temple. And just as the beauty of a portrait leads me in gratitude back to the beauty within the painter, all beauty around me beckons me to seek its Creator with thanksgiving. No wonder, my Father, that "my soul waits for [You], more than watchmen wait for the morning" (Psalm 130:6).

Just as being eternally united to God's perfect goodness is the ultimate of human Happiness, being eternally united to God's perfect beauty is the ultimate of human Joy. For that reason, even now, when we catch a glimpse of God, we experience joy as a token, a pledge, of our final encounter Face-to-face. As Edwards described it, the sweetness of the little joys we experience now are a foretaste, a "prelibation of the joy of heaven," when we will feast at the great banquet of the Lord, and our Joy will be perfect.[3]

But that's true only if our hearts are turned in welcome toward the coming King. We must allow our little joys to be caught up in the great Joy by continually turning with gratitude from the immediate sources of our delight toward the One whose holiness is perfect Delight. When God comes into view, our joy is made full. Thus the little showers of blessing, when they trickle together into the great Spring of living water, will swell Its flow within us. But if they fall alone, they disperse into the sand and evaporate.

No doubt, even that richer, fuller Joy will still be painful, because it longs to be consummated. But as C. S. Lewis has observed, "The very nature of Joy makes nonsense of our common distinction between having and wanting. There, to have is to want and to want is to have."[4] Even the pain of longing for God is more precious than the possession of anything else.

NOTES:
1. Karl Barth, *Church Dogmatics*, Volume 3, Part 4, "The Doctrine of Creation," translated by A.T. Mackay (Edinburgh: T & T Clark, 1961), page 375.
2. Jonathan Edwards, *The Nature of True Virtue* (Ann Arbor, Mich.: University of Michigan Press, 1960), page 14.
3. Edwards, "Religious Affections," in *Jonathan Edwards: Representative Selections*, Clarence H. Faust and Thomas H. Johnson, ed. (New York: Hilland Wang, 1962), page 208.
4. C. S. Lewis, *Surprised by Joy: The Shape of My Early Life* (London: Fontana, 1959), page 135.

They will come and shout for joy on the heights of Zion;
they will rejoice in the bounty of the LORD. . . .
They will be like a well-watered garden,
and they will sorrow no more.
JEREMIAH 31:12

□

I will search for the one my heart loves.
SONG OF SONGS 3:2

□

My commonest attitude is this simple attentiveness, an habitual, loving
turning of my eyes to God, to whom I often find myself bound with more
happiness and gratification than that which a babe enjoys clinging
to its nurse's breast.
BROTHER LAWRENCE

□

I have not yet thought or said, O Lord, how much Your blessed ones will
rejoice. Surely, they will rejoice in the degree that they will love. And they
will love in the degree that they will know. How much will they know
You in that day, Lord; how much will they love You?
ANSELM OF CANTERBURY

CHAPTER 5

A WATERED GARDEN

Joy is a gift, a gracious gift. We can never earn it. Who among us could ever be worthy of the joyous presence of God? Yet despite our rebellion, He has graciously stooped to join us on this desert planet, first in flesh and now in Spirit. No wonder the New Testament Greek word for grace, *charis*, actually comes from *chara*, the word for joy. In that language, grace originally meant "that which causes delight."

Yes, the Spring of God that flows within us flows freely. Nevertheless, the land around a spring doesn't become a garden until it's cultivated. God greatly desires each of our souls to become "a well-watered garden" (Jeremiah 31:12). *He* supplies the water, because His presence brings with it joy (Psalm 21:6). But He calls *us* to prepare our hearts to receive the flow of joy so that we can bear fruit.

This process of cultivation can be described in several stages. First, we must have built in us faith, love, and hope, which I call the three *floodgates* of joy. The perspectives provided by these three essentials of our walk with God release joy from the divine river and open us up to receive it by turning our gaze toward God. Thus we can see, know, and love Him in His mighty acts and His precious promises.

The next stage is what I call digging the *furrows* of joy. Once we have a basic knowledge of who God is, of the beauty of His perfect goodness and holiness, we can "plow" our lives in certain ways that perfect our vision of God, and so allow the waters of joy to be channeled fruitfully. The furrows we dig make a way for joy to flow into every area of our lives.

The next stage (it's actually simultaneous with the second) involves dealing with what I call the *freezing* of joy. Certain attitudes and behaviors tend to obscure our vision of God in one way or another. When we can't see Him in a particular situation, our joy freezes up and ceases to flow.

Next come the *fruits* of joy, those qualities in our character that God delights to find in our "garden." When the soil of our souls has been well watered with joy, we're not only refreshed; we're transformed. This part of the process is especially thrilling, because in it we see God Himself taking pleasure in us; we have the high honor of becoming a contributor to *His* delight.

Finally, we look forward to what I call the *feast* of joy. Our delight in God will be perfected when we at last see Him, not "through a glass, darkly," but instead "face to face" (1 Corinthians 13:12, KJV). In that eternal celebration, we'll know even as we're known, we'll love as we're loved, and our joy will be beyond the telling as we drink from the very fountainhead of the Water of Life and feast on the sweet fruit God has grown within us.

Seeing, knowing, loving, enjoying

Before we explore each of these stages separately, however, we need to understand the inner sequence of events culminating in joy that lies behind each of them. We've already touched on this sequence implicitly, but before we go further we should make it explicit, because I'm convinced it's the key to understanding how joy is discovered in any situation.

You may have noticed that in the process described earlier, each step begins with *seeing the Lord* in one way or another. The floodgates, the furrows, the fruits, and the feast of joy all involve a particular *vision of God*, a certain angle of vision or a perspective that allows us to view Him more clearly and completely. On the other hand, the freezing of joy results from the *obscuring* of our vision of Him.

Jesus spoke of this connection between vision and rejoicing when He comforted His disciples on the night of His betrayal. He told them, "In a little while you will see me no more, and then after a little while you will see me. . . . I tell you the truth, you will weep and mourn while the world rejoices. You will grieve but your grief will turn to joy . . . . Now is your time of grief, but I will see you again and you will rejoice, and no one will take away your joy" (John 16:16,20,22).

For the first disciples as for us, joy comes when we see the Lord, because it's the natural result of being in the presence of someone we love. And just as they continued to see Him even after His body had ascended into heaven—by the works He did through His Spirit—we, too, can see Him if we're willing to look for Him. The resulting vision of God will cause joy to well up within us.

Catherine of Siena, whose writings have instructed and encouraged thousands since the fourteenth century, described with beautiful simplicity the sequence of inner events involved as joy flows from seeing God. Speaking to her about the soul who has sought Him, the Lord said, "Seeing Me, she knows Me. Knowing Me, she loves Me. Loving Me, she enjoys Me, the supreme eternal Good."[1]

That is, in a nutshell, what I would call the "order of joy": seeing, knowing, loving, enjoying. Each activity leads to the next. I believe the order applies to any of our experiences of delight, though at times it all happens so fast that we may not be able to distinguish each step. In any case, if we would drink deeply of *ultimate* Joy, we must necessarily begin with a vision of God. The cry of the psalmist must be our own: "My eyes are fixed on you, O Sovereign LORD" (Psalm 141:8).

This sequence of inner experience should clarify now the reasons for the claim with which this book began: *To discover joy, we must abandon the search for it, and go looking instead for the One who is Himself joy to see, to know, and to love.* Whenever possible, we must look for God's presence in a given situation. If we can see the beauty of His goodness there at work, we will know Him better. Knowing Him better, we will love Him all the more. And loving Him, we will enjoy His presence.

Whatever my circumstances, Jesus, You have promised to be with me. I know You are always near, but I lose sight of You, Lord, when things around me are dark or distracting. And when I lose sight of You, I lose all joy.

Teach me to seek You in the whirlwind, in the earthquake, in the fire, in the still, small Voice. Open my eyes, shine Your light, uncover Your face. You who are the Herald of the Morning, lift up Your countenance, and mine too will brighten, just as the dewdrop sparkles in the glory of the dawn.

Seeing, knowing, loving, enjoying. This "order of joy" is at the heart of our walk with God. It was illustrated for me in a simple way one dreary winter morning in Germany some years ago. The staff photographer of our Christian mission organization was making individual portraits for our newsletter, and my turn for a sitting had come. At the time my heart was full of financial concerns and questions about my future, so my face reflected the inner turmoil. How, I thought, could I possibly fake a smile?

But my friend behind the camera was a wise man. Once I was seated, he gave me one brief instruction: "For just a minute, I want you to think of someone back home you love very deeply."

Immediately my thoughts turned to my mother, and I could see her face in my mind. At that moment, as I "saw" her, I loved her more than ever. Just the thought of her kind, selfless face caused a little spring of joy to well up inside. The joy naturally spilled over onto my face. The photographer snapped the shutter, and the result was the best portrait ever taken of me.

Just as "seeing" my beloved mother in that moment awakened joy in me, so the "sight" of our Lord can create in us a holy delight. In a sense, then, the task before us as we prepare ourselves for joy is actually a matter of *directing our attention*. Like the bride in the Song of Songs, we must search diligently, casting the eyes of our soul in every direction until we find the Bridegroom (Song of Songs 3:1-3). Whatever comes our way, we must look for God's presence if we want to open ourselves to joy.

Jonathan Edwards, who was the great revivalist of the First Great Awakening in America, recognized this principle as it applied to evangelism. Sadly, he's usually remembered as a "hellfire and brimstone" preacher because of his eloquent sermon "Sinners in the Hands of an Angry God." Yet a look at his other writings shows that he could also win people to the Lord by portraying, as he called them in another sermon, "The Excellencies of Christ." In keeping with his understanding of the human will, Edwards was certain that if only he could paint the picture of God's goodness and holiness accurately enough, the loveliness of that divine Portrait would draw men and women to the One portrayed. So through his words he carefully and skillfully turned their attention to the beauty of God.

If even unbelievers can be drawn to Jesus by the sight of His holiness and grace, how much more so should *we* be drawn, who already know and love Him! None of us can see God perfectly, and so none of us has perfect joy. For that reason, however far along we might be in our walk with God, we can all benefit from considering how it's possible to gain a clearer vision of the Lord. We must learn to "fix our eyes" on Him.

This intentional act of looking for God, I'm convinced, is part of what it means to *rejoice*—to participate actively in joy. After all, Paul's famous words to the church at Philippi were a command: "Rejoice in the Lord always. I will say it again: Rejoice!" (Philippians 4:4). That means his friends were expected to respond to the exhortation with some act of the will.

Yet it makes no sense to tell people they *must* take pleasure in something whether they like it or not. Though we can tell a child, for example, to finish her vegetables, we'd be silly to insist that she also enjoy them at our command. Joy is a natural and automatic response to goodness, and therefore beyond our immediate control.

Nevertheless, we *can* make it our continual intention to be open to joy by looking for God in every situation. His goodness is indeed delightful, and will bring us joy once we have Him in view. But the joy will be absent as long as our gaze is turned away from God.

To "rejoice always," then, means (at least in part) to cultivate what A. W. Tozer once perceptively called "the inward habit of beholding God."[2] In the chapters to come we will consider some ways to maintain that habit in a variety of circumstances. But before we do, one other element of the act of rejoicing must be carefully examined. It is, in fact, the element that enriches and completes that act, and makes our joy full. And it deserves its own chapter.

NOTES:
1. Catherine of Siena, *The Dialogue*, translated by Suzanne Noffke (New York: Paulist Press, 1980), page 92.
2. A. W. Tozer, *The Pursuit of God* (Old Tappan, N.J.: Revell), page 96.

You turned my wailing into dancing;
you removed my sackcloth and clothed me with joy,
that my heart may sing to you and not be silent.
PSALM 30:11-12

□

Shout for joy to the LORD, all the earth,
burst into jubilant song with music;
make music to the LORD with the harp,
with the harp and the sound of singing,
with trumpets and the blast of the ram's horn—
shout for joy before the LORD, the King.
Let the sea resound, and everything in it,
the world, and all who live in it.
Let the rivers clap their hands,
let the mountains sing together for joy;
let them sing before the LORD.
PSALM 98:4-9

□

True joy . . . will not be so shut up within the heart that no signs of it
will appear outside. A quiet heart and one which truly believes that God
has been reconciled to us on account of Christ will produce a cheerful
countenance and happy eyes, and it will loosen the tongue for the praises
to God. . . . God is not offended by gaiety.
MARTIN LUTHER

□

When I think upon my God, my heart is so full of joy that the notes
dance and leap from my pen.
FRANZ JOSEF HAYDN

□

O for a thousand tongues to sing my great Redeemer's praise!
CHARLES WESLEY

CHAPTER 6

MAKING MUSIC IN YOUR HEART

On that hot summer day when my friend led me from the Dead Sea to the oasis of En Gedi, I wasn't totally surprised to see the lush vegetation come into view beyond the rocks where we walked. While we were approaching, I'd been given a clue that falls were near: The water sang as it poured into the pool, and its music could be heard some distance away.

That refreshing sound I heard points to yet another metaphor for joy used by the biblical authors. Alongside the imagery of water, and often appearing in the same passages, is that of *music*. Again and again, the response of God's joyous people to His goodness is portrayed as musical, and physically expressive, jubilation: singing, dancing, shouting, clapping, leaping, and playing instruments. At the same time, the exhilaration of this activity is intensified by the awareness that all creation joins in the song (Psalms 5, 33, 47, 96, 98, 150, and many others).

Such boisterous celebration provides us with a vivid picture of a second aspect of rejoicing: the act of *expressing* our joy. When the apostle Paul commanded Christians to rejoice, I believe he was insisting not only that we direct our attention to God's goodness and beauty, but also that we allow the resulting joy to come pouring out of us. "Speak to one another," he urged, "with psalms, hymns and spiritual songs. Sing and make music in your heart to the Lord" (Ephesians 5:19).

In this exhortation, of course, Paul was only echoing the exuberance of Jesus, who had told His disciples that when they rejoice they should "*leap* for joy" (Luke 6:23). In fact, the Lord Himself was standing within a long tradition of biblical people who knew God so closely that they could hardly contain their joy, and expressed it in physical ways. The prophetess Miriam and her fellow Israelites exulted in God's salvation in a dance with tambourines (Exodus 15:20-21). King David and his soldiers danced before the Lord "with all their might," accompanied by music of the loudest variety (2 Samuel 6:5,14-15). Even John the Baptist, while still a baby in his mother's womb, leaped for joy at the sound of Mary's voice (Luke 1:44).

The root meanings of the biblical words for joy themselves reflect this element of rejoicing. One means literally to jump for joy; another means to sound a trumpet. One refers to a loud, ringing cry; still another to the shattering force of exultation. And one was used originally to describe the way spring lambs frisk and skip in the meadow!

The sad restraints of culture
Such a spontaneous demonstration of delight is natural to human beings. The soul is so closely connected to the body that the river of joy, when it springs up in one, necessarily flows into the other. We need only watch young children have fun to realize that we were made to let joy bubble out.

Nevertheless, somehow our culture has concluded that the exuberant physical expression of joy is, in adults, simply unacceptable. Few of us allow ourselves a whoop and a leap when we hear glad news. We've even learned to turn our faces away in embarrassment when some joy erupts from us irrepressibly in tears.

Actually, we do allow adults some physical expressions of joy. But the places where our society says exuberance is acceptable should tell us just how inverted our values are. Many churches, for example, would be horrified to see an enthusiastic expression of joy in the Lord that goes beyond a polite smile or perhaps a quiet "Amen." Yet some of those same folks have no qualms about screaming and leaping and dancing in the bleachers when their football team wins a game. Shouldn't we allow ourselves to get at least as excited about the Creator of the universe as we do about a pigskin?

The prophet Jeremiah foretold a time when the people of God, both children and adults, would rejoice without inhibition because of the goodness of God. The Lord said through him, "Then maidens will dance and be glad, young men and old as well. I will turn their mourning into gladness; I will give them comfort and joy instead of sorrow" (Jeremiah 31:13).

For the sons and daughters of God who have learned that the Kingdom of God belongs to those who are childlike (Luke 18:17), this prophecy has already been fulfilled. Resisting the world's attempt to diminish their joy in the Lord, they've put aside truly childish things—like being afraid of what others will say—and have "girded themselves with gladness" in their celebration of God.

Francis of Assisi was one of those childlike rejoicers. Even on his deathbed, he sang a glad song to God. John of the Cross, one of the wisest Christian teachers of the six-teenth century, was another. As he celebrated Christmas services one year beside a nativity scene, he was overcome with joy at the Advent of Christ. So without giving thought to what others might say, old John took into his arms the carved figure of the baby Jesus from the hay—then began to dance unashamedly and with delight.

In admiring the exuberance of ancient Hebrew worship, C. S. Lewis observed, "I think we delight to praise what we enjoy because the praise not merely expresses but completes the enjoyment; it is its appointed consummation."[1] This reality is apparent whenever we see anything beautiful that gives us delight. Couples in love never tire of telling each other how they enjoy being together. Children call their parents to the window to see a lovely sunset, and exclaim to one another how pretty it is. Whenever we give ourselves "permission" to express gladness openly— whether in word, song, laughter, or even in an exultant leap—we allow our joy to be made full. But when we restrict the domain of our rejoicing to the inside alone, we impoverish our joy.

At the same time, the explicit expression of gladness in God, which most often takes the form of praise to Him, is good simply because it's appropriate. As the ancient liturgy reminds us, "It is *right* to give Him thanks and praise." When the psalmist urged the saints to sing and play before God, he insisted, "Sing joyfully to the LORD, you righteous; it is fitting for the upright to praise him" (Psalm 33:1).

Bringing the river to the surface

For these reasons, then, we must allow the streams of God within us to sing their song. Joining together the two biblical metaphors of water and music in this way, we might describe the expression of joy as the conscious act of *bringing to the surface the river of delight that runs within us, so that the music of its flow can be heard.* A smile or a song, a shout or a leap, a dance or a hand clap, can uncover the joy within us and expose it to the fresh air so that our delight is intensified.

Meanwhile, we should remember that when the ancient Jews returning from exile shouted for joy at the laying of the Temple foundation, "the sound was heard far away"—presumably by their unbelieving neighbors who were curious about what was going on (Ezra 3:13). Just as I could hear from a distance the melody of the waterfall at En Gedi, so also our joy can be heard by others when we bring it to the surface. And if they stand close enough, they themselves may very well be splashed by its refreshing spray.

The act of rejoicing is our high privilege as a people redeemed by the Lord. When we turn our attention to look for a glimpse of God in every situation and then allow the resulting delight in His love to flow out of us, we're making ourselves vessels of heaven's joy. This double nature of rejoicing—vision and expression—should be kept in mind throughout the rest of our discussion of the joyful life. As we attempt to trace the relationship between joy and the other aspects of our walk with God, we'll see that in one form or another, rejoicing as we've defined it is an intentional activity to be carried on in all the areas of life.

"Blessed are those who have learned to acclaim you, who walk in the light of your presence, O LORD. They rejoice in your name all day long; they exult [they leap for joy!] in your righteousness. For you are their glory and strength" (Psalm 89:15-17).

You are by no means deaf, Lord, but neither are You nervous! For ages Your people have let all that is within them bless Your holy name—both their hearts and their flesh have cried out to You, the living God, and the joyful noise has reverberated through all heaven and earth. The mountains rejoice before You with song, Father, and the trees clap their hands. The sea resounds with celebration; the fields are jubilant; the leviathan frolics with delight in the deep (Psalms 96:11-13, 98:4-9, 104:26). Everything that has breath joins the morning stars in shouting for joy. And who, my Lord, could wish to be left out of that glad cosmic chorus?

NOTES:
1. C. S. Lewis, *Reflections on the Psalms* (London: Fontana, 1967), page 81.

PART 2

THE FLOODGATES OF JOY

And now these three remain: faith, hope and love.
1 CORINTHIANS 13:13

□

"Holy, holy, holy is the Lord God Almighty, who was, and is,
and is to come."
REVELATION 4:8

□

There is no love without hope, no hope without love, and neither love
nor hope without faith.
AUGUSTINE

□

When the eyes of the soul looking out meet the eyes of God looking in,
heaven has begun right here on this earth.
A. W. TOZER

CHAPTER 7

"WHO WAS, AND IS, AND IS TO COME"

"No one has ever seen God" (1 John 4:12). In His essence, the "I AM" who is beyond all comprehension has never been beheld by a human being. For how could created eyes ever hope to view the uncreated One, "who lives in unapproachable light, whom no one has seen or can see"? (1 Timothy 6:16).

Yet God in His grace has condescended to be seen, not as He is in His essence, but in ways that we can receive, if not understand. He appeared to Abraham near the great trees of Mamre and to Isaac at Beersheba (Genesis 18:1, 26:23-24). He stood at the top of Jacob's ladder and wrestled with him at Peniel (Genesis 28:12-13, 32:22-30). He spoke to Moses from the burning bush and from the fire atop Mount Sinai (Exodus 3:4-6, 19:18). God led the Israelites through the desert in a pillar of fire and of cloud (Exodus 13:21). His presence filled Solomon's Temple with a cloud of glory (1 Kings 8:10-11). Isaiah saw Him exalted on a throne (Isaiah 6:1) and Ezekiel saw Him above the cherubim (Ezekiel 10:4).

When Christ was born, the fire and cloud became flesh

and blood. "Anyone who has seen me has seen the Father," Jesus told us (John 14:9). In Him God at last had a face the world could touch. Then, at Pentecost, flesh became fire once more, as the Holy Spirit descended into the hearts of the disciples (Acts 2:1-4). Afterward, Paul saw the Lord on the road to Damascus and Ananias saw Him in a vision (Acts 9:3-17). John saw Him on the island of Patmos as He will appear on the Day of Judgment (Revelation 1:12-18).

Through the eyes of each of these people and in the events of their lives, we, too, are able to see something of God. We can see Him at work in our own lives as well. Though it hasn't been granted to many to have a dazzling vision of the Lord, yet in a real sense the eyes of our soul can direct their gaze to find Him in the places where He has invaded, still invades, and will again invade, our world.

In the words of John's revelation, our Lord is the One "who was, and is, and is to come" (Revelation 4:8). As we look in these three directions of time—the past, the present, and the future—we can find Him in all three, waiting for us to see Him, to know Him, to love Him, and to enjoy Him there.

The floodgates must be open

We've spoken of joy as the river of God, and the human heart as a garden that must be cultivated to receive it. Certain godly disciplines and attitudes, when plowed into us, become the furrows through which joy refreshes our hearts. We'll turn our attention to those soon. But just as with any irrigated land, the furrows will never be filled as long as the floodgates remain closed.

I'm convinced that the three floodgates of joy are *faith*, *hope*, and *love*. Without these three, furrows such as prayer, Bible study, or service are dusty and dry—and sterile. Before such disciplines can function as channels of God's river, faith, love, and hope must be built into our lives as the point of entrance for joy's flow.

These three qualities have been the subject of many volumes. Even those who have seemed to understand them best admit that their knowledge is limited. So we obviously have no intention of attempting a comprehensive, let alone an exhaustive, discussion of them in these pages.

Our goal is much more modest. We want to discover specifically how faith, hope, and love contribute to joy in the believer's life. So if seeing God ultimately leads to enjoying God, we might ask our question this way: What is the particular perspective on God provided by faith, hope, or love that allows us to know and love Him in a way that brings joy?

Whatever else they may be, these three aspects of our life in Christ are in a sense *ways of looking to God*. One approach to talking about the nature of the three perspectives involved in faith, hope, and love is to think of them as pointing in the three directions of time where we've said God is waiting to be found. First of all, in an important sense *faith* is directed primarily toward the events of the past. This is not to say that faith isn't exercised in the present, but rather that faith *looks* to the past for its glimpse of God. Our faith is a response to God's perfect faithfulness as we see it demonstrated in the history of the world and of our own lives.

Meanwhile, *hope* is always directed toward the future. While the perspective of faith stretches out toward those things that God has done, believing that they were for our good, hope stretches forward toward those things God has promised to do, believing that they, too, are for our blessing. From the perspective of time, hope is the mirror image of faith. We can look to the future confidently because we can look to the past confidently. "Faith is being sure of what we hope for" (Hebrews 11:1).

Finally, *love* is directed primarily toward the present. Our love response to God's loving-kindness looks to the here and now for ways to express itself. Today is the only day we have to love, and so the angle of love's vision is toward a view of God at work in the present.

In light of these perspectives, then, we can see that faith is being "certain of what we do not see" (Hebrews 11:1). We can't literally see the events of the past in which God was at work. We can read about them or hear about them, but they can never appear before our physical eyes. Only the eyes of the soul can look back at them with trust.

In the same way, "Hope that is seen is no hope at all. Who hopes for what he already has?" (Romans 8:24). Our physical eyes can't see the events of the future in which God will work all things according to His plan. Only the eyes of the soul can look patiently for their fulfillment.

Yet the perspective of love is now, and we *can* see God at work in our lives today. "No one has ever seen God," said John, "but if we love one another, God lives in us and his love is made complete in us" (1 John 4:12). When love searches for God in the present, it finds Him visible in the place where He is working through us and through others.

The disciplines of the Christian life dig little furrows in our hearts by giving us narrowly focused views of God that show us some detail of His character. But faith, hope, and love provide the broad perspective. The three of them together stretch from one horizon of time to the other, allowing us abundant space to see the great panorama of God's goodness.

Between those two horizons, my Lord, You show Yourself to be altogether beautiful, utterly holy. And so "where morning dawns and evening fades you call forth songs of joy" (Psalm 65:8). I rejoice to see You standing there, Jesus, the same yesterday, today, and forever (Hebrews 13:8). In faith, in hope, in love, the eyes of my soul look for a glimpse of You with longing and delight.

Where the vision of the Lord is so great, the joy in the Lord is necessarily a flood. So we must now consider each of these three floodgates in turn.

Burst into songs of joy together,
you ruins of Jerusalem,
for the LORD has comforted his people,
he has redeemed Jerusalem.
The LORD will lay bare his holy arm
in the sight of all the nations,
and all the ends of the earth will see
the salvation of our God.
ISAIAH 52:9-10

□

"I bring you good news of great joy that will be for all the people. Today
in the town of David a Savior has been born to you;
he is Christ the Lord."
LUKE 2:10-11

□

Faith is not a once-done act, but a continuous gaze of the heart at the
Triune God. Believing, then, is directing the heart's attention to Jesus. It
is lifting the mind to "behold the Lamb of God," and never ceasing that
beholding for the rest of our lives.
A. W. TOZER

□

Faith always has as a companion joy in the Holy Spirit.
MARTIN LUTHER

□

Could I behold those Hands which span the poles and tune all spheres at
once, pierced with those holes?
JOHN DONNE

CHAPTER 8

FAITH:
Seeing God's Hand in the Past

The Bible is replete with references to God that speak of what, in a human, would be called, "physical features." We know of course that God is not contained in a physical body. Yet the biblical writers insist on talking about God's eyes (Psalm 34:15), ears (2 Kings 19:16), arms (Isaiah 52:10), face (Numbers 6:25), feet (Psalm 18:9), back (Exodus 33:23), and even nostrils (Psalm 18:15).

Some critics have assumed that such language is at worst "primitive," at best "poetic." According to this understanding, it is simple metaphor. We talk about God's hand, for example, in order to say that His activity resembles in some sense the human hand, just as we talk metaphorically about the heart of a discussion. The human appendage is thus presumed to be the concrete reality, whereas the divine action is its vague, figurative echo.

Now I'd agree that this language about God is metaphorical, but only in a sense that turns the notion of metaphor on its head. If, as the Scripture affirms, we're created in the image of God (Genesis 1:27) and our life here is only a shadow of the substance in heaven (Hebrews 8:5, 10:1), then we're actually using a metaphor in the other direction: We speak of our own human limbs as hands because they somehow echo or parallel the reality in God that is the true Hand. God can extend His power, can shape and move and create; to the extent that we use our upper appendages to imitate His activity, we're employing hands. Thus when we say "God's hand," we're talking directly; when we say "my hand," we're speaking metaphorically.

Or take another example: the phrase "God's eyes." In every sense of the word, God *sees*—all that is, at all times, from every angle. He perceives all things; He's directly aware of their existence. And because He's granted humans a limited portion of that capability—we can perceive whatever reflects light to our eyes within a certain spectrum of electromagnetic frequencies—then we, too, can be said to have "eyes." Our organ of sight is an image of the divine ability of God's eyes.

In either case, God's eyes, hand, or other features are part of the truly hard Reality—the bright, deep, full, solid I AM that makes other modes of being seem pale, shallow, hollow, and flimsy by comparison. Heaven is the substance; we are the shadow. For that reason, I have no hesitation to talk about God's hands or feet or face. As C.S. Lewis sums up the matter, "Grammatically the things we say of Him are 'metaphorical': but in a deeper sense it is our own physical and psychic energies that are mere 'metaphors' of the real Life which is God."[1]

Rather than a crude or poetic approximation, then, such language is closer to the truth of God's reality than any philosophical abstraction or definition could provide. When we speak of the hand of God, I suppose we could say that we mean a certain quality in the divine nature, a pattern of activity in the divine behavior, that is imitated by us humans every time we use our hands to create, to destroy, to hold, to care, to feed, to write, or to extend our energy in any other manual way. But see how much power, beauty, and accuracy is immediately lost in our statement as soon as we try to use more abstract rather than biblical language.

So we will speak of the hand of God. It is that hand, I believe, that we see so clearly with the eyes of faith as we look to what God has done in the past. And it is the hand, as well, that we take in ours through faith. For as the Puritan preacher Thomas Hooker reminded us, "Faith is the hand of the soul; it takes hold of that mercy which God hath provided for us in Christ Jesus."[2]

What is revealed in God's hand

The vision of faith is first of all the vision of a *creative* God. When we see His hand in the beginning, it's dusty from the work of shaping the soil into a living creature (Genesis 2:7). He scatters out the stars across the heavens and counts them (Psalm 147:4). He labors to form each one of us as a potter forms the clay (Isaiah 64:8).

The vision of faith is also the vision of a *mighty* God. His hand, sang Moses, is "majestic in power" (Exodus 15:6): We see it hurling back the waters of the Red Sea (Exodus 13:9). It holds the tumultuous depths of the ocean and carves out a place for the continents (Psalm 95:4-5).

The vision of faith is as well the vision of a *holy* God. His hand, sang the psalmist, is "filled with righteousness" (Psalm 48:10). We see it rebuking the oppression of Pharaoh (Exodus 3:20) and smashing the idolatry of the Philistines (1 Samuel 5:1-6). God's hand wrote the laws of holiness on stone (Exodus 31:18), and it pours a bitter cup of judgment on the wickedness of the earth (Psalm 75:8).

Yet the vision of faith is above all the vision of a *loving* God. In His hand is "the life of every creature" (Job 12:10), and it upholds each of us (Psalm 63:8). It plants His people tenderly like a vine (Psalm 80:15); opens freely to feed all creatures and satisfy their desires (Psalm 145:15-16); protects the human race as a shepherd protects his sheep (Psalm 95:7).

God has demonstrated His creativity, power, holiness, and love throughout the events described in the Old Testament. There we find His hand extended on behalf of the world, sometimes in entreaty, sometimes in rebuke, always in desire for our good. Seeing God in this way helps us to know Him in these glorious qualities; knowing Him, we love Him. Loving Him, a joy springs up in us, because we delight in a God who is so creative, so powerful, so holy, so loving: "For you make me glad by your deeds, O LORD; I sing for joy at the works of your hands" (Psalm 92:4).

Even so, the vision of faith finds its focal point, not in the Old Testament, but rather at that juncture of history where God's hand once and for all ripped open the veil between heaven and earth. In Christ, God actually did take for Himself a body, and so the hand of God comes into flesh-and-blood clarity as the hand of Jesus. Yet in that flesh we see the most startling of sights: The hand of God is scarred.

How can it be? A powerful and holy hand, we had expected. A creative and loving hand, we had anticipated. But a vulnerable and wounded hand? He'd told us that our name was written on His palm (Isaiah 49:16); but we're dazed to find that the word is inscribed there in blood—*His* blood.

And so the eyes of the soul, when they look back in faith, fill with tears. How can it be? Eternity has poured Himself into an agonized moment; the Potter has climbed inside His fractured clay; the Hand that grasps the galaxies opens freely to receive the nail's malice and cover the nail with its blood.

Lord Jesus, that Blood alone would have been enough to earn all our love. That broken Clay lying in the tomb would have been for us in itself the great "treasure, hidden in a field," so precious that we would sell all we have to make it ours. Just to know that our Maker loved us enough to die for us would have filled us with joy. What language shall I borrow to thank You? What song shall I find to tell of the delight that is my gratitude, the sweetness that is my praise?

It was the greatest possible Gift from the greatest of Givers. What more could He have done to secure our joy?

"God," Augustine said of Christ, "in His infinite wisdom, knew not how to give more; God, in His infinite power, could not have given more; God, in His infinite riches, had not more to give."

And yet there was more; the Cross was only the unbelievable beginning. "For the joy set before him"—the joy of returning to His Father, whom He had loved eternally—Jesus endured the Cross and despised the shame (Hebrews 12:2). So when Sunday morning dawned and the Father cried, "Arise!" no power in heaven or on earth could have kept the Son in the grave. He was on His way home. The hand of God hurled away the stone, and the empty tomb became the site of a floodgate, releasing into the world a deluge of joy that the world cannot contain.

Because of what happened there, we, too, are on our way home. Looking back on that morning with the grateful eyes of faith, who could fail to rejoice?

NOTES:
1. C. S. Lewis, *Miracles: A Preliminary Study* (New York: Macmillan, 1947), page 94.
2. Thomas Hooker, *The Poor Doubting Christian Drawn to Christ* (Grand Rapids: Baker Book House, 1981), page 127.

Now we see but a poor reflection . . . then we shall see face to face.
1 CORINTHIANS 13:12

□

*Praise be to the God and Father of our Lord Jesus Christ! In his great
mercy he has given us new birth into a living hope through the
resurrection of Jesus Christ from the dead, and into an inheritance that
can never perish, spoil or fade—kept in heaven for you, who through
faith are shielded by God's power until the coming of the salvation that
is ready to be revealed in the last time. In this you greatly rejoice.*
1 PETER 1:3-6

□

*"Do not rejoice that the spirits submit to you, but rejoice that your names
are written in heaven."*
LUKE 10:20

□

*Now hope is the faculty of the soul to look out for mercy. As a man that
is in expectation of the coming of his friend, goeth to the top of the hill,
looks round about him, to see if he can understand anything of his
friend; so the soul hopes and waits, and stretches itself out for mercy.*
THOMAS HOOKER

CHAPTER 9

HOPE:
Seeing God's Face in the Future

Handed down among the ancient Christian communities of Egypt was a story of the revered old teacher Evagrius, who had been raised by parents that loved and served God. One day he was approached by a messenger with the words, "Your father has died."

"Stop blaspheming," replied Evagrius. "My father cannot die."[1]

That laconic response affirms the foundation of our immovable hope as believers. "If only for this life we have hope in Christ, we are to be pitied more than all men" (1 Corinthians 15:19). But we who know the Lord cannot die. The stars will grow old and fall like withered leaves, the sky itself will wear out and roll up like a tattered scroll (Isaiah 34:4); still we will live on. Though the sun above our heads and the earth beneath our feet are ancient, and though they may dance together across space for thousands of years more, yet their dance will someday come to an end. Meanwhile, you and I will just be beginning the wedding celebration of the Lamb.

That thought was a great comfort when my own father

was dying of cancer a few years ago. He knew the Lord, so he was confident of going home, and his confidence was a great joy in spite of our sorrow. We rejoiced to know not only that he would be with the Lord, but also that we would see him there again someday; and we talked about the future freely.

One afternoon I asked Dad to give me his paternal blessing as the Old Testament patriarchs had done when they were dying (Genesis 49). I believed that the Lord was anxious to grant the godly prayers of a departing father for the children he would leave behind, and I wanted to know what was in my father's heart about my future. So Dad laid his hands on me as I knelt by the bed, and he prayed.

Never in his life had my father been so eloquent. In that moment, the eyes of my soul looked along with his joyfully to the future, as he prayed for years of ministry, years of fruitfulness, years of walking ever closer to Jesus. But one prayer, his closing request, stood out in my mind, and it has continued to be a source of joy. Dad said, "May you reach out and touch the face of God."

The face of God. Not just His hand, but His face: the very countenance of the One whose eyes behold all things with love, whose ears hear every prayer ever whispered, whose mouth spoke the worlds into existence. In the moment my father prayed, I looked at his own radiant face, and was overcome with joy in the love I had for him. How much more so will we one day be overjoyed to see the face of the Eternal Father?

Eternity itself is not the cause for joy
The promise of everlasting life is glorious, but eternity in itself is not what we seek. The misery of hell is also eternal. Life forever is worthy of our hope only because "we will be with the Lord forever" (1 Thessalonians 4:17).

The vision of hope is thus the vision of God's face in the future. In a sense, we all share in the revelation to Stephen, the martyr, as he was being stoned to death: We who look for the Lord "see heaven open and the Son of Man standing at the right hand of God," ready to receive us (Acts 7:55-60).

Only the prospect of seeing God's face and having His name written on *our* faces (Revelation 22:4) makes the promise of heaven a floodgate of joy. The city of gold and the crystal sea will be beautiful, so they will contribute to our joy (Revelation 4:6, 21:18). But their beauty will only be derivative, for they will merely reflect the dazzling light of God Himself (Revelation 22:5). Our reunion with the saints who have gone on before us will give us cause for celebration. But their primary attention, and ours, will be turned toward the Lamb (Revelation 7:9-17). The crowns of glory we receive as our reward will be a cause for rejoicing (2 Timothy 4:8). But we will cast those crowns at the feet of the One who sits on the throne (Revelation 4:10-11). All joy will flow from that throne, and anything else we rejoice in will make us glad only because it points back toward that throne.

What will it be like to see Him?
What will it be like to see in its full majesty the face of God? We can only make feeble guesses. But one of my speculations is that in His eyes we will see the depths of His love for us.

The Lord told His people through Zechariah that "whoever touches you touches the apple of [my] eye" (Zechariah 2:8). Though we've retained the sense of that expression—"the apple of my eye"—to mean something precious, I think we've probably lost the original intensity of the image. The apple of the eye is the English equivalent of "the little man of the eye" in Hebrew. Both of them refer to the eye's black center, or pupil. The Hebrew expression refers to the little reflection of ourselves we can see in the eyes of a person facing us.

For us to be the apple of God's eye, then, suggests to me two realities that will be utterly apparent to us when we look at last on God's face in heaven. The first is that every day of our lives, though "the eyes of the LORD range throughout the earth" (2 Chronicles 16:9), our portrait nevertheless remains at the center of His field of vision. We're the little man or woman reflected in His pupils because His face is turned toward us.

The second truth we'll realize as we gaze into God's eyes is that just as He was always watching us, He was also guarding us as ferociously as we guard our own precious eyesight. In the same way that you or I go to extreme lengths to preserve our vision, God has taken extreme measures to protect us on our journey home. That much, and much more, we'll see in the face of God.

Aside from our speculations, however, the Scripture assures us of one thing. To see the Lord will be to share in His glory (Romans 8:17-18, Colossians 3:4). However we may understand that mysterious word "glory," I believe it means, at least in part, that when we see His face, it will be smiling.

Glory, after all, means not only brightness, but also fame. Not the fleeting fame, of course, granted by other people in this life, the fame that gives the phrase "glory seeking" its ugly sense. Rather, we mean the only kind of fame with any value: fame with God. The atonement of Christ has made possible our reconciliation with Him. On the Cross God's wrath has been spent. The frown of God has become a smile.

The only acclamation worth seeking is for the Creator to know our name and our good works done in His name.

So our highest joy at last will be to see the approving smile of God and to hear the call of glory, "Well done, good and faithful slave. . . . Enter into the joy of your master" (Matthew 25:21, NASB). And in the meantime, the eyes of hope look toward the future and rejoice to see there the welcoming face of God.

When I look to the past in faith, my Father, I see Your mighty hand at work, majestic in power. And when I look to the future, Your face shines in glory and fills my face. I love You, You who are waiting for me at the end of my journey, and who even now watches over me, protecting me as Your precious treasure. That love gives birth in me to joy.

Make me a good and faithful slave—even more, an obedient son—so that in the vision of hope I can taste increasingly the joy of Your smile, and hear You say, "Well done." Then, when that eternal Morning dawns, "In righteousness I will see your face; when I awake, I will be satisfied with seeing your likeness" (Psalm 17:15).

NOTES:
1. "The Sayings of the Fathers," *Western Asceticism*, ed., Owen Chadwick (Philadelphia: Westminster Press, 1958), page 37; Evagrius Ponticus, *The Praktikos & Chapters on Prayer*, translated by John Eudes Bamberger (Kalamazoo, Mich.: Cistercian Publications, 1981), page 40.

How beautiful upon the mountains are the feet of him who brings good tidings.
ISAIAH 52:7, RSV

☐

He now showed them the full extent of his love. . . . Jesus knew . . . that he had come from God and was returning to God; so he got up from the meal . . . and began to wash his disciples' feet.
JOHN 13:1-5

☐

Unless You show us Your own true way, no man can find it. Father! You must lead. So breathe those thoughts into my mind by which such virtue may be bred in me that I may tread in Your holy footsteps. Unbind the fetters of my tongue that I may have power to sing to You, and sound Your praises everlastingly!
MICHELANGELO

☐

It is impossible to fulfill the law concerning love for Me, God eternal, apart from the law concerning love for your neighbors. These are the two feet of affection on which you must follow the commandments and counsels given you by Christ crucified.
CATHERINE OF SIENA

☐

It is always springtime in the heart that loves God.
JOHN VIARNEY

CHAPTER 10

LOVE:
Seeing God's Feet in the Present

When we first "fall in love" with someone, we tend to see our beloved as if through a glowing mist. The face, the hands, even the feet of the one we love are beautiful in our sight. And if a flaw should appear, we usually ignore it or else view it as somehow fitting into the attractiveness of the loved one's overall portrait.

Should the relationship continue, however, the rosiness of our perspective eventually fades. More and more we notice the irritating details, the less-than-lovable qualities of the one we had once nearly worshiped. Then we're faced with the choice of either "falling out of love" or continuing to love in spite of what we see.

Once the "honeymoon" is over, we assume that we've finally awakened from the illusion of romance that had clouded our vision. Now we see "reality"; now we perceive the beloved as he or she *truly* is. Now our vision is clear.

How sad it is that we would speak of falling in and out of love as if love were a lounge chair available for our pleasure. Yet it is sadder still that we should consider the complimentary perspective on another person false and the uglier perspective "real."

In a sense, of course, the latter view *is* real. When the lover's "cloud" has dispersed, we do tend to see things to which we'd been blind before.

And yet there's something about that initial romantic vision that reflects a deeper reality in a way the ugly picture does not. For when we see someone through the eyes of such overwhelming, appreciative love, we're seeing beyond faults to the way God sees. That rosy gown with which our eyes dress the beloved, however flimsy in itself, is a faint parallel to the robe with which the prodigal son was clothed by his father—covering a body that smelled of the pigs! (Luke 15:11-32).

Faith and hope, we've said, see what is invisible in the past and the future. But the perspective of love, although in the present, sees *in spite of* what is visible in the present. It's a looking beyond appearances to see as God sees, to behold others as the beloved creatures of God whom He desires for Himself, despite their brokenness. Love is a vision of the divine intention, of the potential that is present in others because of the love that is actual in God.

A sermon from a Christian teacher of the ancient Middle East describes this viewpoint with simplicity: "If you see a man with one eye . . . look upon him as if he were whole. If a man is maimed of one hand, see him as not maimed, the lame as straight, the palsied as whole. This is purity of heart, when you see sinners or sick people, to have compassion on them and be tenderhearted towards them."[1]

The divine humility

To see others as God intends them to be is of course not easy. It requires, above all, *humility*—the virtue that, as Charles Spurgeon put it, gives us a "right estimate" of ourselves.[2] That estimate is simply this: We, as well as all other human beings on this thirsty planet, are so loved by God that He would give His only Son for us. Even while we were yet sinners, God Himself laid aside His glory and walked the dusty roads of earth.

"What wondrous love is this, O my soul!" You, Lord Jesus, are truly humble of heart. Though being in very nature God, You did not consider equality with God something to be grasped, but made Yourself nothing, taking the form of a servant. And being found in appearance as a man, You humbled Yourself (Philippians 2:6-8). And so I find, my Lord, in the divine humility the pattern for love.

His feet first touched the earth in a dirty stable, and they walked their last tortured steps beside thieves to a garbage heap. The vision of love, then, is the vision of those humble feet of God, for to love is to look for them in spite of the grime of life. To find them, we ourselves must follow in the steps they leave behind.

Rarely do we consider feet beautiful, especially calloused, dusty feet. Yet "how beautiful on the mountains are the feet of those who bring good news" (Isaiah 52:7). From the viewpoint of love, every pair of human feet in the world is beautiful, because each brings with it a reminder of the great Good News: God Himself has taken feet—to walk the path of righteousness; to carry the Cross of atonement; to tread the clouds in victorious Ascension; to stand at the right hand of the Father in intercession for us.

When we see the feet of God in love, following them wherever they might lead us, we learn the reality of the name Immanuel: "God with us." That vision of God fills us with delight in His humility and becomes the third floodgate of joy. In every moment, in every place, if we look we can see God, walking with us and before us. And in His presence is fullness of joy.

I understand now, Jesus, why You could stoop to wash the feet of Your disciples. You knew that You had come from God and were returning to God (John 13:3): You had the double perspective of faith, looking to the Father's mighty hand in the past, and of hope, looking to His welcoming face in the future. So in faith and hope You were joyously free to see His feet in the present, and to wash them; to love Your disciples as the Father had loved You (John 15:9).

Now I also understand, my Lord, why You said that whoever "has had a bath needs only to wash his feet" (John 13:10). For You have cleansed us in the waters of baptism and called us home. But it remains for us to stoop in humility to wash one another's feet from the dust of the journey. Seeing our beginning and our end in You, we too are free, Jesus, joyously free, to see You in our present, to lay aside our garments of pride, to love because You first loved us.

Seeing Your feet in the feet of our fellow travelers, Lord, we will love You all the more, and that love will be our delight. For Your feet are "like burnished bronze" (Revelation 2:18), glowing with the gladness of love, a burning lamp in the darkness "to guide our feet into the path of peace" (Luke 1:79).

NOTES:

1. *Fifty Spiritual Homilies of Macarius the Egyptian*, translated by A. J. Mason (London: SPCK Press, 1921), Homily XV, page 109.
2. Robert C. Savage, *Pocket Quips* (Wheaton, Ill.: Tyndale House, 1984), page 69.

PART 3

THE FURROWS OF JOY

"Break up your unplowed ground and do not sow among thorns."
JEREMIAH 4:3

□

All discipline for the moment seems not to be joyful, but sorrowful; yet to those who have been trained by it, afterwards it yields the peaceful fruit of righteousness.
HEBREWS 12:11, NASB

□

I do not want to leave the impression that the ordinary means of grace have no value. They most assuredly have. Private prayer . . . Bible meditation . . . church attendance . . . service and work and activity; all are good and should be engaged in by every Christian. But at the bottom of all these things, giving meaning to them, will be the inward habit of beholding God. A new set of eyes . . . will develop within us enabling us to be looking at God while our outward eyes are seeing the scenes of this passing world.
A. W. TOZER

□

When we carry out our "religious duties," we are like people digging channels in a waterless land, in order that when at last the water comes, it may find them ready.
C. S. LEWIS

□

It is certainly required of man that he should hold himself in readiness for joy.
KARL BARTH

CHAPTER 11

DISCIPLINE:
Narrowing Our Focus on God

Faith, hope, and love—what we've called the three flood-gates of joy—are the foundational perspectives on God that allow us to see, know, love, and delight in Him. But the water that flows in through these gates, however refreshing, will only spread aimlessly across the ground of our hearts, soon running off or evaporating, unless we dig furrows to channel it. These furrows might be called the *disciplines* of the Christian life.

Now, breaking up unplowed ground in the soul is at best a painful endeavor: "All discipline," said the writer of Hebrews, "for the moment seems not to be joyful, but sorrowful" (Hebrews 12:11, NASB). Only later, he adds, do we see the fruit of our labor. As another ancient Christian teacher described it, discipline is like lighting a fire whose warmth and light we'll enjoy. We must work hard to get the fire going, and in the meantime we get smoke in our eyes.[1]

Sooner or later, joy *should* flow through the channels of discipline. But sadly enough, many folks set to work digging furrows yet never see water run into them. Discipline hardens into a dry routine, a legal obligation, a joyless duty.

How does it happen that the furrows should remain dry? In light of our claim that joy in the Lord follows from seeing the Lord, I'm convinced that *we lose delight in our discipline when we fail to keep God in sight as we labor.* If we plow with our eyes toward the ground, we'll probably never connect the furrows with the floodgate—and we might just end up with a crooked row as well.

My grandfather was a farmer all his life. He once told me what he considered to be the only way to make sure a row was plowed straight. Choose an object at the far end of the field, he recommended, and set your sights on it as you plow. If you look down at the plow itself as you go, you'll always end up off course.

I think the labor of discipline is much like plowing in that regard. If our eyes aren't constantly on the Lord—the reason for our labor—then we'll go astray. More probably, we'll succumb to thirst from a lack of joy and give up our work altogether.

"Where there is no vision," says Proverbs, "the people are unrestrained"—or, to use a synonym, they are undisciplined (Proverbs 29:18, NASB). Vision and discipline must go together. As someone has wisely said, without discipline, a vision is only a fantasy; but without a vision, discipline is only drudgery. Laboring for God without the joy of *seeing* God becomes legalism. Or to use our garden imagery, *a furrow without water is just a rut.*

A narrowing of focus

The following chapters will describe some of the disciplines of Christian life that make room in our lives for joy—*if* we keep our eyes on the Lord as we form them. Keep in mind that our discussion is not intended to be comprehensive in each case, nor even to provide details about how to establish a particular discipline. That kind of guidance is available from a number of other sources by Christians much wiser and more disciplined than I am.

Our intent here, rather, is simply to show in each case how the discipline can become a channel of joy by opening our eyes to some particular aspect of God's goodness that will enable us to see, know, love, and delight in Him more deeply. In that sense, then, we'll view discipline as *a narrowing of our focus on God.* Such focus allows us to see more clearly, for example, His faithfulness, His wisdom, or His power.

The disciplines addressed here are far from being a complete list. You'll probably have others to add that have been important to you in seeking the Lord. At the same time, you may be puzzled by the inclusion here of some activities you've never thought of as discipline—witness, for example, or play and humor. But I hope that by the time you've finished reading, you'll be convinced that all the disciplines we've listed do indeed deserve that title.

I've avoided any attempt to order them according to relative value, though I see the Scripture as foundational for our knowledge of God, and worship as the central act of our life with God. But the disciplines are necessarily all of one piece. If we were to give them any kind of rough grouping, it would be to associate each "furrow" with one of the three "floodgates."

By this we mean that the joy arising from the perspectives on God granted by faith, hope, and love are most often channeled by particular disciplines. Of the ones listed here, we could view Scripture study, meditation, and witness as disciplines of faith; worship, play, and humor as disciplines of hope; and prayer, obedience, service, fellowship, and work as disciplines of love. But more about that will come as we turn to each one individually.

A final word about the discussion in this section: Some

of the following chapters, as well as the later chapter on suffering, would not appear here if I were writing only from experience. During the last few years I've made progress in digging some useful furrows in the areas of worship, meditation, and fellowship. But in other areas, my hoe has only scratched the ground. So my thoughts on these latter subjects are offered on the basis of a few scattered drops of joy I've tasted whose source I think I recognize. My goal is to point you to that source.

On my knees, Lord of Holiness, in the dusty soil of my soul, I dig a trench, wipe the sweat, and look up to You in thirst. My garden is already full of ruts, Lord. Teach me to plow furrows instead. Break up the rocks, pull up the weeds, as I open up the ground. And I will rejoice to know that You discipline me for my own good, that I may share in Your holiness (Hebrews 12:10).

NOTES:
1. "The Sayings of the Fathers," page 46.

Sing to him a new song; play skillfully, and shout for joy. For the word of the LORD is right and true; he is faithful in all he does.
PSALM 33:3-4

□

When your words came, I ate them; they were my joy and my heart's delight, for I bear your name, O LORD God Almighty.
JEREMIAH 15:16

□

The Bible is not an end in itself, but a means to bring men to an intimate and satisfying knowledge of God, that they may enter into Him, that they may delight in His Presence, may taste and know the inner sweetness of the very God Himself in the core and center of their hearts.
A. W. TOZER

□

Not with doubtful but with sure knowledge do I love You, O Lord. By Your Word You have transfixed my heart, and I have loved You.
AUGUSTINE

□

Beyond the sacred page I seek Thee, Lord;
My spirit pants for Thee, O living Word!
MARY A. LATHBURY

CHAPTER 12

SCRIPTURE:
Seeing God in Black and White

John Calvin, one of the chief architects of the Protestant Reformation, was fond of comparing the Scriptures to a pair of "spectacles." He often said that even though we could know something of God from the creation that surrounds us, such knowledge was fuzzy and incomplete without the aid of the Bible, through which we can see God in brilliant clarity. Calvin insisted that just as people with failing vision need glasses to read even the most beautifully printed volumes, we who are fallen creatures must look through the Scripture to "read" the beauty of God in the sharp, distinct lines of His verbal self-revelation.[1]

In this sense, the vision of God offered by the Scripture might be called a view of Him *in black and white*. When we go to the Scripture looking for the Lord, we find that our blurred, generalized notions of Him are clarified by what He reveals about Himself there. We discover, for example, that His goodness is more complex than our typically shallow, innocuous ideas of goodness—that He's not only loving and merciful, but also holy and just.

When we search Scripture habitually to learn about the

beauty of God's nature and the graciousness of His activity on our behalf, we're digging a furrow for the joy of faith to come flooding in. The more we see of God in the Bible, the more we learn to love Him and the more we take joy in His great goodness. Reading the Word of God becomes like reading a love letter from our closest friend. In each line we can taste the pleasure of knowing the One we love.

Fascination with the lens

I once saw a toddler playing with a pair of eyeglasses she had discovered in a desk drawer. I'm sure she'd seen people wearing such glasses before, but because these were folded up, she evidently failed to realize what they were. For her, they were only a fascinating gadget that could be manipulated in novel and interesting ways. Her "toy" provided a full ten minutes of entertainment (quite a long while for a toddler to maintain attention) before she moved on to something else. Yet by the time she did move on, she had never once put them before her eyes to look through them.

Sadly enough, I think we sometimes act like that little girl when we take up Scripture. At times we treat the Book as if it were the end itself, instead of a means to the true end of seeing, knowing, and loving God. Rather than using the Bible as "spectacles" for a clear view of God, we sometimes focus on the glasses themselves. We fail to put them on and look in His direction.

That was the mistake of many in Jesus' day who challenged His authority. "You diligently study the Scriptures," He told them, "because you think that by them you possess eternal life. These are the Scriptures that testify about me, yet you refuse to come to me to have life" (John 5:39-40). Evidently, Jesus was speaking to a religious audience who knew the Scriptures well and held them in high regard. Yet they had failed to allow those sacred written words to point beyond themselves to the One about whom they testified.

How often do we who know Jesus as Lord make a similar mistake? I must confess that at times I've treated the biblical text as a sort of truth machine whose crank I can grind to churn out propositions that are sound, reasonable, consistent—and utterly without life, unless I allow them to point me toward a personal encounter with God. Like that child, I've been guilty of manipulating Scripture into an interesting and novel "system" or doctrine that might be intriguing but that fails to connect meaningfully to my practical walk with the Lord. And I've seen many others do the same.

Assent versus consent

In part, I believe, the problem comes from our frequent failure to distinguish between the activity of the mind and that of the heart—that of our intellect and that of our will. This distinction is perhaps summed up in two terms, *assent* and *consent*, which Christian thinkers of the past such as Aquinas and Edwards were careful to explain in their discussion of godly behavior.

Aquinas put it this way: To assent is simply to *agree with something else*. Thus it implies some sort of analytical distance from the thing to which assent is given. But to *consent* is to *sense along with*. This implies a kind of "union" with whatever we give our consent to. Using the picture of the intellect and the will we described before, when the intellect perceives something as true, it *assents* to what it perceives, but makes no "movement" toward it. On the other hand, when we *consent* to something, our will reaches out to it, is drawn toward it, and attempts to be in a kind of "unison" with it.[2]

Assent, then, is the yes of the head, while consent is the yes of the heart. We assent to biblical truth when our intellect nods approval, but we consent to biblical truth when our will actively reaches out for Truth Himself in desire and obedience. That, said James, is part of what distinguishes us from the demons, who also assent intellectually to the God of Scripture—but they "believe . . . and *shudder*" (James 2:19).

When we allow the meaning of statements in Scripture to be the end of our search, we may be *assenting* to the truth we find there with our intellect but we're failing to *consent* to the One who stands behind the text. As Edwards so beautifully described it, "Thus there is a difference between having an opinion, that God is holy and gracious, and having a sense of the loveliness and beauty of that holiness and grace. . . . The former may be obtained by hearsay, but the latter only by seeing the countenance. . . . The former rests only in the head . . . but the heart is concerned in the latter." When the heart consents, added Edwards, it's drawn toward the beauty of God that it sees, and the result is an inner sweetness—joy in beholding the Lord.[3]

When we become enchanted, then, by the mere study of a biblical text and fail to go on in a search for the God revealed by that text as we pray and obey, we are only toying with our "spectacles." But fascination with the Scripture itself is not the only reason we sometimes merely play around with it. A second reason, I believe, is that we're a bit fearful of what we might see were we to look through the lens to the God who is standing behind it.

If the vision of God provided by Scripture is indeed a view in black and white, then the hard clarity of that vision may be a bit startling and even intimidating. God doesn't always look the way we might want Him to look. Through the Scriptures we may see Him behaving and speaking in ways that challenge our assumptions or undermine our comfort, just as Jesus' words and actions were a threat to many of the Scripture readers of His day.

Whatever the reason, if we make it a habit to focus our vision on Scripture instead of the God who calls to us from Scripture, we'll find the joy that arises from faith draining away instead of increasing as we study. For if a vision of the Lord leads to joy in the Lord, then even Scripture, when it blocks our vision, will stifle our joy. As Edwards pictured it, we may read about the sweetness of God's honey, but we won't be able to taste it ourselves.

Learning to focus on God in Scripture

How do we go about looking through Scripture to seek the Lord Himself standing behind it? My own experience has been that we encounter the Lord first of all by joining our study intimately to prayer. Whenever we approach the Bible, we should take time to invite the Author to read it aloud over our shoulder.

That means we allow our reading to become a conversation. If you had me in the room just now as you read and came across a statement on these pages that didn't make sense (I hope they would be few), you most likely wouldn't fret long over the interpretation. Instead, you'd turn to me and ask me what I meant.

In the same way, when we don't understand a text of Scripture, we shouldn't merely sit and puzzle. We should ask God directly to explain the text. Though we may not receive an immediate answer, just the act of asking Him in prayer keeps our attention on Him. It also lessens our frustration because we're reminded that whatever our confusion, the ultimate goal is to glorify Him, not necessarily to understand Him. In the meantime, He'll give us enough light to meet whatever expectations He has for us.

A second way to seek God through the text is to keep in mind several questions as we read. For example, "What does this passage tell me about God's character and behavior?" Better yet, we can address the question to Him in the second person: "Lord, what does this tell me about You?"

As that question is answered, we can transform the answer into specific words of thanksgiving and praise. In thanksgiving, we tell God our gratitude for what He's done; in praise, we tell Him our appreciation for who He is. We thank Him for His activity and His promises; we praise Him for His nature and His character.

Finally, we seek God through Scripture by asking Him, in light of the text we're reading, what response He calls for on our part. Having gained specific insights into God's character and behavior, we put down the Book and set out to be conformed to that character and behavior.

Such a focus on God sooner or later releases the streams of joy. Though at times our study may be dry, it will rarely be fruitless. As we pray through the biblical text, we'll find that our vision of the Lord becomes not only clear but even three-dimensional as the realities of His Word become solidified in our lives. The Friend who wrote us His love letter will Himself appear at our door, and we'll rejoice to see the Word again made flesh.

Settling for a fuzzy vision
Meanwhile, some of us must be careful of a tendency that is the opposite of paying too much attention to the Book itself. At times we may tend to focus on God in prayer and obedience without viewing Him habitually through the lens of Scripture. When this happens, our neglect of Bible study leaves our vision of God fuzzy. The picture we have of Him may become distorted by influences from a secular culture that is blind to Him. Consequently, our well-intended prayer and obedience may take a turn in the wrong direction without the healthy corrective lens of God's Word.

The result in this case is also a loss of joy. To enjoy God, we must love Him, and to love Him, we must know Him—for, as Augustine once observed, "Nothing is loved unless it is known."[4] Without the sharp, black-and-white view of God presented to us in Scripture, we won't know Him well. And to the extent that we're ignorant of the Lord, we'll find our love for Him and our joy in Him diminished.

For that reason, the study of Scripture is a critical discipline of faith. In the Bible we see with clarity the God who has acted to create and redeem us, and that view provides a furrow to channel the joy from faith's floodgate into the various areas of our lives where faith is applied. Without the furrow of Scripture, the joy arising from faith scatters and evaporates, for as the ancient Bible scholar Jerome noted, "Ignorance of the Scripture is ignorance of Christ."

God has given teachers

When we speak of the discipline of Scripture study, we must of course include the habit of placing ourselves under sound biblical teaching. The arrogant individualism of our society chafes at the notion of humbling ourselves to learn from those who are wiser than we are. Yet Christ has graciously given teachers to the Church as one of His gifts for maturing the saints (Ephesians 4:7-16). We dare not refuse so great a gift.

Learning from the teachers God has given us means more than simply hearing sound instruction from the leaders of our local church every week. That discipline, of course, is essential. But in addition we must give ourselves, when possible, to reading the great teachers of the faith God has given to the Church at large, both those of today and those of the past.

Reading Christian teachers of the past is especially

critical, because each age has its own blind spots. As a student working toward a doctorate in historical theology, I might be expected to make this claim, but I hope that the usefulness of such study is amply reflected in this book. What seems obvious to us today may have been hardly noticed by people who lived a few hundred years ago—such as our universal conviction that human slavery is wrong. Meanwhile, the common assumptions of our own period (in particular, our bondage to rationalist ways of thinking inherited from the Enlightenment) often come to light most clearly when we read the thoughts of a Christian whose own society's assumptions were different from our own.

In addition to reading Christian teaching of the past, reading Church history itself is also useful. An ancient Greek philosopher once said that history is philosophy teaching by example. I would adapt that insight to insist that Church history is theology teaching by example. The accumulated experience of faithful believers in a variety of circumstances can illustrate which biblical interpretations have been sterile and which have born fruit, so that we don't waste our time attempting to reinvent the theological wheel.

In a sense, we might say that studying a variety of Christian teachers and traditions is like looking through a series of lenses that allow us to see the "spectacles" of Scripture itself more clearly. A classical historical example of that principle, I think, was John Wesley's experience at Aldersgate, which directly transformed his life and indirectly influenced the lives of thousands of Methodists who were to follow him in his quest for God. The spark that ignited Wesley that day was in fact his hearing of Martin Luther's *Preface* to Paul's Epistle to the Romans.

Something Luther had written about the scriptural text allowed Wesley in that moment to get its truth about faith in focus for the first time. Then, once Scripture was in focus, it clarified his vision of God's grace. The result was the planting of a seed of joy—or, as Wesley himself put it, his heart was "strangely warmed."[5] In a similar way, the two sets of glasses—Scripture and Christian teaching about the Scripture—can strengthen each other for our use as well, yielding a clearer picture of the One we seek.

Word of God, in Your written Word I hear You speaking. It's at once Your autobiography, Lord, and Your love letter to me. There, between the awesome fluid walls of the divided Red Sea, I see You standing and holding them in place. In the dusty hay of the stable I see You clinging in terrible humility to a human breast. Through the streets of Jerusalem I see You sweep in a Firestorm, exploding on Your people and roaring outward from there to consume the hearts of men and women across all the continents.

Again, in the teachers of Your Word, Lord, I hear You: Your voice speaks in many languages and accents, each pointing to a detail of Your portrait I might otherwise have neglected. And I see You at work in Your Church as well, You who have been faithful for two thousand years despite our rebellion and our coldness of heart.

In Your Word, Lord, and in the echoes of Your Word, I see You, and my heart is transfixed by Your wisdom. Seeing You there, I love You, and I taste Your sweetness. For You, Lord, are the Honey, and Your Word is the Honeycomb.

NOTES:

1. John Calvin, *Institutes of the Christian Religion*, translated by Ford Lewis Battles (Philadelphia: Westminster Press, 1960), I. vi. 1, pages 69-71; I. xiv. 1, pages 160-161.
2. Aquinas, *Treatise on Happiness*, page 137.
3. Edwards, "A Divine and Supernatural Light," *Selections*, page 103.
4. Augustine, *On the Trinity*, X, page 1.
5. *John Wesley*, ed., Albert C. Outler (New York: Oxford University Press, 1964), page 66.

"Ask and you will receive, and your joy will be complete."
JOHN 16:24

□

I have set the LORD always before me. Because he is at my right hand, I will not be shaken. Therefore my heart is glad and my tongue rejoices. . . . You will fill me with joy in your presence, with eternal pleasures at your right hand.
PSALM 16:8-9,11

□

Always and everywhere, a person should aim to live as if God were visibly present. So Elijah and Elisha used to say: "As the Lord of hosts lives, before whom I stand." Such alertness requires that we turn our minds fully and decisively to the Lord. The angels, wherever they may be sent, never stop gazing upon God; in the same way a virtuous person, as much as he can, always keeps the memory of God in his heart.
BONAVENTURE

□

Think of the time as lost when you have not been aware of God.
BERNARD OF CLAIRVAUX

CHAPTER 13

PRAYER:
Seeing the Nearness of God

One of the most disturbing parables Jesus ever told concerned the Pharisee and the tax collector. In that story, you'll remember, the Pharisee prayed proudly and self-righteously; the tax collector prayed humbly and penitently. Only the tax collector "went home justified before God" (Luke 18:9-14).

What disturbs me most here, even more than the concluding judgment that the Pharisee left unjustified, is a remark all the more chilling for its understatement. Jesus said, "The Pharisee stood up and *prayed to himself*" (verse 11).

The implications of that remark haunt me sometimes. I wonder how often I may be praying as that Pharisee did—which is to say, not really praying at all. In the final analysis he was only talking to *himself* rather than to God. He looked to heaven and saw only a mirror. He listened for heaven, and heard only an echo of his own voice. Both he and the tax collector were physically in the Temple. But in his spirit, he never got farther than the gate of the outer court, while the spirit of the tax collector was ushered into the Holy of Holies.

It was pride that kept the Pharisee from genuine prayer. But the same result might have followed from any attitude—legalism, apathy, anxious preoccupation—that would have turned his attention away from God. For whenever the external eyes are looking to heaven but the inner eyes are looking elsewhere (or perhaps nowhere in particular), we might rightly confess to be praying to ourselves.

This isn't to say, of course, that in prayer we should be thinking only of God. Prayer, by its nature, involves bringing petitions to Him about matters of concern. But even then, we must approach the Throne with the hands of our spirit holding our petitions while the eyes of our spirit focus on Him. As Catherine of Siena described it, to intercede for another person is to hold up that person's soul in the presence of God.[1]

God wants our eyes on Him as we pray, because He desires prayer to be an intimate conversation. But all too often we approach it instead as an exchange of business memos. We make our lists and add our signature on the bottom line, perhaps with a deadline. Then we send it off with all the detachment of a warehouse clerk.

Teresa of Avila once pointedly described such "prayer" when she spoke sadly of those who attempt to pray without experiencing a genuine encounter with God. Those prayers, she said, lacked life-giving substance, and were like the inns for the poorer travelers through Spain in her day. Though you might be hungry, you wouldn't be served food there. All you'd have for a meal was whatever you happened to bring along with you.

Not surprisingly, prayer focused on something or someone other than God Himself is utterly joyless. When we fail to keep the Lord in view as we pray, our love for Him is diminished, and our joy dries up. But what is that particular view of God that prayer provides as a source of delight in Him?

His name is Immanuel

When John Wesley, the founder of the Methodist movement, lay on his deathbed, he was heard repeating softly a phrase that reflected a lifetime of earnest meditation on the Christian life. In his last hours, Wesley said simply, "The best of all is, God is with us."[2]

Those words, I'm convinced, displayed the wisdom of a great veteran of prayer, for the vision of God we receive in genuine prayer is *the vision of His nearness.* Jesus was called Immanuel—"God with us"—because through Him, we who were "far away" have been given "access to the Father by one Spirit." We're no longer strangers in the house of God (Ephesians 2:17-19). Because of Christ's sacrifice, in prayer we can "draw *near* to God with a sincere heart in full assurance of faith" (Hebrews 10:22).

God has answered the agonized cry of the psalmist: He has split open the heavens and come down to us (Psalm 144:5). The veil of the Holy of Holies was torn, and its tear ran from top to bottom because it was accomplished by the hand of God (Matthew 27:51). Now, through His indwelling Spirit, the Lord is as close to us as our own breath. And because the Spirit Himself prays within us (Romans 8:26-27), we can truly say with the Christian poet George Herbert that prayer is "God's breath in man returning to his birth."[3]

No doubt God has always been truly everywhere, for "by him all things were created" and "in him all things hold together" (Colossians 1:16-17). To use the metaphor of the ancient Christian theologians, God is a circle whose center is everywhere and whose circumference is nowhere. We can agree with the apostle Paul, who said even pagans know in a limited way that "in him we live and move and have our being" (Acts 17:28).

Nevertheless, only in prayer offered with the eyes of our heart toward the risen Christ do we see God standing, not only with mighty arms upholding the world but also with nail-scarred hands extended to receive us. He is nearby in a way never dreamed of by the ancient Israelites, who stood trembling at the foot of Mount Sinai while God thundered at its peak (Exodus 19:16-24). No wonder, then, that when we see the lovingkindness of an incarnate, crucified God so near at hand as we pray, the resulting vision of His goodness and mercy awakens joy in us.

Of course, even with our inner gaze remaining on the Lord, not all our times of prayer will be immediately joyous. Sometimes we have to pray despite the sense of dryness, a "dark night of the soul," as John of the Cross described it. The most seasoned men and women of prayer throughout the ages have seemed to agree almost universally that this is the case.

But most of them also have agreed that if we persevere in turning our hearts to God as we converse with Him, recognizing the reality of His presence despite appearances or feelings, in time that view of the Lord will lead us to joy in the Lord. Like the other "furrows" we're describing, the dry soil must be plowed before the water can flow in.

"On earth as it is in Heaven"

When Jesus taught His disciples to pray, He offered several specific petitions as models for the various kinds of requests we might make. But I believe that all He taught us to pray for is summed up in those awesome words, "Your kingdom come, your will be done on earth as it is in heaven" (Matthew 6:10).

This, I think, is the ultimate petition, the heart cry of genuine prayer. We address here a Father "in heaven," yet He's also near. In these words we recognize that the kingdom of the world in which we live has been invaded by another Kingdom; that the indwelling Spirit of God has established here, in us, an outpost of heaven; and that it's God Himself who works in us "to will and to act according to his good purpose" (Philippians 2:13), so that His will may be done on earth.

Such prayer to a God close at hand, who walks beside us and lives within us, helps make our highway straight for His feet, our dwelling place fit for His presence. For that reason, prayer to the God who is near is a discipline of love, a furrow that channels the joy of love's perspective on God into the areas of our lives where God's footprints need most of all to be seen.

In prayer, Father, I look for You in the present, inviting You to be at work in the world and finding You already busy there. I come to You, Lord, with the needs of the world in my hands, holding them in Your presence. Then You take them from me, load them like a precious burden onto Your own back, and carry them Yourself along the dusty roads where You journey beside me.

As I travel with You there, Lord, I find a deep and abiding delight in the continuing fellowship of One who's so humble, so faithful. Your companionship comforts and strengthens me. Having given up my own burdens, I can gladly take Your burden instead, and I find that Your burden is joyously light (Matthew 11:30). What began as petition, Jesus, is thus completed in action as I bear others' burdens, for I recognize them now as Yours.

Learning to focus on the Lord in prayer

Each of us must find our own ways to keep our eyes on the Lord as we pray. But I've personally found it most helpful to begin times of prayer with words of specific thanksgiving and praise whenever possible. That establishes immediately the direction of our gaze, with a focus on His character and faithfulness.

When we sense, after a time of thanksgiving and praise, that we've come into "the Throne room," with an assurance that He's near and listening, that's the time to lift our petitions to Him. In light of the specific qualities we've been grateful for, we can pray more confidently: "Because of Your great mercy, Lord, I come to You confessing. . . . " "You're just and You love justice, Father, so I ask You to act on behalf of these people who have suffered injustice. . . . " "You're our Healer, Jesus, and I bring my sick child before You. . . ."

A second way we can keep the Lord in view is by remembering that He wants a conversation—and that means dialogue, not monologue. We must spend some time in silence to give *Him* a chance to speak to *us*. And we should freely ask questions, fully expecting answers (though not always immediately).

A third way we can remain aware of God's nearness is to speak with Him as we would to our earthly father, or some other respected and beloved friend. That may sound trite, but I'm still amazed to see how many people stiffen when they begin to pray, switching to formal and artificial language they would never use with a friend.

We must never forget that Jesus called God "Abba," which is actually not "Father," but rather "Daddy." He assured us that our Daddy was concerned about not only large matters but also the little ones, like the number of hairs on our head (which is admittedly more important to balding men like me than to others).

At the same time, we should remember that in the seventeenth century, when the King James version of the Bible was first published, the pronoun "thou" was *informal*, used especially for family and friends. The word "you," on the other hand, was used to address superiors and strangers. The translators' choice of "thou" for presenting biblical prayer thus emphasized our closeness to God rather than our distance. But sadly enough, a twist in the connotations of these words over the last few centuries has resulted in the irony of our using "thou" as a term of distance in a formal address to God.

A fourth way to keep our focus on God is to minimize distractions as we pray. In simplest terms, that may mean finding a quiet place or at least learning how to disengage from surrounding sights and sounds. The Anglican pastor and poet John Donne said it in verse this way: "Churches are best for Prayer, that have least light: To see God only, I go out of sight."[4]

Keeping a note pad handy also helps. When thoughts unrelated to specific prayer, yet nevertheless important, cross our minds, we can write them down and put them aside for the moment, assured that they won't be forgotten later when we can act on them.

If the distraction is more persistent—a preoccupying worry, for example, or anger over someone's offense—then we need to take that distraction and make *it* the subject of our prayer, looking at God as we bring it before Him, and asking, "What do I do with this?" When we cease to be submerged in a difficulty, and instead get a critical, "clinical" distance on it by handling it with prayer, the problem loses much of its power over us.

Another way to remain mindful of God's nearness is to keep track of answered prayers and then rejoice in them as a sure sign that He's with us. Jesus said, "Ask and you will receive, and your joy will be complete" (John 16:24). A written, ongoing list of answers to prayer that we take with us when we go to our knees can provide the foundation for our time of thanksgiving. We can even ask others about answered prayers in their own lives, repeating their "testimonies" to the Lord and sharing their gratitude.

Finally, we can "set the LORD always before [us]" (Psalm 16:8) by cultivating a habit of turning our inner eyes toward God whenever possible, whatever we're doing. That may be the most practical way to "pray continually" (1 Thessalonians 5:17). Bonaventure, a thirteenth-century leader of the Franciscan Order and an extraordinarily busy man, described it this way: "Of course we cannot continually concentrate on the Lord in profound meditation; but at least we should remember his presence and direct the gaze of our hearts at him. When a sculptor obtains the material for a statue, he studies it from every angle; then, when an opportunity comes, he is ready to give it the proper shape. So too, mindfulness of God will be shaped into meditation or prayer when the opportunity comes."[5]

In each of these ways we train ourselves to say to the Lord with the psalmist Asaph, "I am always with you; you hold me by my right hand" (Psalm 73:23). Digging the furrow of prayer in this way, we strengthen our vision of the God who is near, who has humbled Himself to walk beside us, dwell within us, and act on our behalf. As we see Him reaching out to us, our hearts reach out to Him in gratitude and desire. Delight wells up inside us just to have our Beloved so close. And we rejoice simply because "it is good to be near God" (Psalm 73:28).

NOTES:
1. Catherine of Siena, *The Dialogue*, page 195.
2. Stanley Ayling, *John Wesley* (New York: William Collins, 1979), page 315.
3. George Herbert, "Prayer (I)," in *Herbert* (New York: Dell, 1962), page 65.
4. John Donne, "A Hymne to Christ, at the Author's Last Going Into Germany," *The Complete Poetry and Selected Prose of John Donne* (New York: The Modern Library, 1952), page 258.
5. St. Bonaventure, *The Character of a Christian Leader*, translated by Philip O'Mara (Ann Arbor, Mich.: Servant Books, 1978), page 69.

Shout for joy to the LORD, all the earth.
Serve the LORD with gladness;
come before him with joyful songs.
Know that the LORD is God.
It is he who made us, and we are his;
we are his people, the sheep of his pasture.
PSALM 100:1-2, NIV (1978 Version)

□

Yet a time is coming and has now come when the true worshipers will
worship the Father in spirit and truth, for they are the kind of
worshipers the Father seeks.
JOHN 4:23

□

When I look into Your holiness,
when I gaze into Your loveliness,
when all things that surround
become shadows in the light of You;
when I find this joy of reaching Your heart . . .
I worship You;
the reason I live is to worship You.
WAYNE & CATHY PERRIN

□

Fully to enjoy is to glorify. In commanding us to glorify Him, God is
inviting us to enjoy Him.
C. S. LEWIS

CHAPTER 14

WORSHIP:
Seeing God on the Throne

The psalmist Asaph apparently struggled, as we all have, with the seeming injustice of life. In the Seventy-third Psalm, he poured out his heart in confusion and complaint about "the prosperity of the wicked" (Psalm 73:3). Those who rebelled against God and trampled other people underfoot seemed to act with impunity, even blessing: They were healthy, wealthy, and carefree (verses 2-12).

Meanwhile, Asaph agonized, people like us who try to keep our hearts pure end up suffering (verses 13-15). So when he attempted to understand it all, he found the whole matter "oppressive" (verse 16). But then Asaph took an important step: He "entered the sanctuary of God" in order to worship (verse 17).

At that point the psalm takes a major turn in tone, because Asaph's attention took a major turn in direction—away from the circumstances and toward the Lord. In worship, the psalmist focused the eyes of his heart on the Throne of heaven, thus renewing his vision of a sovereign God. Such a vision changed his whole viewpoint of things on earth as well. He could see the wicked from a totally new perspective: "Then," he declared, "I understood their final destiny" (verse 17).

By that point in his thinking, Asaph had moved from a third-person lament over the world to a second-person prayer addressed directly to God. "Surely you place them on slippery ground," he realized; "you cast them down to ruin" (verse 18). The victory of justice that once seemed so far away was now viewed as coming "suddenly" (verse 19). Before, wickedness seemed to be the concrete reality and God's activity a vague illusion (verse 11), but now everything was reversed. The Lord, he affirmed, was the final reality, and the rebellion of the wicked was only a fading dream, with no more ultimate substance than a fantasy (verse 20).

I've often had an experience similar to that of Asaph. Once, I remember, I was standing alone at an uncovered bus stop as the gray, shrouded sky above me began to drizzle. It was a frustrating moment: I was exhausted from a long day, I had no umbrella, and I was coughing from the fumes of eight lanes of rush-hour traffic. That morning the computer had broken down, losing hours of my work; the rest of the day's labor had been fruitless; I'd missed my regular bus; and now I knew I'd be late to dinner. It was the end of a grueling Friday, an appropriate finale for a whole week of frustration that had preceded it.

Of course, my complaints were hardly as serious as those of Asaph. My problems at the time were rather petty, primarily matters of inconvenience rather than injustice. Even so, my eyes, too, were focused on circumstances rather than the Lord of circumstances. As the rain began, it seemed as if all the minor anxieties and irritations of many months settled on my shoulders in one great weight. I was so burdened I wanted to cry.

But just then there filtered into my mind the strains of a song we'd been singing in church the Sunday before, whose lyrics were from Isaiah. The repeated words of the chorus grew increasingly louder in my head until at last they captured my attention: "Our God reigns! Our God reigns! Our God reigns! *Our God reigns!*"

I didn't feel like singing. In fact, I wanted to indulge in a bit of self-pity. But that little chorus somehow demanded I join in, and so I sang: aloud, to the world around me, and to myself. As I sang, louder and louder with each chorus, I lifted my eyes up toward the gray sky.

At the same time, I lifted up the eyes of my heart. In my mind I could see beyond those clouds to a blue firmament; and beyond that to a shining host of stars; and beyond that to "a door standing open in heaven" (Revelation 4:1). I remembered what John had seen through that door in his vision: a crystal sea spreading out before the Throne of God. And in that moment I knew I was joining in heaven's own chorus: *Our God reigns!*

At that point I did begin to cry, but not with discouragement. I was crying for joy. The tears, in fact, came tumbling out with laughter that I couldn't contain. I must have been an entertaining sight to those weary motorists caught in traffic and in problems of their own: singing my heart out in the rain, laughing, and finally clapping my hands. But I really didn't care what they thought. I was in the presence of God, and I was rejoicing.

For you see, above all the ugly, silly, burdensome circumstances of that day, I had caught once more a vision of the King on the Throne. The sight of His sovereignty filled me with relief and delight, and set me free to express my joy in His reign.

Asaph's experience in the Temple and mine at the bus stop, despite the greater seriousness of his situation, have this in common: Both reflect how the discipline of worship leads to joy. For the characteristic vision of worship is, in a phrase, *a view of the Throne.* When we consciously turn our attention to God's infinite and eternal nature, we begin looking for the King. And when we see Him there, reigning in splendor, we can only rejoice.

At the same time, the vision of worship is a view *from* the Throne. When the eyes of our heart search for God's rule beyond apparent circumstances, then we're recognizing that "God raised us up with Christ and seated us with him in the heavenly realms in Christ Jesus" (Ephesians 2:6). If Christ is in control and we are in Christ, then we can relax and trust that the outcome of all things is in His hands.

From the perspective of the Throne, we see things as *God* sees them—which is simply another name for wisdom. We're reminded that wickedness will come to an end and God's goodness will triumph. We see that much of what the world calls great is actually small, and what the world calls small may indeed be great. Where the world sees weakness, we see strength; where the world sees foolishness, we see wisdom; what the world despises as undesirable, we treasure as beautiful (1 Corinthians 1:18-31, 1 Peter 2:4-8).

Having gained a view from the Throne, we gain with it not only wisdom, but comfort, release, and—consequently— joy. From the eternal perspective our mountains are truly molehills and our oceans are a puddle. To see Christ there, high above the universe and maintaining it by His power, shows us a liberating reality of which my wife enjoys reminding me: "There are only three Persons in the Blessed Trinity, dear, and you're not one of Them. So quit worrying about how the universe is run."

In this way, the vision of worship beautifully complements the vision of prayer. In prayer, we rejoice to see the *nearness* of God, a nearness that assures us of His *desire* to work in all things for our good (Romans 8:28). But in worship, we rejoice to see the *sovereignty* of God—a sovereignty that assures us of His *power* to work in all things for our good. Prayer shows us that God is willing; worship shows us that He is able. We need assurance of both in order to walk in joy.

The nature of worship

Though we tend to think of worship exclusively in terms of formal church services, biblical examples make it clear that worship can take place anywhere, anytime—as Jesus said, not just on the mountain or in the Temple (John 4:21-24). When Abraham's chief servant learned from a stranger that God had led him right to the place he was seeking, he stopped in the middle of his conversation by a spring and worshiped God (Genesis 24:26-27). When the Magi found Jesus, they worshiped Him in the house where He was staying (Matthew 2:11). The disciples worshiped the Lord in their boat when He calmed the storm (Matthew 14:33), on the way from the empty tomb (Matthew 28:9), and on the mountain where He ascended into heaven (Matthew 28:17).

On the other hand, we can participate in formal services without genuine worship at all. That was the rebuke God gave His people through Isaiah when He told them, "These people come near to me with their mouth and honor me with their lips, but their hearts are far from me. Their worship of me is made up only of rules taught by men" (Isaiah 29:13).

Jesus went to the heart of the matter with His prophecy to the woman at the well: "A time is coming and has now come when the true worshipers will worship the Father in spirit and truth, for they are the kind of worshipers the Father seeks" (John 4:23). These words are rich with many meanings, but I believe they tell us at least two things.

First, true worship is a matter of the *spirit*. The root

meanings of several Hebrew and Greek words for worship suggest some form of *prostration* before God, and so I believe that to worship in spirit is less an activity of the body than *a posture of the spirit*. Worship is at its heart an attitude, a "bowing" of our spirits before God, which can take place whether we're singing in the congregation or singing at the bus stop.

The essence of an inner posture is well illustrated by the story of the rebellious little boy who refused to sit in the corner as a disciplinary measure. When more serious measures were threatened, he finally cooperated. But as he sat in the chair and turned to face the wall, he issued one last defiant declaration: "I may be sitting down on the outside, but I'm standing up on the inside!"

The example is a negative one, but the point is the same. We may be standing or sitting, or even lying down, for that matter, on the outside, but if we're bowing on the inside, we're worshiping. Our inner posture is one of submission to God, of laying aside every distraction, of forgetting ourselves and turning our attention totally toward Him.

Perhaps the best way to describe the attitude of worship is as an intentional act of *self-abandonment*. When we genuinely enter into worship, whoever we might be, we consciously abandon ourselves, our needs, and our surroundings, and lose ourselves in an overwhelming awareness of God's presence. While prayer asks from God, worship offers to God. The classic example of such joyous self-forgetfulness is King David, dancing down the road before the Lord in his underclothes (2 Samuel 6:1-22).

All this is not to say, of course, that our outer posture is unimportant. Though our spirits should lead the way for our bodies, sometimes our bodies can help our spirits along. In fact, it seems easier for me to bow my spirit when I'm kneeling, or to lift my heart's eyes toward heaven when my physical eyes and hands are raised as well. In the same way that the act of rejoicing is completed by the physical expression of joy, the act of worship can sometimes find a certain fullness in corresponding physical postures. But the attitude of the spirit is primary.

Worship in truth

Jesus said we must worship both in spirit and in *truth*. To me, this means that we must know accurately Who it is we're worshiping. This insight is reflected in Jesus' comment to the woman at the well that her people, the Samaritans, worshiped Someone they didn't know (John 4:22).

If we attempt to worship, for example, a god who's only a benevolent heavenly grandfather, we won't worship truly. He won't even be worthy of our respect, much less our adoration. On the other hand, if we try to worship a god who is all wrath—distant and hostile and keeping a scoreboard of sins—then our spirits will turn away from heaven in fear rather than toward it in love. That's why it's so important that our worship be informed by knowledge of God's self-revelation in the Scripture. To adapt Augustine's remark quoted earlier, nothing can truly be worshiped unless it's truly known.

By increasing our knowledge of who God is, we increase our ability to offer praise (that is, to confess the particular aspects of His character and power) as well as thanksgiving (to confess the particular deeds He has done). Focusing on Him in this way, we gain a new view of the One on the Throne, and of the earth below the Throne.

No wonder, then, that Teresa of Avila, an extraordinarily joyous teacher and worshiper of God in the sixteenth century, always referred to the Lord as "His Majesty." She had learned to live her whole life with a vision of the reigning King.

Learning to focus on the Lord in worship

As with prayer, we all probably have our own ways of focusing on God in worship. But I can offer a few insights from my personal experience that might be helpful.

First of all, the principle that worship is primarily in *spirit* should keep us aware that all we do externally as we worship ought to serve the purpose of establishing or expressing the correct inner posture. When we approach worship, we must each ask, "Will this activity or this item help focus my attention on God, or will it distract me?"

This concern, I think, should provide the central criterion for forms of worship. Will this particular ritual, this liturgy, this hymnal, this type of music, these instruments, this order or format, even this building, point us toward God or attract attention to itself? Does it move us from a third-person frame of mind about the Lord (or other things) to a second-person encounter with the Lord?

Of course, the answer to these questions often depends on the individual's intentional choice. I can choose to sing from a hymnal in such a way that the words are read mechanically, and my mind wanders. Or can I choose to sing the very same song, meaning the words as I read them, and allowing that meaning to turn my attention to the Lord. The hymnal is a vessel. Will I fill it with an awareness of God? Or will I leave it empty, either because I'm too interested in how the vessel itself is crafted or because my heart is turned in a different direction altogether?

I'm not saying, of course, that everything happening in a church service or a private devotional time must fit this criterion. We must have public announcements, for example, or private times of Scripture memorization, that direct our attention purposefully elsewhere. But that's only to say that worship is only one of the things we seek to do in church gatherings or personal devotions. Whenever we desire, however, to move from other activities that are necessary into a genuine encounter with God in worship, then I think the criterion applies.

A second insight into worship that has been useful to me is similar to our earlier suggestion about prayer: Thanksgiving and praise provide the natural starting point for worship. The psalmist said, "Enter his gates with thanksgiving and his courts with praise" (Psalm 100:4). I don't want to make too much of this simple metaphorical statement, but I must say that for me it's a reminder about where I can find the entrance into God's presence.

Thanking God for what He's done and praising Him for who He is naturally lead me from self-awareness into God-awareness so that I turn the eyes of my heart toward Him. In my own devotional times, I may begin with songs that tell about the Lord, but I usually move into songs that are addressed directly *to* the Lord. The move from third-person to second-person, it seems to me, is a critical turn in the direction of our thoughts and feelings if we could truly enter into worship.

A third insight has helped me avoid any notion that God demands worship because He has a big ego—a notion that can undermine any motivation to worship at all. Though few would say it so bluntly, I've often encountered folks who hold this assumption implicitly. Consequently, they place little value on worship because they can't imagine that God really "needs" it.

In one respect, they're correct. God doesn't "need" worship, or anything else, for that matter. But worship is, after all, the *appropriate* response of a creature to a Creator, so it's just as right that we worship as it is that we tell the truth. Righteousness, Micah told us, includes acting justly, loving mercy, *and* walking humbly with God (Micah 6:8). The last of those three is as fundamental an ethical orientation as the first two—and it's worship above all that places us in that position of humility before God.

At the same time, glorifying God is for our good. As we've said before, putting ourselves in an inner posture of submission leads to wisdom and joy and much more. Of course, it would be right to praise God even if we received no benefit from it, and the benefit to us should not be our focus as we worship (that would be the very opposite of worship). Yet remembering that it's for our good as we approach worship keeps us from thinking that God selfishly demands worship only for His own sake.

Closely related to these insights is the realization that our praise—both here and in heaven—isn't simply a matter of telling God things He likes to hear about Himself. The biblical picture of heaven as a worship-filled place would be a nightmare if that meant we would spend eternity as flattering sycophants around a powerful tyrant, saying tediously again and again, "Well, God, You sure are big. Yes, You're certainly powerful. And You've got everything figured out, too."

Instead, we should view our praise to God—both here and in heaven—as the kind of verbal admiration lovers have for one another. As we noted in an earlier chapter, when we're enchanted by the inner and outer beauty of another person, we can hardly stop telling that person how beautiful he or she is, and how delighted we are to be in his or her presence. Such praise is not felt as a burdensome duty, but rather as a response to the beloved so fitting that to fail to praise would be unthinkable. Though it's at most only a parable of a reality we'll someday know in full, I think the image of a lover bubbling over with joyous praise of the beauty in the beloved is the best image to keep in mind as we think about worshiping God.

And that brings us back again to the reason for this

rather lengthy discussion of the nature of worship. My intent has not been to give some comprehensive definition, nor some complete guidelines for structuring our worship. Rather, I've attempted to show the connection between worship and joy that is so often lacking in our churches.

My claim is simply this: When all is said and done, with whatever forms of worship we might choose, our worship must at its heart be a personal encounter with a sovereign God if it's to be genuine. Anything less than that will be only motions or emotions, and will rob us of the transforming vision of God on the Throne.

When we worship "in spirit and truth," however, the result is inevitably joy. To see the Creator reigning even now awakens in us as creatures an immense joy that all things are in His hands. To see the Beloved enthroned forever stirs in us lovers a delight that we'll be in His presence eternally. In worship we rejoice to know that His power secures His promise.

Thus worship is a discipline of hope. Through the glimpses of God it gives us, it channels the joy of tomorrow's ultimate vision of Him into the thirsty soil of today.

Reign on, King Jesus. Someday I will see You face-to-Face, and "join the everlasting song." But for today, let me prepare, Lord God, by tuning the strings of my heart in praise. I thirst for a foretaste of the joy prepared for us.

When I look at Your holiness in worship, when I gaze at Your beauty in wonder, I love You more than ever, Bright Morning Star. I rejoice to know that You're on the Throne, and that I abide in You.

Since the creation of the world God's invisible qualities—his eternal power and divine nature—have been clearly seen, being understood from what has been made.
ROMANS 1:20

□

I meditate on all your works and consider what your hands have done. I spread out my hands to you; my soul thirsts for you like a parched land.
PSALM 143:5-6

□

For, quite clearly, the mighty gifts with which we are endowed are hardly from ourselves; indeed, our very being is nothing but subsistence in the one God. Then, by these benefits shed like dew from heaven upon us, we are led as by rivulets to the Spring itself.
JOHN CALVIN

□

We pursue . . . the inner meanings of what is created, for the sake of attaining to the Lord who has created them.
EVAGRIUS

□

Any thought, therefore, not centered on God is stolen from Him.
JOHN OF THE CROSS

CHAPTER 15

MEDITATION:
Seeing God in His Creation

When Eastern religious thought made new inroads into American culture in the sixties, the word "meditation" became suspect in some Christian circles. Many who understandably feared the influence of unbiblical ideas on young believers assumed that any talk of "Christian meditation" was a misguided attempt to syncretize biblical terms with Hindu or Buddhist practices. They were especially concerned that the Eastern style of meditation, which attempts to empty the mind, opened the door wide to demonic spiritual influences that would seek to fill the vacuum.

I, too, would fear for someone who opens himself or herself in this way. I know personally a number of people who encountered much more than they bargained for when they attempted to gain "enlightenment" along the path of Eastern religious teachings. When we use the word "meditation" in this chapter, however, we're speaking of something very different, and quite biblical.

Many definitions could be given for the term "meditate," perhaps the most general being "to ponder." But the meaning we'll assign to it here is narrower and more specific. When we speak of meditation, we'll mean by that word *the habit of thinking deeply about things and events in the world around us in such a way that they turn our thoughts to God.* The goal of such a habit has been beautifully expressed by the Puritan writer David Dickson, who said we "meditate on our making, that we may fall in love with our Maker."[1]

Asaph the psalmist said to the Lord, "I will meditate on all your works and consider all your mighty deeds" (Psalm 77:12). Not surprisingly, he and the other psalmists seem to have cultivated this habit and allowed it to blossom into wise and beautiful poetry. Especially rich examples are Psalms 8 and 19, where David tells how "the heavens declare the glory of God"; Psalm 104, where the writer's mind surveys the earth, sea, and sky for testimonies to God's goodness; and Psalm 136, where the speaker weaves a powerful litany of thanks to God for His part in the events of Israel's history.

In fact, almost any place a psalmist compares God's nature or behavior metaphorically to something on earth, we see the fruit of meditation, of a pondering that has led the mind from the things around it to the things beyond it. We can easily imagine, for example, how a young shepherd boy's meditation on his work could turn his thoughts toward the great Shepherd (Psalm 23). Or a musician's meditation on his craft could beautifully illustrate for him how all creation could be said to sing praise to God (Psalm 98).

Yet this spiritual discipline is not at all confined to the psalmists. The book of Ecclesiastes, for instance, is one long meditation on the meaninglessness of things and events in the world when not considered in the light of eternity. Many of the Proverbs offer the distilled wisdom of those who "applied [their] heart to what [they] observed and learned a lesson from what [they] saw" (Proverbs 24:32), studying intently the world around them to find moral and spiritual lessons reflected there.

In the New Testament, Jesus urged His disciples to meditate in this way when He told them, "Consider the lilies of the field," and then used the flowers to make a point about God's nature (Matthew 6:28-30, KJV). Paul, like other New Testament writers, frequently recognized that natural objects and events point toward spiritual realities, as when he compared the Christian life to that of a soldier or an athlete (2 Timothy 2:4-5).

This long tradition of meditating on the creation as a way of seeing the Creator more clearly has continued down through the ages in the life of the Church. A more recent example of it I've found especially compelling is Jonathan Edwards' image of the precariousness of human life. We walk, he told his congregation, like a spider on a thin filament of web over a blazing fire, and only the grace of God keeps the thread from dissolving and us from falling. The image of the spider was in fact one of his favorites, appearing in several of his works. Edwards' writings from his early childhood show that he'd spent many hours, even at an early age, closely observing and meditating on the life of that fascinating creature.[2]

Meditation's angle of vision on God

Paul told the Roman Christians that God's invisible qualities can be seen through what He has made (Romans 1:20). Just as it is with human art work, the masterpiece tells us volumes about the Master. Combined with a thorough knowledge of Scripture, which brings the creation into proper focus, meditation on the world around us can help us see God more clearly in at least two ways.

First, the vision of God as seen through creation reveals many of His attributes: wisdom, creativity, omniscience, omnipotence. (Personally, I think some of God's handiwork, such as the ostrich or the duckbill platypus, also tells us of His sense of humor.) The deeper we go as we meditate, the more amazed we sometimes are at what we discover about the depths of God.

Many examples could be offered here. I still remember how, as a young Christian, I stopped one morning in the yard to admire a dark crimson rose, and my thoughts naturally turned in praise to God for His gift of beauty. But then I went a step further and thought how wonderful it was that He would have created the color red itself, and what a delightful basic element of creation it is. Next I realized that even the notion of *any* color at all was infinitely wise and kind. God could have chosen to place us in a black-and-white world, but instead He's allowed us all the visual pleasures of red, blue, yellow, and all their mixtures. The deeper I went into the created object before me, the more awesome I saw God to be.

A particularly powerful season of meditation in my personal life came when my wife and I first discovered that our daughter was on her way, and began reading books about a child's development in the womb. Birth is such a common event that we tend to take it for granted. But after that time of studying conception, pregnancy, and birth, I'll never again view the process as anything less than miraculous. The more complexity I discovered, the more I was driven to my knees to tell God how wise He is and, with the psalmist, to praise Him because we're "fearfully and wonderfully made" (Psalm 139:14).

With my daughter's arrival, my meditation often took a new direction as I contemplated the natural parent-child relationship, and compared it to our life with our heavenly Father. Growing into my role as a dad, I began to discover all kinds of new insights into God's love for us and how He expresses it through care and correction. Many of Jesus' words took on richer meaning, as when He said, "Which of you, if his son asks for bread, will give him a stone?" (Matthew 7:9).

In this way, then, meditation is like an inner poem that moves our minds from concrete images to deeper meanings. In fact, we could describe meditation in the same way Robert Frost once described poetry: A poem, he observed, "begins in delight and ends in wisdom."[3]

When we meditate, we begin with the delight of a rose, or a new life, or a father's care, and we end in deeper wisdom about the nature of God. As Frost also noted, that motion is the same as the motion of love. It turns our hearts, as love does, in the Lord's direction, with gratitude and a desire to be united to Him.

God's principles in the creation

In addition to seeing some of God's attributes through creation, we can also discover there many of His *principles*. In a number of ways the world's physical laws reflect spiritual and moral laws, so that the patterns we discover in one can be applied to our understanding of the other. Meditation on these patterns must always be evaluated within the context of Scripture so that we don't apply them to the wrong spiritual realities. But we find in the Bible itself many examples of how the comparison can be fruitful.

The classic example, of course, is Jesus' statement that "unless a kernel of wheat falls to the ground and dies, it remains only a single seed. But if it dies, it produces many seeds" (John 12:24). The principle of life, death, resurrection, and fruitfulness found its cosmic summit in the Incarnation. But the principle occurs throughout creation on countless levels: in the farmer's field, in our conversion to the faith, in our growth in holiness, in our ambitions for ministry, in the consummation of earthly history to come.

In addition to the example, Jesus' parables often find their application in the parallels between the spiritual and the natural worlds. The Kingdom of God, for instance, begins small, but grows large, like the mustard seed. And even while it's small, it exerts a great influence on its surroundings, like yeast in dough (Matthew 13:31-33). Paul insists that the principle of sowing and reaping is as fixed in the spiritual world as it is in the natural (Galatians 6:7-10). And James reminds us that just as a little spark can ignite a forest fire, so a little tongue can destroy a whole life or even a community (James 3:5-6).

Wisdom that ends in delight

Meditation thus acts as a mental staircase that takes our thoughts from earth to heaven, from what has been made to the One who made it. When what we observe is beautiful or fascinating, then meditation, like a poem, "begins in delight and ends in wisdom."

Yet in reality, a true meditation doesn't end there. The reason we've devoted a chapter to meditation in a book about joy is that the wisdom we gain—that is, a clearer vision of God—should itself lead us on to appreciate and enjoy Him. Meditation finds its consummation when it comes full circle, beginning with delight in creation, leading to wisdom, and ending with delight once more: delight in the Creator.

Consequently, meditation is the discipline by which we can allow the many little joys in life to participate in the great Joy in the Lord. When our delight in creation is turned by an act of the will and intellect toward a search for the Creator, the river of delight in God begins to swell. We've compared the disciplines of the Christian life to furrows that channel joy. But in a sense, meditation is more like a rain barrel that collects the daily refreshing showers of blessing that fall from heaven throughout our lives. Such showers, if collected, can fill the furrows. But if allowed to scatter and fall alone, they dry up quickly without a trace.

For this reason, meditation should become a spiritual *discipline*—a cultivated habit. Most of us have probably at times engaged in it spontaneously. It's only natural for spiritual ears to hear echoes of heaven on earth. But if we learn to meditate as a way of life, we'll find our view of God, our love for God, and our joy in God enriched immeasurably.

Cultivating the habit
How do we go about cultivating the habit of meditation? It's more a frame of mind, I think, than anything else—an alertness to what God might be saying in the everyday circumstances of our lives. When the psalmist said, "Teach us to number our days aright, that we may gain a heart of wisdom" (Psalm 90:12), I believe he meant more than remaining aware that our time on earth is short. The Hebrew verb translated "to number" here means literally "to weigh." As we meditate on the days of our lives, we learn to give them their proper "weight" by seeing them in the light of eternal matters.

But only a grounding in biblical truth provides the proper "scales" for weighing what fills our days. As Calvin said, with the Bible, creation's picture of God comes into focus; without it, the view is fuzzy. For that reason, the mind prepared to meditate is the mind that has steeped itself in Scripture.

In addition, the mind ready for meditation echoes always with one important question: "What might this thing or event tell me about God?" An old saying suggests that "joy is seeing a sunset and knowing the One to thank." For the mind cultivating the discipline of meditation, the shadow of that One continually falls over everything around it.

If someone who loves You can learn to see You even in the humble spider, my Lord, how great a panorama of Your glory must be waiting for us in this wide earth! Make the opaque things of this world transparent, Lord God, so that my sight passes through them to glimpse You standing behind them and upholding them in love.

Let every object, every event, be a stained-glass window through which Your light shines, each one a scene from sacred history where Your hand is displayed at work. Through faith, my Lord, those visions of Your hand will color and warm the inside of my temple, filling it with wisdom and joy, making it a place where Your Spirit is pleased to dwell.

NOTES:
1. *The Golden Treasury of Puritan Quotations*, compiled by I. D. E. Thomas (Chicago: Moody Press, 1975), page 187.
2. Edwards, "Sinners in the Hands of an Angry God," pages 162-165, and "Of Insects," pages 3-10, in *Selections*.
3. Quoted in the introduction to *The Treasury of American Poetry*, ed., Nancy Sullivan (New York: Doubleday, 1978), page xxxiv.

The prospect of the righteous is joy.
PROVERBS 10:28

□

*"Whoever has my commands and obeys them, he is the one who loves me.
He who loves me will be loved by my Father, and I too will love him and
show myself to him. . . . I have told you this so that my joy may be in
you and that your joy may be complete. . . . You are my friends if you do
what I command. I no longer call you servants."*
JOHN 14:21; 15:11,14-15

□

Avoid sin for the simple reason that Christ loves you.
ERASMUS OF ROTTERDAM

□

*O Lord our God, grant us grace to desire You with our whole heart, that
so desiring, we may seek and find You; and so finding You we may love
You; and loving You we may hate those sins from which
You have redeemed us.*
ANSELM OF CANTERBURY

□

Obedience is the opener of eyes.
GEORGE MACDONALD

CHAPTER 16

OBEDIENCE:
Seeing God as Our Friend

In the parable of the talents, Jesus told of a master who entrusted each of three servants with a different amount of money while he was away on a journey (Matthew 25:14-30). The first two invested their talents and were rewarded with a profit. So the master commended them, promoted them, and invited them to enter into his joy.

The third servant, however, merely buried his money and profited nothing. His master was understandably displeased, and the servant was punished.

Considering that Jesus intended this story as a parallel to our relationship with God, we ourselves might well profit by paying close attention to the third servant's reason for his fruitlessness: "'Master,' he said, 'I knew that you are a hard man, harvesting where you have not sown and gathering where you have not scattered seed. So I was afraid . . .'" (Matthew 25:24-25).

I was afraid. The unprofitable servant viewed his master as a hard, unreasonable man, and that view paralyzed him with fear, making his labor sterile and preventing him from entering his master's joy. Sadly enough, the same can be said about many of us who seek to serve our Master. We labor in fear, lacking joy in our service. For just as seeing God as a kind Father moves us to love Him and thus to enjoy Him, so, too, seeing God as a hard taskmaster moves us to fear Him and empties us of joy.

Judging from the parable, the fear that comes from viewing God as a hard taskmaster is ungrounded. This insight is confirmed by John's insistence that "there is no fear in love. But perfect love drives out fear, because fear has to do with punishment" (1 John 4:18).

Nevertheless, we have a problem here: The fear of God appears as one of the most constant themes throughout Scripture, alongside the love of God. It's praised as the key to righteousness. To make matters even worse, we're told by Isaiah that the Messiah would be One who *delights* in the fear of the Lord (Isaiah 11:3). How could joy and fear possibly coexist that way? If we're to solve this seeming contradiction, then we must first examine what the biblical writers mean when they speak of fearing God.

Different kinds of fear

A quick survey of most scriptural references to the fear of God reveals that the phrase implies, above all, *obedience*. Fearing God means serving Him, walking in His ways, following His laws, shunning evil (Deuteronomy 6:13, Joshua 24:14, 2 Chronicles 6:31, Job 1:1, Psalm 128:1). Admittedly, in many cases, dread of threatened punishment from God is what stimulates such obedience, at least initially.

Even so, on the night of His betrayal, when Jesus exhorted His disciples to obedience He pointed them toward *love* as the necessary motivation. Such love was possible, He said, because He was no longer calling them servants, but rather friends (John 15:15). Henceforth they would be expected to obey Him because they loved Him: "If you love me, you will obey what I command" (John 14:15).

Teachers of the Church down through the ages have pondered this passage carefully, as well as the biblical commands to fear God. Many have come to the conclusion that Jesus' words in this text provide the key to understanding how Scripture can say both that we must fear God and that perfect love drives out fear. Dorotheos of Gaza, a sixth-century writer, was not the first or the last to offer such an explanation, but I think his is perhaps the most helpful.

Dorotheos resolved the biblical paradox by suggesting that there are two kinds of fear toward God: what he called *preliminary* and *perfect*. Preliminary fear, he said, is the starting point of our relationship with the Lord, as it was for so many in the Bible. It's the fear of punishment, of condemnation—the fear that motivated the Israelites to obey the Law when God threatened curses if they disobeyed (Deuteronomy 28:15-68).

On the other hand, said Dorotheos, when we have what John called "perfect love" for God, such love drives out that preliminary fear. For John tells us specifically that the fear he's talking about is the kind that has to do with punishment (1 John 4:18). A person who has grown into a "perfect" love for God, Dorotheos claimed, finds his or her preliminary fear giving way instead to *perfect* fear—a desire to keep God's will, "not for fear of punishment, not to avoid condemnation, but. . . because he has tasted the sweetness of being with God; he fears he may fall away from it."[1]

In this regard, Dorotheos and other Christian teachers such as Basil, Gregory of Nyssa, and Catherine of Siena identified what they considered three stages of motivation for our obedience to God. The first is the stage of slavery, in which, like the servant in the parable, we obey because we fear punishment from the master. Such "slavish" fear is necessary as a beginning point, but we must move on beyond it if our labor is to be fruitful and joyous.

The second stage is that of the wage earner or mercenary. In this stage of motivation, we obey God primarily because of what's in it for us. We seek to earn God's blessings and rewards as the due "wages" of our labor. We look for the gifts rather than the Giver.

The third stage is that of the friend of God. This is the place of obedience Jesus described when He said His disciples were no longer servants but friends, and should obey Him in love. In this stage, we obey God, not for fear of punishment nor desire of rewards, but because we love God Himself and know we're loved by Him.[2]

Nevertheless, at this stage of maturity, we don't cease to fear God because we love God; rather, perfect fear and perfect love coincide. In perfect fear, however, we're not afraid of punishment. We're afraid instead of offending or hurting the One we love, afraid of putting distance between ourselves and a God who has become so precious to us. As Gregory summed it up, "We regard falling from God's friendship as the only thing dreadful and we consider becoming God's friend the only thing worthy of honor and desire."[3]

The vision of obedience

In light, then, of this understanding of the fear of God, I'm convinced that the vision of mature obedience is *the vision of God as our Friend*. The kind of submission to His will we're describing here results not from the cowering fear of the third servant in the parable, a "slavish" fear of punishment based on a view of God as a hard taskmaster. Instead, we mean a submission to the Lord out of the "perfect fear," as Dorotheos called it, that shuns the thought of insulting or offending our Beloved. And even though the most mature of Christians may at times obey God for lesser reasons, I believe that this attitude is the ideal.

Such obedience, Jesus told His disciples, will allow Him to show Himself to us (John 14:21). The more we do His will, the more we're able to see of Jesus, for "without holiness no one will see the Lord" (Hebrews 12:14). Our obedience makes us more like Him. We think His thoughts, we feel His feelings, we walk His ways; and so we're more likely to recognize Him, and to find ourselves where He is. Gregory described the connection this way: "To follow God wherever He might lead is to behold God."[4]

In this way, we imitate the obedience of Jesus to the Father as He described it: "My Father is always at his work to this very day, and I, too, am working. . . . I tell you the truth, the Son can do nothing by himself; he can do only what he sees his Father doing, because whatever the Father does the Son also does. For the Father loves the Son and shows him all he does" (John 5:17, 19-20).

With such a vision of the Lord resulting from obedience, it's no wonder that the psalmist would cry, "Direct me in the path of your commands, for there I find delight" (Psalm 119:35). Obedience leads to joy because it keeps before our eyes our best and most beloved Friend, the One who showed His love for us by laying down His life (John 15:13). "Obedience," John Wesley observed, "is the performing of all the ordinary actions of life with the single eye and the pure heart."[5] That single eye of the heart is fixed on Jesus. When we obey Him for fear of losing our closeness to Him, His joy is in us and our joy is truly complete (John 15:11).

In this way, obedience is a discipline of love. By placing us alongside the Lord, it channels the joy that arises from a view of God at work in the present into the daily decisions of our lives. There, as Zechariah prophesied, we can "serve him without fear in holiness and righteousness before him all our days" (Luke 1:74-75).

"O my Strength, I watch for you; you, O God, are my fortress, my loving God" (Psalm 59:9-10). I watch for You daily, Lord, and I find You standing at the crossroads where I must choose to obey or not to obey. The sight of You waiting there in love gives me strength to choose Your way, the way in which I can walk and work alongside You, the only way of joy. Grant me grace, Father, to choose always friendship with You, and to shun every evil that would come between us. For "You are my Lord; apart from you I have no good thing" (Psalm 16:2).

NOTES:

1. Dorotheos of Gaza, *Discourses and Sayings*, translated by Eric P. Wheeler (Kalamazoo, Mich.: Cistercian Publications, 1977), page 109.
2. Dorotheos, *Discourses*, pages 110-111; Catherine of Siena, *The Dialogue*, pages 111-116.
3. Gregory of Nyssa, *The Life of Moses*, translated by Abraham J. Malherbe and Everett Ferguson (New York: Paulist Press, 1978), page 137.
4. Gregory of Nyssa, *The Life of Moses*, page 119.
5. John Wesley, "Single-Mindedness," *The Nature of the Kingdom*, ed., Clare George Weakley, Jr. (Minneapolis: Bethany House, 1979), page 211.

Serve the LORD with gladness.
PSALM 100:2, NIV (1978 Version)

□

If you spend yourselves in behalf of the hungry
and satisfy the needs of the oppressed,
then your light will rise in the darkness,
and your light will become like the noonday.
The LORD will guide you always;
he will satisfy your needs in a sun-scorched land
and will strengthen your frame.
You will be like a well-watered garden,
like a spring whose waters never fail. . . .
Then you will find your joy in the LORD.
ISAIAH 58:10-11,14

□

"Then the righteous will answer him, 'Lord, when did we see you . . . ?'
The King will reply, 'I tell you the truth, whatever you did for one of the
least of these brothers of mine, you did for me.'"
MATTHEW 25:37,40

□

From our neighbor are life and death. If we do good to our neighbor, we
do good to God: if we cause our neighbor to stumble,
we sin against Christ.
ANTONY

□

The soul of one who serves God always swims in joy, always keeps
holiday, and is always in the mood for singing.
JOHN OF THE CROSS

CHAPTER 17

SERVICE:
Seeing God in the Least of His Brethren

When I was a child, the story of Jesus' birth sometimes left me a bit sad. I was glad to know the Lord was born, but the circumstances of His coming seemed cruel. I fretted about the noise and dirt and cold of the stable, and the rejection Mary and Joseph must have felt in being turned away from so many places. I wished I could have been there to help in some way. With typical childish confidence, I thought, *"Even someone my age could have given up his own bedroom for the night, or brought some blankets, or kept the animals quiet."*

Only years later did I realize that if I'd been there, I might well have been as selfish and unconcerned as everyone else in Bethlehem that night. But at the same time I grew to recognize that ever since that first Nativity, the needs of Christ continue. Even today, I have a chance to ease His suffering.

A memorable Christmas
Perhaps I saw that reality most clearly one Christmas Eve a few years ago. Our home was buzzing with anticipation: It was the first Christmas for our first baby, and her proud

grandmother had come from far away to help celebrate. My brother, his wife, and their daughter were driving in from out of state as well, bringing with them an older single man who would have been alone otherwise. The house was bursting with delicious aromas, colorful lights, and nostalgic music. It was one of the most exciting Christmas Eves I'd ever known.

As we were setting the table for the feast, the phone rang. It was the young mother of a refugee family from Vietnam whom we and another family had "adopted." For several months, we'd been spending most of our free time with them and other refugee families we'd met through them. We collected food, clothing, and furniture for them; took them shopping, job hunting, and for medical care; and taught them English as a second language in a weekly class we began in their home.

Given the circumstances, a call from this young woman was nearly a daily occurrence, so I wasn't surprised. Since they were a Buddhist family, this day was like any other for them. I knew they were unaware we were celebrating. With the guests due to arrive anytime, I thought I'd wait a minute to be polite, and then offer to call back later.

My heart sank, however, when I heard her say the phrases she'd had to learn almost as soon as they came to our city: "Baby sick. Go doctor." Her poor little daughter, only a year old, had been plagued with recurring ear infections and sore throats for months. We had taken her to the doctor many times before.

I wish I could say that at that moment I was glad to have another chance to help these friends in need. But that wasn't the case. I answered, "I'll be there soon," but only with half a heart. Then I told my wife gloomily, "If I'm not back in time, go on without me."

"It's *Christmas Eve*, Lord," I mumbled. "Our guests will

be here soon. Why tonight?" The doctor's office was closed, so that meant finding a hospital emergency room or a twenty-four-hour clinic, and scraping up the cash to pay for it. I grumbled all the way out the door.

In the car on the way to their home, however, I came face-to-face with my own selfishness. My eyes began to burn. I was angry at myself for having such a shallow love. It wasn't the first time our commitment to these new friends had been tested by inconvenience, but somehow the contrast of my frustration next to the joy of the season brought into sharp clarity the limits of my caring. I was ashamed, and I prayed for forgiveness.

As it turned out, we found a clinic rather easily, and the child only had a minor throat infection. After a stop by the drugstore to fill the prescription, I took them home, explained the prescribed dosage, and hurried home myself. There I discovered that my brother's family was running several hours late, and hadn't arrived yet. I was even more ashamed for having worried.

The evening, when it finally got going, was warm and happy, one I'll long remember. But longer still I'll remember the grateful look on that mother's face, and the peaceful look of the child as she fell asleep in relief. And I could never forget what the Lord said to me that night as I was dropping off to sleep, words I had to write down:

Son, you've often thought what joy it would be to see Me in the flesh and care for My physical needs. You've wished you could have lived when I walked the earth, so you could walk with Me.

Tonight, you had your wish fulfilled. I walked the earth again in that frightened mother. I cried out again in the flesh of that suffering child. Tonight, your town was a Bethlehem, their home was a stable. And when I had nowhere else to lay My head, your arms were My manger. I was sick and a stranger, and you took care of Me.

Though you acted with only half a heart, with the eyes of your whole heart you can see Me now. I was waiting for you to find Me in the least of these My brethren. Don't ever forget what you saw tonight. For wherever you go, Bethlehem is all around you.

That night I knew that just as Scripture says, I saw the Lord in the needs of people I served (Matthew 25:34-40). And because of such a vision, that Christmas turned out to be the most joyful ever.

Even so, that wasn't the last time we saw the Lord in our Vietnamese friends. I remember well the evening I went to visit that same young mother, who was quite ill in the hospital. I prayed for a miracle, and when I finished praying, her face was radiant with the light of the Lord. By the next day she was healed and at home again. Then, only a few days later, she and her husband called us to come over and tell them the good news about this Jesus who had healed her.

The last time we saw them before a new job took us three thousand miles away was at a farewell dinner they held for us. When we first entered their tiny apartment, we could hardly believe our eyes: The entire Southeast Asian neighborhood had brought their chairs and tables and their finest native dishes to lay out a royal spread for us.

We had to fight back the tears, because we knew it was a banquet purchased with the widow's mite. They had so very little, and yet with joyous abandon they had lavished it all on us. That night I thought of another glad Banquet that is yet to come, of how very much it also cost the Host. And once again, I saw Jesus in their faces, and rejoiced.

Finding the place to serve
You can imagine how our joy grew in serving and being served by these precious people. Each glimpse of the Lord we caught in them stirred in us a deep and abiding delight.

We came to realize that even if the Lord had no direct needs in Himself, we could nevertheless meet His needs in those for whom He'd laid down His life. Through them we learned that the vision of service is *the vision of God in the least of His brethren.*

Even so, in the years since then, it has not always been easy to recognize the least of Christ's brethren, that is, the people we should be serving. That's not to say that the world isn't full of need, for it is. In fact, the magnitude of the need is precisely the problem. It often paralyzes us because we don't know where to begin, and we can't do it all. Or we may plunge ourselves into the needs around us indiscriminately, then rapidly burn out. Either way leads eventually along a joyless road.

I suppose it's a matter of calling, though many use that idea as an excuse to do nothing: "I just don't feel *called* to feed the poor." My wife and I would never want to make a standard out of our experience, but we've come to two simple conclusions as we've sought to serve God joyfully.

First, we believe that everyone is called to serve. However vague at times the Lord's leading may seem to be, it's better to be doing something than nothing—unless, of course, God has instructed us to take an intentional, well-defined season of rest. Otherwise, a life of minimal service is a life of minimal joy.

Second, we've found that when we seek the Lord's will diligently in prayer, fasting, and scriptural study, He makes it clear to us how we're to be serving. Instead of assuming that we're to say yes to every opportunity that comes along— especially the typical "busy" work that can so easily fill church programing—we try to imitate Jesus by doing only what we see the Father doing (John 5:17,19-20).

The way we came to know those Southeast Asian families provides a useful example of how God can work. One day we and another Christian family set aside a day to pray and fast, asking God to place us in ministry to someone truly in need. We'd recently realized that most of our free time had been swallowed up by our church's activities—things that were perhaps good but were all directed inward, for the benefit of the church. We were beginning to sense that our service had become mostly selfish, and thus joyless; so we were looking for an opportunity to turn outward.

Within three days, God slowly began opening a door. First we read in the local paper that our city had refugee families who had escaped from Southeast Asia with nothing more than the clothes they were wearing. Then our friends bought a water bed and gave us their old bed, so that we had an extra to give away. When we called the social agency working with the refugees and offered them the bed, they asked if we could deliver it to a family ourselves. We agreed, and arranged to meet them in the housing project where many of the refugees were located.

Still not realizing that God was answering our prayer, we arrived at the Vietnamese family's apartment—and were horrified by the poverty we found. That night we gathered up all the clothes and household items we didn't need, loaded up some bags of groceries, and went back with a small truck full. Day by day, we learned of new needs, and gradually we became collecting agents for things needed by people in the neighborhood. Before long, we were providing transportation, looking for jobs, teaching English, and praying more than we'd ever prayed before.

It wasn't long before we knew that we'd been called to the work we were doing. We hadn't planned it, though we'd sought it. God honored our willingness to serve by opening the right door. Knowing that we were doing what we saw the Father doing gave us a great joy as we labored. It kept us from being overwhelmed or from burning out.

Someone has wisely said that the place where God calls us is that place where our great gladness and the world's great need come together. By the same token, I think, the place where God has *not* called us may be a place of the world's need, but it won't be a place of gladness as we attempt to serve. My wife and I know, because we've tried it both ways.

This isn't to say that joyless service for a season is necessarily misguided; we often have to sow in tears before we can reap in joy (Psalm 126:5). But avenues of service chosen haphazardly or in desperation, without seeking God's plan for our lives, will almost certainly lead to frustration. We'll have a hard time finding the Lord in it all, and thus a hard time rejoicing in Him.

Who are the least of His brethren? We must ask Him to show them to us. My wife and I have found them among refugees whose poverty was material, and among American families whose poverty was spiritual. We've found them among handicapped children whom we've cheered in the Special Olympics, and confused college kids who've come for counseling. We've found them among the Christians in Soviet prisons for whom we send our letters and our prayers, and among the young believers we've invited to live in our home for a season of discipleship. Truly, Bethlehem is all around us.

In each of these places, because we've seen the least of God's brethren, we've seen God as well. The vision of service is in fact a vision of the Lord because being a servant takes us to the very place where Jesus is already at work in the world. "Whoever serves me must follow me," He said. "And where I am, my servant also will be" (John 12:26).

When we care for the least of the Lord's people, we find our feet fitting into His footprints behind Him, and we rejoice at the sight of Him serving with us. Thus our service is a discipline of love. It channels the delight from our view of God at work to the borders of our garden, where He wishes to extend the area of our cultivation out into a thirsty planet.

The world turns in darkness, Lord, longing for light. Make me Your star in their night, a bright sign that You've heard their cry and invaded their place of need. Make my soul a stable, though it may be poor, so that the least of Your brothers and sisters may seek You and find You in me, even as I find You in them. Lord Jesus, come walk in our streets, and make our home the site of Your continuing Nativity, so that we, too, might bring "good tidings of great joy."

Glorious things are spoken of you, O city of God. . . . Then those who sing as well as those who play the flutes shall say, "All my springs of joy are in you."
PSALM 87:3,7, NASB

□

For where two or three have gathered together in My name, there I am in their midst.
MATTHEW 18:20, NASB

□

Now you are the body of Christ, and each one of you is a part of it.
1 CORINTHIANS 12:27

□

Suppose we were to . . . draw the outline of a circle. . . . Let us suppose that this circle is the world and that God Himself is the center; the straight lines drawn from the circumference are the lives of men. . . . The closer those lines are to God, the closer they become to one another; and the closer they are to one another, the closer they become to God.
DOROTHEOS OF GAZA

□

I needed this support, this nearness of those who really loved Christ so much that they seemed to see Him. I needed to be with people whose every action told me something of the country that was my home: just as expatriates in every alien land keep together, if only to remind themselves, by their very faces and clothes and gait and accents and expressions, of the land they come from.
THOMAS MERTON

CHAPTER 18

FELLOWSHIP:
Seeing God in His Body

For many years I used to muse about how Jesus' face must have looked when He lived on earth. Evidently, many others throughout the centuries have speculated as well. Countless "portraits" of Christ adorning the art galleries of the world testify to their imaginings.

Some in our day have wondered whether the famous Shroud of Turin actually carries what might be called the Lord's miraculous self-photograph. Others of long ago, like the third-century theologian Origen, came to the rather odd conclusion that Jesus' face appeared different to every person who saw Him, according to that person's particular needs. In any case, though I used to puzzle about it myself, about two years ago I stopped wondering. It happened one evening at church when I discovered, I believe, something of how the Lord's face looked when He lived on earth, and how it will look when we see Him in heaven.

Now you may be thinking I'm like that little boy who once told his mother he was drawing a picture of God. When she suggested gently that no one knew what God looks like, he insisted flatly, "They will when *I* get through."

That's not at all what I mean: I don't lay claim to any special visions of Jesus.

That evening in church, however, something caught my eye as the saints came together to worship. A close friend of mine, as godly a man as you'll ever find, glanced at me with a radiance in his face that looked utterly familiar; and yet I knew it wasn't his radiance. Or perhaps it's closer to the truth to say that it was both his radiance and the radiance of Someone else shining through him.

I turned to my family sitting beside me, and there it was again. It shone as well from the folks on the next pew, from the worship leader, from the pastor. In that moment I knew I was seeing in all of them a Face I'd seen a thousand times before: each from a different angle, perhaps, or in a different stage of growth. But all the same, it was a single, familiar Face, and it called forth from me a glorious flood of joy.

I don't mean to sound mysterious; it seemed, in fact, not a mystery, but rather the resolution of a mystery—as if at long last I could say, "So *that's* it! I should have known all along!" It was like being introduced to a man whose appearance struck me as curiously familiar, only to discover later that he was the brother of an old friend. It was, after all, a family resemblance I was seeing in the ones "Jesus is not ashamed to call . . . brothers" and sisters (Hebrews 2:11).

The resemblance was in some ways actually physical. The smile, of course, was one of its basic elements; but also the preponderance of laughter lines rather than worry lines; the attentive eyes with their look of compassion; the ear inclined to listen with concern. Their voices, though varying in quality, shared a certain warmth of tone. And even their gestures of touching one another were the same: affirming hugs, comforting pats, confident handshakes.

I may be wrong, but that night I concluded that when we finally see Jesus in heaven, His face will be surprisingly familiar. The light in His eyes, the smile on His lips, the tone of His voice, even His gesture of welcome, will have met our eyes countless times before. When at last we do see Him, then, we'll know that the joy we tasted in Christian fellowship on earth was a foretaste of the joy we'll have in seeing His face eternally. For the vision of fellowship is *the vision of God's Body—the Body of Christ.*

Meanwhile, the delight we experience in fellowship is intensified and enriched by the very fact that we share it with others. Just as expressing our joy allows it to come to the surface, so participating in joy with others allows it to surround us and sweep us up together into the same life-giving current. Solitary joy is like a refreshing spring within us, but joy in fellowship is much more. It breaks over us like the waves of a great ocean where we frolic together on the shore.

More than His face
In the Church, then, I've seen the face of Christ shining in the faces of His people. Yet a body is more than a face. In Christ's Body, we can see much more than His countenance. With its variety of members, each doing his or her appointed work (Ephesians 4:16), the Church in its wholeness presents to us as rich and complete a portrait of the Lord as we can expect to have in this life. For that reason, if we wish to see Jesus in the world so that we can love and enjoy Him there, then we must look beyond our own little member of His Body.

I once visited a small art gallery with two major photographic exhibits. The first was a collection of endearing portraits showing children in all their various moods and activities: eating and sleeping, playing and studying, laughing and crying. The second was a series of intriguing prints in which the photographer had focused the camera exclusively on close-up shots of his own hands, feet, arms, legs, and face.

The second exhibit was fascinating and at times entertaining. Yet the result (which I think the artist intended) was a depersonalized, fragmented view of a human body. In fact, from such a narrowed, isolated series of perspectives, the subject became something less than an organism, something more like a mechanism or an abstraction.

Of course, I enjoyed the unique perspective of that second exhibit, and learned through it to view the human body in new and interesting ways. But perhaps the most important lesson it taught me came from its close proximity to the first exhibit. For even though the children's portraits weren't nearly as daring or original, by contrast I saw through them in a new way the captivating and joyous beauty of the human creature considered as a dynamic whole.

The parallel of that incident to our view of the Body of Christ should be obvious. When we search for a glimpse of the Lord in ourselves alone, or in our little part of His Church, the view we gain will be narrow and fragmented. Seen in isolation, the individual members of the Body may seem static, two-dimensional, and abstract, rather than dynamic, full-bodied, and concrete.

If my congregation or denomination, for example, focuses on sound teaching, then keeping our eyes on it may give us a close-up view of the "mouth" of Christ's Body. But unless we look as well to see how Christ's "hands" are being extended in other places, or where His "feet" are headed, our perspective on the Lord's activity in the world will be impoverished. And to the extent that our vision of God is impoverished, our joy will be necessarily diminished.

Seeing the whole picture of Christ's Body also allows us to find joy in the midst of brokenness in our particular congregation. When factionalism or even schism appear, our joy in the Church is understandably undermined by the sorrow we feel. Yet maintaining a broader view, keeping us aware that God is still at work through His people in every place, can strike at least a spark of joy in us during such seasons of turmoil.

Widening our view

We might say, then, that we broaden the furrow of fellowship, making a wider channel for joy, whenever we widen our view of Christ's Body. In practical terms, that means first of all commitment to a community of faith where we can serve and be served, encourage and be encouraged (Hebrews 10:24-25). Only when we recognize our need for other members of the Body—even those we don't particularly enjoy in themselves—can we rejoice in the life that flows through them to us, making up for our lack and providing the conditions necessary for maturity (1 Corinthians 12, Ephesians 4:11-15).

Though we're often reluctant to admit it, we can't serve God adequately alone. In fact, we can't even take care of ourselves alone. That truth became real to me one night soon after my conversion when I was deeply troubled by a particularly difficult situation.

As I prayed about the problem, I came to the simple conclusion that more than anything else, I needed a hug from Jesus. So with the boldness of faith that comes so easily to new converts (and is lost so easily soon after), I prayed, "Lord, I don't know exactly how You'd do it short of a miraculous appearance, but would You please come down and give me a real, flesh-and-blood hug?"

Nothing happened immediately, and it was time to go to a Bible study. So I grabbed my Bible and left. But all evening I thought about that request and wondered what would happen.

At the end of our study time, we stood in a circle and joined hands to pray. When the last "amen" was spoken, and I was about to open my eyes, suddenly I felt a pair of strong arms around my chest, and I was pulled into a long, warm bear hug.

I was almost afraid to look, but I did. Of course it was one of the students in the group; yet I hardly knew him, and neither he nor anyone else in that room had ever hugged me before. When he let go, he said simply, "The Lord just told me to pass that along to you from Him."

You'll never convince me that that was not in fact a flesh-and-blood hug from Jesus. In that moment, the risen Christ abiding in that believer moved through him to minister to me physically, to give me a hug I couldn't give myself. The Body of Christ touched me in that man's arms just as surely as His physical body had once touched the apostles. And you can imagine the joy I felt in that moment, not only to know He cared for me, but actually to see and feel Him in the flesh.

Beyond our own fellowship

Beyond simply seeing ourselves as members of a local community of faith, we must also widen our view of Christ's Body by looking beyond our own group. That means, first of all, having some kind of regular fellowship, on a formal or informal basis, with believers of other traditions and communions. It also includes giving at least prayer support and perhaps other types of support to those groups that are accomplishing what our own group cannot. And it involves, above all, learning everything we can from those Christians whose walk with God has given them experiences that are different from ours, and thus complement ours.

The believers I know who find the most joy in fellowship are those who have the clearest and broadest view of the Lord at work in His Church. They avoid what I call "the Elijah syndrome"—the fearful, paralyzing assumption the prophet made that he was "the only one left" who was faithful to God (1 Kings 19:9-14). Joyous members of the Body see themselves, not in competition, but in cooperation, because they know Christ is not divided (1 Corinthians 1:10-13).

If we want to see the Lord in His Church and find joy in Him there, then like Paul we must be grateful for others' partnership in the gospel (Philippians 1:3-6). We must recognize with him that whenever any part of the Body is honored, every part should rejoice with it (1 Corinthians 12:26). We, too, should be thrilled to hear reports of what God is doing in ministries others have established and nurtured, and anxious to provide those other ministries any service we can (Romans 1:8-11).

When Paul's perspective on the Church becomes our own, then with him we'll be able to affirm, "The important thing is that in every way . . . Christ is preached. And because of this I rejoice" (Philippians 1:18).

Despite our blemishes and our brokenness, Lord, I delight to see Your beauty shining through Your Body, robing us in Your righteousness, adorning us with the gifts of Your Spirit. Teach me, Lord, to see You from head to foot, and not to be so preoccupied with a hand or an eye or an ear that I forget the rest of You. When I become entranced by a single note, break the trance with the thunder of Your full symphony; when I become fascinated with a detail, draw me back to view the full-length portrait. Open the eyes of my heart to see "the riches of [Your] glorious inheritance in the saints" (Ephesians 1:18), until I, too, can say of Your people, "from Zion, perfect in beauty, God shines forth" (Psalm 50:2).

The LORD will lay bare his holy arm in the sight of all the nations, and all the ends of the earth will see the salvation of our God.
ISAIAH 52:10

□

"But I, when I am lifted up from the earth, will draw all men to myself."
JOHN 12:32

□

Who can blot out the Cross? . . .
Swim, and at every stroke, thou art thy Cross;
The Mast and yard make one, where seas do toss;
Look down, thou spiest out Crosses in small things;
Look up, thou seest birds raised on crossed wings.
All the Globe's frame, and spheres, is nothing else
But the Meridians crossing Parallels.
JOHN DONNE

□

Now seeing that He is the Word of God Almighty, who in an unseen way in our midst is universally extended in all the world, and encompasses its length and breadth and height and depth . . . in [these four directions we see] crucified the Son of God, inscribed crosswise upon it all . . . summoning all that are scattered in every quarter to the knowledge of the Father.
IRENAEUS OF LYONS

□

How could He have called us if He had not been crucified, for it is only on the cross that a man dies with arms outstretched? Here, again, we see the fitness of His death and of those outstretched arms: It was that He might draw His ancient people with the one and the Gentiles with the other, and join both together in Himself.
ATHANASIUS

CHAPTER 19

WITNESS:
Seeing God on the Cross

Karl Barth, the famous Swiss theologian who lived in the first half of our century, is said to have had in his study one day a guest who asked an unusual question. The visitor said to him simply, "Who are you?"

In response, Barth quietly walked over to a wall of the room where there hung a painting of the Crucifixion. In a lower corner of the picture stood John the Baptist, looking upward at Jesus on the Cross and pointing his finger toward Him. Barth reached out and pointed his own finger toward that of John.

"Who am I?" he said. "I am that finger."

The vision of God we gain and maintain in our witness is the same vision John had in that painting, and Barth had in his career. It's *the vision of God on the Cross*—a God whose arms are extended in a bleeding and urgent invitation. In those arms we behold a divine welcome, an offer of forgiveness, and a humble entreaty. The sight of such a God compels us to confess Him as Savior, to add our testimony to those of countless saints who have gone before us, pointing to the Cross by their words and their lives.

Yet we also see in the crucified arms of God a gesture of victory. I once visited an old chapel in rural France that dated from the early medieval period, and was surprised to find that the Christ portrayed on the Cross was not dead. Instead, His head was erect, His eyes were open on a triumphant countenance, and He wore a king's garb: a golden crown and a royal purple robe. Though His hands and feet bore the marks of His crucifixion, they were stretched out, not in pain, but in power. His arms looked as if they were extended to receive the homage of His people and to gather in the treasures of a world that belonged to Him.

I've since learned that such a crucifix was once common in Western European churches, and is still found in many Eastern Orthodox churches. It's called the *Christus Victor*—Christ the Victor. This triumphant cross, I'm convinced, is also part of the vision of witness. Because Jesus is Lord of all, and Victor over sin and death, there is no place that should be without testimony to His power and grace.

In both of its aspects, our vision of the Lord on the Cross awakens in us delight in a loving and mighty God. Because His arms are extended there in pardon and victory, witness is a channel for the joy of faith. Through it flows our celebration of all that has been accomplished by the hands of God. And when we tell of what we've seen Him do, we "make our joy complete" (1 John 1:1-4).

To undertake witness as a discipline, we must make a habit of pointing to the God on the Cross through our words and our actions. By digging furrows through the three fields of witness—our own hearts, the Church, and the world—we channel joy not only into our own lives, but also into the lives of fellow Christians and of those who need so desperately to see the Lord. We might even say that because the habit of confessing Jesus as Savior and Lord keeps our vision of Him clear, it sweeps away the debris that tends to collect in all the other furrows of joy, allowing the refreshing water to move more freely there.

Our witness within our own hearts

The joy that flows through witness springs up in us first when we initially encounter the reality of the gospel—the good news that the same Jesus who was crucified for our sins has been made "both Lord and Christ" (Acts 2:36). When that truth apprehends us, then "the Spirit Himself bears witness with our spirit that we are children of God" (Romans 8:16, NASB). In this way, the Holy Spirit's testimony within us provokes a great gladness, because it banishes our slavery to fear (verse 15).

Our confession of Christ then becomes the external expression of that internal witness. Just as vocal praise completes the joy of worship, vocal confession completes the joy of witness; it is itself, in fact, a form of praise (Hebrews 13:15). Confessing aloud that Jesus is Lord and Savior confirms what has happened in our hearts, and points us toward the God on the Cross (Romans 10:9-10).

Even so, our initial testimony is only the beginning. For the furrow of witness in the field of our own heart to remain clean of debris, we must continue to bear witness to Christ. Especially in times of trouble, when fear or doubt assails us, we need to affirm to ourselves the reality of the God on the Cross, who "took up our infirmities and carried our sorrows," whose punishment brought us peace, and whose wounds have healed us (Isaiah 53:4-5).

In practical terms, this habit of witnessing within ourselves means that we turn our attention to the things God has done. Like David, we command our souls to recount God's faithfulness: "Praise the LORD, O my soul, and forget not all his benefits, who forgives all your sins and heals all your diseases, who redeems your life from the pit and crowns you with love and compassion" (Psalm 103:2-4). The discipline of witness thus restores the joy of our salvation in troubled times by renewing our vision of the crucified and conquering God.

Our witness in the Church
A second area in which we dig the furrow of witness is the field of the Church. Again, David provides our model: "I will declare your name to my brothers," he insisted. "In the congregation I will praise you" (Psalm 22:22). He prayed to be able to declare God's praises "in the gates of the Daughter of Zion, and there rejoice" in the Lord's salvation (Psalm 9:14).

This witness to other believers can take many forms. We witness, for example, when we affirm our faith together through one of the creeds. I don't mean, of course, an empty recital of a creed, but rather a triumphant declaration that invests every word read or memorized with the "yes" of our hearts as well as our mouths.

When I first came to the conclusion as a twelve-year-old that God was only a creation of the human mind, I realized that I could no longer say the Apostles' Creed with integrity in the church where my family attended. I felt a bit empty on the following Sunday when I stood silently as the others repeated the Creed. But for years after, I maintained that silence. You can imagine my great joy, then, when six years later I came again to the place of faith, and was able to proclaim in celebration with another congregation, "*I believe in God. . . .*" The joy of affirming that creed has abided with me ever since that glorious day.

We also witness in the Church when we sing together the great hymns or popular choruses that tell of what God has done (again, assuming that we mean what we sing). In this way, songs of witness complement songs of worship. In the music of worship, we speak *to* God rather than *about* Him. In the music of witness, we "speak to *one another* in psalms, hymns and spiritual songs" to awaken glad and grateful music in our hearts (Ephesians 5:19).

Still another way we witness in the Church is by our spontaneous personal testimony to the Lord's faithfulness. Some churches set aside time especially for such witness, often in evening services. But even when they don't, we hardly need a public forum to tell of God's grace. We can make it a habit to tell other Christians what God is doing in our lives whenever we talk with them, particularly in those times when we sense that their faith needs a boost. I keep a written list of answers to prayer especially for that purpose, as a reminder of all the little "testimonies" that accumulate daily through God's goodness.

In all these ways, we encourage one another to "hold unswervingly to the hope we profess, for he who promised is faithful" (Hebrews 10:23-25). The furrows of delight we've dug in our own gardens connect up with those in the gardens of other believers, so that water flowing through one flows through the others as well. Like the woman who found her lost coin and called her neighbors together to celebrate, through our witness in the Church, we issue the invitation, "Rejoice with me!" (Luke 15:8-9). When such joy in the Lord is shared, it is inevitably multiplied.

Our witness in the world
Irenaeus of Lyons, perhaps the greatest Christian theologian of the second century, once wrote beautifully of how the Cross of Christ is imprinted on all creation. He suggested that when we look at the four directions of the compass, we should see there the symbol of our faith. On that universal Cross, said Irenaeus, we should behold Christ

extended throughout the world, calling all people in every place to Himself.[1]

I think that that picture, offered by a man whose great desire was to see the gospel preached everywhere, provides the best understanding of the vision of God we gain in witness to the world. When we declare His global invitation to receive the redemption and lordship of Christ, we point toward a God whose hands stretch out in welcome from horizon to horizon. We also affirm that one day the kingdoms of this world will become "the kingdom of our Lord and of his Christ, and he will reign for ever and ever" (Revelation 11:15).

The stories of God's faithfulness reported in the newsletters of mission organizations that my wife and I support have prompted me in recent months to spend more time in prayer for other nations. In fact, as I was interceding one morning not long ago for Soviet Christians imprisoned for their faith, the Lord told me to get a world map and hang it on my office wall so I could visualize the places involved in my prayers.

Now when I pray for other countries, I stand before that map, holding up in the Lord's presence the planet it represents. As I look at the markings for the four compass directions, I think of Irenaeus and that universal Cross, extending the love of God across the globe. Then, like the Christian poet John Donne (whose words are quoted at the beginning of this chapter), at the places where the lines of latitude and longitude come together, I see the emblem of our salvation. And when I do, I hear the Lord whispering, "Here, too, lives someone who is thirsty for Me."

One of those little crosses on the map lies near my home city. It reminds me of the friends, neighbors, and business associates all around me who may never look at my God on the Cross unless I become a finger to point their gaze in that direction. Just as Bethlehem is all around me, so also Calvary is all around me, if I'll only look for it.

The cycle of witness and joy

Another of those little crosses lies near Frankfurt, West Germany, where I once served as a musical evangelist with a mission organization that targeted youth. It reminds me of the night one particular young man, who had dissipated his life in alcohol and drugs, responded to the good news we preached by coming forward to where we stood and kneeling to pray for a new life in the Lord.

I put my arm around him and joined him in prayer; and when he looked up, his face was brilliant. I could see the Lord in him already—his new countenance was a wordless testimony to the Spirit's witness inside him. In that moment, the joy of my witness to the world was as sweet as I can ever recall it being, because that young man reflected so radiantly the light of the God on the Cross who had saved him.

Interestingly enough, his first words to me sounded like an echo of my own thoughts. "When I first saw you come into this room," he said through his tears, "there was such a light on your face that I thought Jesus Himself had walked in. I just couldn't turn away from the joy I saw in you."

That night I realized that our witness and our joy create a glorious cycle: When we testify to the Lord, delight is stirred inside us. And when that same delight comes spilling out, it bears witness to God in itself. As Samuel Shoemaker once observed, "The surest mark of a Christian is not faith, or even love, but joy."

That insight was confirmed years later when I was talking to a college friend who had recently come to Jesus. I'd usually been rather free about referring to the Lord in conversation with nonChristian students, and she knew many of the people in my dorm with whom I'd spoken. So I asked her to tell me honestly what those people thought of my faith.

"Well," she admitted, "you're so relentlessly joyful that most of them have decided one of two possibilities must be true: Either you're totally crazy, or you're on to something they want to know more about."

Ours is indeed a thirsty planet. Considering how desperate that thirst is, the exciting truth about the river of joy flowing through witness is that it seems to have its own power to plow furrows. Once it's flowing, it can break out of the channels we've dug for it and carve new ones for itself.

Lamb of God, who takes away the sins of the world: Your salvation and Kingdom and power have vanquished the Accuser; Your blood has hurled him down. And we have joined in Your triumph by the word of our testimony. No wonder the heavens and all who dwell in them are rejoicing! (Revelation 12:10-12).

You have chosen us for Yourself so that we might "declare the praises of him who called [us] out of darkness into his wonderful light" (1 Peter 2:9). Shed Your beams on us from the Cross, Lord Jesus: beams of humility and lovingkindness, of power and glory. Then burn brightly through us as well. Cause Your face to shine upon us, that Your ways may be known on the earth, Your salvation among all peoples, till all the nations are glad and sing for joy (Psalm 67:1-4).

NOTES:
1. St. Iranaeus, *The Demonstration of the Apostolic Teaching,* translated by J. Armitage Robinson (New York: Macmillan Company, 1920), pages 101-102.

The LORD your God will bless you in all your harvest and in all the work of your hands, and your joy will be complete.
DEUTERONOMY 16:15

□

"My Father is always at his work to this very day, and I, too, am working. . . . I tell you the truth, the Son can do nothing by himself; he can do only what he sees his Father doing, because whatever the Father does the Son also does."
JOHN 5:17,19

□

I think the grace the brothers have comes from their work, which keeps them perhaps (when properly done) from getting too obsessed with themselves and their spirituality.
THOMAS MERTON

□

To sing is the work of a lover.
AUGUSTINE

CHAPTER 20

WORK:
Seeing God's Acts in Our Own

Work is one discipline most of us don't have the luxury of neglecting. But even though the majority of us can't choose not to work, I'm convinced we can nevertheless choose in most cases to work with some degree of joy.

Obviously, some kinds of work simply aren't joyful. Certain types of labor can be oppressive and demeaning, or tedious and numbing. But I believe that whatever we do for a livelihood, any potential it has for genuine joy will lie in our ability to see somewhere in it that we are *echoing the work of God Himself.*

Conforming our work to God's work
Of course, before we can see God's labor in ours, we must do all we can to make sure our labor practices conform to the standards of His character and behavior. We see this necessity illustrated especially throughout the book of Deuteronomy. That rather earthy volume is filled with dirt and sweat, household routines and vocational labors, along with joyous celebration.

Again and again we find here in God's instructions to

the people of Israel that the very fabric of their lives in the field and in the home was to be woven into a tapestry picturing what God had done for them. Their domestic routine, their child rearing practices, their clothing and architecture, and even the conversation on their way to the pastures and the marketplace, were all to reflect the work of God (Deuteronomy 6:4-9; 22:5,8,11-12). Their houses and fields and wells and cities were to remind them of His mighty acts (6:10-12). Their agricultural methods were to symbolize their separation to Him as a holy people (22:9-10).

God's own nature and character could also be seen in the work done according to His Law. Hospitality and the treatment of employees reflected the Lord's own kindness and care (Deuteronomy 5:14, 10:18-19, 15:12, 24:14-15). Liberality in business, displayed through canceling debts, lending freely, and leaving gleanings for the poor, was to mirror His generosity (15:1-11, 24:19-22). The rulings of the courts had to abide by God's standards of justice and mercy (17:8-13, 24:17). And business dealings had to measure up to the criterion of divine integrity (25:13-16).

If the people were careful to conform their works to the works of God in this way, Moses promised that they would find joy: "The LORD your God will bless you in all your harvest and in all the work of your hands, and your joy will be complete" (16:15). Thus Deuteronomy is also a book of celebration. The people were in fact commanded to set aside special times for the expression of their joy: They were to "rejoice before the LORD" in the Feast of Weeks and to be joyful at the Feast of Tabernacles (16:10-14).

Aside from the feasts, however, the Israelites who sought to reflect God's activity in their own would find His joyous reward in the daily routine of their labors. God would bless the mundane moments and everyday items of their lives: their travel, their crops, their livestock, their baskets, their barns—even something as humble as their kneading troughs (28:1-12).

On the other hand, if their work didn't conform to the divine work, it would be joyless, and worse—it would become a curse (28:15-68). Especially if they left God out of the picture, claiming that their prosperity had come from themselves, then they would be headed for destruction (8:17-20). Moses warned that if they didn't labor with God in joy and gladness, they would labor instead for their enemies in sorrow (28:47-48).

In the end they would be consumed—a much more terrible fate than what we mean by "burn out." To use Isaiah's frightening metaphor, "The mighty man will become tinder and his work a spark; both will burn together, with no one to quench the fire" (Isaiah 1:31).

Like the ancient Israelites, however, we can choose to work in such a way that our labor reflects God's acts and character. When we do, we too are turning our hearts in love toward Him, listening to His voice, and holding fast to Him (Deuteronomy 30:10). Then, with our hearts facing His direction, we see the works of God in our own works—and we rejoice, as they did, to see Him there.

Looking for echoes of God's acts

The first step, then, to discovering joy in our work is to make sure that we see in it a reflection of God's character. But even when our work meets God's ethical standards, we sometimes have difficulty seeing what our labors have to do with His labors. What, we may ask, does washing dishes have to do with Him?

It helps, I've found, to think of God's own work in four ways: as His *creativity*, His *productivity*, His *activity*, and His *thought*. Our particular line of work might then more easily be viewed as echoing His by placing what we do in one of those same categories.

Creative work that reflects God's own wise and beautiful creativity includes some obvious professions: writing, music, painting, and the other fine arts; architecture, broadcasting, graphic design, and the other applied arts. Yet we could also place in this category such work as gardening, computer programing, even traffic engineering. That's because whenever our work requires the creation or invention of something new—even an intangible new thing, such as an educational strategy—it shows that the divine attribute of creativity is evident in us, for we are made in God's image. When we create at all, we participate in His work of creation, and we can see Him working there through us if we're willing to look.

The same is true of any productive work, because it reflects God's own productivity. God laid the foundations of the earth to fashion humankind a home, and a building crew takes part in that labor when they lay the foundation of a particular house (Psalm 102:25). God gives all creatures their food, and farmers and ranchers participate in that work as they raise crops and livestock (Psalm 104:27). The seamstress, the factory worker, the carpenter, and the welder all labor to produce what we need, just as God has produced what we need. Thus His productivity is found in theirs.

Most of the service professions would fall into the third category, whether they're exalted or humble by human standards. The doctor and nurse take part in God's work of healing (Exodus 15:26). The righteous judge and public official participate in God's own government and administration of justice (Psalm 7:11, Isaiah 9:7). The parent, teacher, and daycare worker who care for children take part in God's own parenthood, instruction, and protection

(Deuteronomy 1:30-32, 4:5). And the janitor, plumber, electrician, and mechanic, who maintain buildings or cars, are involved in the Lord's own labor of sustaining the world (Hebrews 1:3). They reflect the One in whom "all things hold together" (Colossians 1:17).

Finally, the laborers involved in information and communication reflect the act of God's thought. When they do their work well, they can be viewed as thinking God's thoughts after Him. The Lord has counted and named the stars, and the astronomer echoes His work (Psalm 147:4). The Lord weaves the human being in the womb, and the physiologist and psychologist find out how (Psalm 139:13). God speaks through Scripture and through history, and the theologian and historian try to interpret His thoughts there (Hebrews 1:1-2).

God in a meat market

This rather extensive list of examples should serve as sufficient evidence that almost any kind of work can be seen as a participation in God's work, if we look closely enough. Even if our particular vocation is difficult to categorize, we can probably find within it duties or responsibilities that reflect the Lord's labor, and can therefore be a source of joy.

For me, the best examples of this approach to work are my own parents. Dad was one of those people who had little choice about his vocation. When he was still a young teenager, he had to help support his family, and so he trained for the available job in his neighborhood that paid the best at the time: a meatcutter's assistant. Years later, after he had a wife and five children to support, he considered it too late to change careers. Then, because he had established a family business, my mother, my siblings, and I found ourselves in the same situation. To survive financially, we all had to cut meat.

I must say that for several years my work in that family market was rather joyless. Meatcutting can be a tedious and tiring labor. But eventually I noticed that even though my parents felt the same way about this trade, they were able to find joy in certain aspects of it, and then concentrate on those aspects.

When my father made sausage, for example, he made delicious sausage, even *beautiful* sausage, according to his own criteria for what would bring pleasure to the eyes and tastebuds of his customers. His filet mignon was a model of symmetry, and every crown rib roast was by meatcutters' standards a masterpiece. He thus taught me by his behavior that meatcutting could be a joyful art in which we participate in God's creativity.

More importantly, Mom and Dad both tended to turn their primary attention, whenever possible, to the people with whom they associated. They genuinely cared whether or not the food they sold met the needs of their customers, and always inquired about their satisfaction. They saw themselves as providing an essential service. As Dad always said, "Everybody's gotta eat."

Most importantly, my parents focused on becoming encouragers, exhorters, even counselors of a sort. My father was a master of the thoughtful compliment that could brighten a day for a troubled youth. My mother listened countless times with great patience and love to the ramblings of lonely and elderly people. They helped employees with family and financial problems. And they quietly added extra meat without charge to the packages of poor people, keeping the gift a secret in order to maintain the customers' dignity.

In all these ways they found joy in their work, because they saw what they did as participating in God's own labor of nourishing the world—both physically and spiritually.

Unlike the workmanship, say, of a sculptor, the work of their hands disappeared quickly. But because they could see their labor in the context of God's activity, it nevertheless possessed a certain permanence, evidenced by the love and gratitude of hundreds of people who came weekly to the market—many of them, not to buy, but to be refreshed.

I believe that our work, too, can be a furrow of joy. If we look for God in it, labor can channel the delight from our view of God at work in the present into those forty or more hours that occupy so much of our weekly schedule. Then for us, as it was for my parents, our vocation can be much more than a livelihood; it can become a discipline of love.

"Establish the work of our hands," Lord, *by taking our labor up into Your labor (Psalm 90:17). Give us the privilege of contributing to Your workmanship, of seeing Your hands busy in ours.*

Our works in themselves are like "the new grass of the morning" that fades so soon; our days "quickly pass, and we fly away" (Psalm 90:5-6,10). But You teach us, Lord God, to weigh our days rightly in wisdom by seeing our small labors added in the scales to Your own infinite and eternal works. In that vision, we see the true significance of our work, and Your unfailing love expressed there causes us to "sing for joy and be glad all our days" (Psalm 90:14).

A merry heart hath a continual feast.
PROVERBS 15:15, KJV

□

There is a time for everything . . . a time to mourn and a time to dance.
ECCLESIASTES 3:1,4

□

Should we not see that lines of laughter about the eyes are just as much marks of faith as are the lines of care and seriousness? Is it only earnestness that is baptized?
HELMUT THIELICKE

□

We can take our own tears more lightly than we could take the tremendous levities of the angels. So we sit perhaps in a starry chamber of silence, while the laughter of the heavens is too loud for us to hear.
G. K. CHESTERTON

□

Play is a taste of the Paradise from which we came, a foretaste of the Paradise we will enter.
GEORGE SHEEHAN

CHAPTER 21

PLAY:
Seeing God's Abundance

The parable of the prodigal son, it seems to me, might just as well be known as the parable of the prodigal father. The son, of course, was prodigal in that he wasted his wealth in reckless living. But the father was more prodigal still in that he lavished *his* wealth on his penitent son in reckless love.

That parent was no doubt a generous soul, and his generosity was the source of his extravagance. Yet the generosity couldn't have found such immense expression had it not been for the immensity of *abundance* in the father's house. Despite the youth's squandering of half the inheritance, when he came home there were still robes and rings and fatted calves to spare. Thus it was the father's bounty that made possible the playful merriment of the feast that followed (Luke 15:11-32).

Jesus taught this joyous parable, I believe, to picture the depths of God's forgiveness and restoration. Yet the story provides as well a fitting portrait of the vision of play, for in play we make merry in view of *the abundance of God*. We too must "celebrate and be glad," because we who were dead are alive again; we who were lost are found (verse 32).

Though all of us have sold ourselves out to sin, the Father has purchased us back. And despite the infinite price of that redemption—the very life of God's Son—still heaven's treasure house is overflowing with "God's abundant provision of grace and of the gift of righteousness" (Romans 5:17).

The gift of Christ includes all that we'll ever need, and infinitely more. For "he who did not spare his own Son, but gave him up for us all—how will he not also, along with him, graciously give us all things?" (Romans 8:32). Whatever lack we may suffer now, we're nevertheless free to celebrate, because in the end, all things belong to us, and we belong to Christ, and Christ belongs to God (1 Corinthians 3:22-23, NASB). Thus play is a discipline of hope: It channels the joy from our vision of God's face in the future—when He will welcome us to the celebration of the Lamb—into the tired and somber areas of our lives today that need refreshing.

Like the restored son of the parable, we can afford to make merry even now because we have a prodigal Father ("prodigal" not in a wasteful, reckless sense, but in the sense of His lavish generosity). In our play, we affirm that the God we serve has time to spare for something other than work. He Himself took the seventh day off (Genesis 2:2-3). If the servant is not above his or her Master (Matthew 10:24), then we're to imitate the Lord's example in what novelist George MacDonald has called a "sacred idleness."[1]

To be "sacredly idle," I think, is to disengage ourselves from our labor for a season in order to "waste" time and energy in "nonproductive" ways that refresh us and restore a healthy perspective on life. Through play, we proclaim that our calling is to be good stewards, not good misers; to live life with an open rather than a closed hand; to be liberal with our hours rather than to hoard them. We can afford to play because we don't have to worry that in the end our labor won't have been enough.

The feasts of Israel

The ancient Israelites knew well how to make merry, for God had commanded merriment. Each year when they'd finished the labor of harvest, and again when they'd completed the labor of threshing and pressing, the people of Israel were to set aside freewill offerings to God. These gifts were symbols of the abundance God had given, a declaration that they had plenty to spare.

Along with the offerings there came each time a feast—the first of Weeks, the second of Tabernacles—when the people were to play together in view of God's abundance. Surrounded by stacks of food that betokened the Lord's generosity to them, they ceased their labors and "wasted" time just having fun together. Such recreation, the Scripture tells us, made their joy "complete" (Deuteronomy 16:9-15). In those feasts, I believe, we find a good example of the joy that comes from "sacred idleness."

It was the same assurance of God's abundant power that set Miriam and her Hebrew sisters free to dance and make merry beside the Red Sea, even though they were facing a long desert trek (Exodus 15:20-21). Despite the apparent scarcity of physical provision, their celebration pointed prophetically to the abundant water, manna, and quail that God was to serve generously on their wilderness table. That supply would always be sufficient, even for the weekly day of rest when they took time off from gathering it (Exodus 15:22-17:7).

On the other hand, it was Israel's ultimate failure to keep the abundance of God in view that finally robbed them of the celebration He'd planned for them. Despite God's repeated faithfulness, they stopped looking to the skies where His abundance had rained down, and looked, rather, at the rocks and dust. When they discovered giants in the Promised Land, they forgot God's abundant power displayed in their deliverance from Egypt. Instead they looked at their own size, feared that they had insufficient strength, and refused to cross the Jordan. In this way, "They were not able to enter, because of their unbelief" in God's abundance (Hebrews 3:19).

The elder brother

Sadly enough, many Christians fail to recognize that play is a discipline we must cultivate. Our focus tends to be on the work to do, the needs to meet, the goals to achieve. Like the elder brother in Jesus' parable, we sometimes remain in the field when we should be at the feast (Luke 15:25).

Certainly, that brother's primary reason for avoiding the feast was his bitterness toward his younger sibling. Yet the fact remains that in all his years of serving at home, before he had any reason to resent his father's generosity, that son had never asked for a feast for himself. He had "slaved" in the fields (verse 29) without any seasons of merriment—despite the obvious abundance of his father that could have made a feast possible. For that reason, I suspect that the elder brother might have been what we now call a "workaholic."

If that's indeed the case, then many of us are too often like him. We rarely stop to make merry. Our anxious, ceaseless labor has blinded us to our abundance. If only we would realize that we're always free to celebrate (verse 31) because all the Father has is ours!

Needless to say, when we play the role of the elder brother, we shut ourselves out from the joy of God's "party." We also tend to judge those who have the vision of abundance we lack. Like the folks who called Jesus "a glutton and a drunkard" because He enjoyed merriment, we're like pouting children who want others to mourn to the tune of our dutiful dirge (Matthew 11:16-19).

The nature of genuine play

Our society, someone has said, tends to work at its play, play at its worship, and worship its work. Anyone who has observed how common is the grim seriousness of training for organized sports on all levels, the spiritual games played in many church services, and the idolatry of careers, must sadly agree. For that reason, we who have the vision of divine abundance must learn to cultivate the discipline of genuine play as a sign to an overearnest and often joyless world.

To do that, we must learn first of all to distinguish genuine play from its counterfeits. Real play—as opposed to work masquerading as play—is characterized by *self-forgetfulness*, an absorption in the activity at hand. In this attribute, we see the kinship of play to that other discipline of hope: worship.

In both play and worship we abandon ourselves for a while. Then, when we return to ourselves, we find that the "vacation" has given us a new and wise distance on the things we previously viewed as overwhelming. No wonder that time spent in prayer has been called by some theologians *recreatio mentis in Deum*: a recreation (or re-creation) of the mind in God.

Work concentrates on goals, achievements, products. But play simply rejoices in the fullness of the moment, having fun for the sake of the immediate pleasure and refreshment it brings. When we forget the distinction, our play often turns into work.

I've seen countless examples of that sad transformation. A sport that was originally taken up for pleasure may succumb to intense competition aimed at producing a winning score. A hobby may become an exacting second job. A child who wants to adapt a game for the fun of it may be told by a parent who's "playing" along that the rules can't be

changed. Or perhaps all the Christmas toys a family pur-
chases must have some "educational objective."

To avoid such work that pretends to be play, we may
need to make some changes in our forms of recreation. My
wife and I, for example, sometimes play a parlor game or
board game without keeping score so we can simply enjoy
the demonstration of wit or skill involved in the play itself
without worrying about who "wins." When we direct games
with groups (Leisa was a recreation major, so we get that
assignment regularly), we choose mostly cooperative rather
than competitive games. And when we select toys for our
daughter or her friends, we don't always insist that they
have "instructional value." By keeping our focus on the fun
rather than maintaining some hidden agenda, we try to
prevent play from becoming joyless work in disguise.

Qualities of playfulness

Once we learn to recognize true play when we see it, we
must make ourselves ready for play; that is, we must develop
an attitude of playfulness. Such an attitude, I think, is com-
posed of a number of qualities.

Most important of these is the confidence of *hope*—our
trust that in the end, God is in control, all the truly important
work will get done, and His abundance assures our provision. Admittedly, most Christian workaholics believe in
their heads that God will provide, yet their hearts seem
unable to let themselves play. I know, because I've been
there.

The roots of addiction to work are so complex that we
couldn't possibly analyze them here, and I'm not qualified
for such an analysis anyway. But I can offer one suggestion
from my own experience: It's easier to start discovering joy
in play by letting ourselves go in little situations, where
we're not risking much at first.

If we normally don't feel free to play, we may, for example, consider a two-week vacation or even a weekend away simply out of the question. Yet we might be able to risk half an hour this evening to toss a ball with the kids or play a game of solitaire, because we know that, if necessary, we could make up the work time by stealing it from our sleep. That's how I began recovering daily playtime with my daughter when the grueling schedule of a doctoral program and a full-time job demanded all my waking hours.

Sometimes for me it's been a matter of even smaller portions of time. I've taken Lydia on errands, for example, and in the moments when I usually plan my schedule as I drive, we sing silly songs instead. Or we stretch out a daily routine with a little fun. Instead of just walking with her upstairs for bedtime prayers, we've begun "wasting" an extra minute each evening by making it a "camel-back ride," complete with hobbles and cudchewing.

Interestingly enough, as I've risked the time I've found that somehow the work still gets done—or else that what goes undone isn't as important as I'd thought. Each time that proves to be the case, my hope in God's provision grows a little stronger, and I let go a little more. Last weekend I spent a whole day with my daughter at the zoo even though I needed desperately to finish this chapter; next fall we're planning a four-day weekend in Florida in the *middle* of a semester. I'm convinced this reforming workaholic is growing bolder all the time because my confidence in God's abundance is increasing.

A second quality of playfulness is *humility*. Only when we set aside our pride can we laugh at ourselves and our shortcomings, see the world from a child's playful perspective, and quit worrying about "what people will think" if we act a little silly or get a little dirty. I couldn't play camel every night if I were worried about my "image" at home.

Nor can I let concern for my public "image" keep me from play. Neighbors have seen me frolicking in a clown costume for my daughter's birthday party, and dancing in a circle with her friends. They've watched me join her on the playground swings and chase her around the apartment complex in a water pistol battle. If I were to listen to the voice of pride in such situations, we'd miss out on loads of fun.

A third necessary quality is *imagination*. That's what transports us beyond the routine of what life *is* to the excitement of what it *could be*. Imagination is essential for a child's game of pretending, and for our play as well.

Fourth is *alertness*. When we remain open to play, even in the midst of our work, we soon become aware of countless playful moments that spring up with potential for fun. In our family, for example, a slip of the tongue is often turned into a play on words or a nonsense rhyme. If we get caught in the rain without an umbrella, we count the puddles by jumping in them.

Spontaneity, a fifth quality, spurs us to seize those moments before they pass, whatever our previous plans might have been. It also spawns surprise, an important element in play.

Someone has said that play makes breathing room for the spirit. *Flexibility*, a sixth quality, makes elbow room for play. Being flexible allows us, for example, to put down the newspaper for a wrestling match on the carpet with our kids.

Finally, *liberality* is the quality that encourages us to lavish our "precious" time on others in play. Because of God's abundance, we have freely received, and we can freely give (Matthew 10:8). In God's economy, our investment of time in play somehow allows us to "give freely, yet gain even more," so that all the truly important work still gets done. And when we've refreshed others by joining them in play, we find that we ourselves have been refreshed (Proverbs 11:24-25).

Play as a sign of heaven

When all is said and done, we must realize not only that we can afford to play, but that we can't afford *not* to play. God's abundance is more than sufficient for us. If we remain blind to that abundance, then, like the elder brother, we'll be trading our joy for a grim and dutiful scowl.

Certainly, we may find that play has a price: It may require giving up some goals we discover to be less important than we'd thought. At the same time, we can't be always at play, nor would we want to be. As we've seen, work itself can be a furrow of joy as well.

Even so, we mustn't neglect the discipline of merriment, if only because it gives us a glimpse of the world to come. The old spiritual from slave days asks poignantly, "How can I play, when I'm in a strange land?" Our answer must be that in the very act of playing, we affirm that this "strange land" is in fact not our home.

Playful activities, as C. S. Lewis has said, are in a sense "frivolous, unimportant down here; for 'down here' is not their natural place. Here, they are a moment's rest from the life we were placed here to live. But in this world, everything is upside down. That which, if it could be prolonged here, would be a truancy, is likest that which in a better country is the End of Ends. Joy is the serious business of heaven."[2]

"Serious business" it is indeed—and even now, in the joy of playful moments, we must be about our Father's business.

Open my eyes, Lord God, to the One "who is able to do immeasurably more than all we ask or imagine" (Ephesians 3:20). If Your love is the lavish Feast set before us, then I delight to be called, as Jesus was called, "a glutton and a drunkard"—for I want to be filled with You, intoxicated with You, merry with the music of Your gladness. In those moments when You summon me to Your banquet, Lord, give me grace to let business go (Luke 14:15-24), and to accept the invitation with a joy in the abundance of my prodigal Father.

NOTES:
1. Quoted in C. S. Lewis, *George MacDonald: An Anthology* (New York: Macmillan, 1947), page 109.
2. C. S. Lewis, *The Joyful Christian: 127 Readings* (New York: Macmillan, 1977), page 228.

There is . . . a season for every activity under heaven . . . a time to weep, and a time to laugh.
ECCLESIASTES 3:1, 4

☐

This is what the LORD says: "Heaven is my throne, and the earth is my footstool."
ISAIAH 66:1

☐

The One enthroned in heaven laughs; the Lord scoffs at them.
PSALM 2:4

☐

Man is the only animal that laughs and weeps; for he is the only animal that is struck with the difference between what things are and what they ought to be.
WILLIAM HAZLITT

☐

The well known humor of the Christian is not a way of denying the tears, but rather a way of affirming something which is deeper than tears.
ELTON TRUEBLOOD

CHAPTER 22

HUMOR:
Seeing God's Footstool

Some years ago I had the privilege of singing at the funeral for the grandmother of one of my closest friends. She was a godly woman, and had lived like Job to be "full of days" (Job 42:17, NASB). But even though her death lacked the bitterness of an unexpected or untimely loss, sadness hung like a heavy veil over the little wood-frame church building where we gathered to say goodbye.

Fighting the tears, I struggled to finish my song, and then sat down to hear the pastor's sermon. He began mournfully, reflecting the emotional landscape inside all of us. But suddenly his words took what seemed to me an odd turn, in the direction of humor. He recalled a few comical anecdotes, and then he joked that we could be glad our friend wasn't like the atheist whose tombstone read, "All dressed up, and no place to go."

It took us a while to move with him from grief to amusement, but soon we were smiling and even chuckling. The humor of the message finally reached its climax when he told of how a funeral should remind us that we who were still on earth should view ourselves and others with humility, for "dust thou art, and to dust returneth." "Can you imagine!" he finally shouted, with a comical facial expression of mock disdain. "Here we are: One speck of dust, looking down its nose at another speck of dust, and saying, 'I'm better than you!'"

The congregation roared with laughter, and for a moment you'd have thought we were anywhere but at a funeral. Yet in that moment, the veil of sadness was torn, and the light of eternal life shone brightly into that little church. Is it any wonder that the service ended with a joyous victory celebration unlike any other I'd ever seen?

Though his strategy seemed at first inappropriate, what that wise pastor did in his sermon was to present us with a new viewpoint that lifted us out of our sorrow. Through his joking, he had in fact granted us in a nutshell the profound vision of humor—which is, I believe, *the vision of earth as God's footstool* (Isaiah 66:1). In the clarity of perspective provided by his jest, we could laugh at the silliness of taking ourselves and our present surroundings too seriously; of thinking this world is the crown for which we reach, instead of a place to stand higher so that we can reach further still.

With such a perspective, we could go on from laughter to celebration, knowing that our friend had left God's footstool to ascend to His throne. We could stand with the apostle Paul at the hollow tomb, and scoff at death's pretensions: "Where, O death, is your victory? Where O death, is your sting?" (1 Corinthians 15:55).

Only later did I discover that the pastor's sermon actually stood in a noble and ancient Christian tradition called the *risus paschalis*, the "Easter laughter." Even among the most dry and somber of preachers in centuries past, the custom at one time was to begin every Easter sermon with a joke, a token of the Christian's scorn for the devil's pre-

tended victory in death.[1] In the words of the Irish poet
Patrick Kavanaugh, the resurrection of Jesus was truly "a
laugh freed forever and ever."[2] That laughter has ever since
echoed through the lives of the saints, as it did when Thomas More joked with his executioner on the way to his
martyrdom—and to his crown.

In that unusual funeral service, then, I learned what
the Church has long known: Humor is a discipline of hope.
It channels the joy of our vision of God's reign in the future
into the sad or tedious ruts of today. In a sense, humor
clears the ground for worship, that other discipline of hope;
for the vision of God's footstool is just a step below the
vision of God on the throne. By setting this world in its
rightful and therefore humbled place, humor pushes us to
look beyond immediate appearances to see the ultimate
reality of God.

For that reason, theologian Reinhold Neibuhr could
insist that "humor is, in fact, a prelude to faith; and laughter
is the beginning of prayer." To use his beautiful imagery,
laughter is found in the outer courts of the temple, and its
echoes should resound in the sanctuary. Then, in the Holy
of Holies, "laughter is swallowed up in prayer, and humor is
fulfilled by faith."[3]

The nature of humor

What exactly is it about humor that can clarify our vision so
effectively, and thus lead us to joy? For centuries people
have attempted to define the nature of the comic, from the
ancient Greek philosopher Aristotle to contemporary international conferences on the topic. Though many claim that
to analyze humor is to kill it, a brief look at the wellsprings
of laughter reveals an intimate connection between humor
and our vision of God.

No one seems to have provided a comprehensive definition, but many agree that the central feature of most humor is the element of *incongruity*, the seemingly inappropriate joining of things that are inconsistent or irreconcilable. The claim of the German philosopher Arthur Schopenhauer, confirmed by such Christian theologians as Soren Kierkegaard and C. S. Lewis, is that "laughter is the sudden perception of incongruity" between our ideals and the actualities that are before us.[4]

A glance at most jokes or humorous situations provides ample evidence for this analysis. The preacher's "dust" remarks, for example, were comical because in them we recognize the inappropriateness of creatures acting proudly as if they were gods. The joke about the atheist's tombstone elicits laughter (even, I trust, from atheists) because of the incongruity of dressing up a body that is destined for nothing more than disintegration.

The humor inherent in certain biblical stories reveals itself through this analysis as well. In the eighteenth chapter of Genesis, for example, we find Abraham engaging in the traditional Oriental style of haggling, so typical even now of the Middle Eastern marketplace. What makes the scene comical (despite the great issues at stake) is that he, a mere mortal, dares to bargain that way with Almighty God. When I read how old Abe slowly ups the ante, I find myself laughing—not only *at* him, but *with* him, because I catch myself at times doing the same.

The inappropriateness of bargaining with God is what makes us laugh at this situation. The vision of that incongruity then reminds us of who we are. Such an enlightening vision of the world and of ourselves appears in other biblical stories as well, such as that comical episode in which Balaam receives a divine rebuke from his pack animal (Numbers 22:21-35). In our minds, we've established sharply defined categories that separate heaven from earth, or the human from the beast. So when Balaam's donkey speaks, or Balaam himself acts asinine, the inappropriateness makes us laugh—and we see ourselves more clearly.

The subtle humor of our Lord Jesus provides the classic example, I think, of how laughter can uncover pretense or sham, thus cleansing our vision of the world, God's footstool. Most of His barbs were directed at the Pharisees or other religious leaders who had deceived themselves into thinking that they had earned a ticket to the throne of heaven. If any of them were ever able, by God's grace, to let Christ's humor have its intended effect, then I believe they discovered through His words how inverted their perceptions were.

Jesus' joking comments about the hypocrites of His day focus on the incongruity of their self-righteousness and their pride. The humor, I think, appears most sharply when we try to imagine such people taking part in the acts the Lord described. The image of a blind man leading another blind man into a ditch (Luke 6:39) reminds me of bumbling episodes from slapstick television comedians. The hypocrites blowing trumpets to announce the jingling of their pennies evokes a similar picture (Matthew 6:2-4).

I smile at the thought of dill leaves in the offering plate (Matthew 23:23), lamps under the bed (Mark 4:21), and prim diners eating from spotless dishes filled with rotting garbage (Matthew 23:25-26). I must say that I even laugh aloud at the absurdity of a camel squeezing through the eye of a needle (Matthew 19:23-24), an eye doctor with a log sticking out of his own eye (7:3-4), and a gnat-free Pharisee with a camel's hoof stuck between his teeth (23:24).

I laugh, but the laughter is redemptive only when I place myself alongside the Pharisees and see my own pretensions made the butt of the Lord's jokes. To be a corrective for vision and thus a discipline of hope, humor must go beyond scorn of another's shortcomings to a recognition of our common predicament. When it does, it prods us to reexamine ourselves, convicts us of our need for continuing salvation, and allows us to seek God's rescue from ourselves.

The gospel as humor

Those comical remarks of the Lord, though certainly significant in themselves, point beyond themselves to a more profound reality. In a sense, the entire gospel is permeated with the liberating vision of humor.

The human dilemma is, after all, a paradox, an incongruity resulting from the Fall. We are mortals who flourish and fade like the grass (Psalm 103:15), and yet we have a sense of eternity placed in our hearts that makes us hope for immortality (Ecclesiastes 3:11). We have the universal moral law written inside us (Romans 2:14-15), but we all sin and fall short of even our own moral standards, not to say the glory of God (Romans 3:23). We crawl on earth and hope for heaven. So how do we reconcile these terrible opposites of our existence?

The resolution of the paradox comes in the good news that God is God, and we are beloved dust. If we're willing to listen, then far above the mud in which we're swallowed, from beyond the skies for which we reach, we'll hear a cosmic tumult. And though it comes to shake the earth like thunder, it won't be thunder. It will be the sound of laughter.

From His throne, the Lord of the galaxies looks down at His footstool to behold the specks of dust there claiming lordship of their lives, and sometimes of the earth itself. Not surprisingly, the absurdity of our pretense breaks the divine Countenance into mirth, and "the One enthroned in heaven laughs" (Psalm 2:4). If we're willing to lay aside our pretenses, that heavenly laughter can cleanse and awaken us to repentance. It will quake our faulty foundations, tumble us from lofty (and dangerous) places, and rip away our masks.

In His great faithfulness, the Lord follows His chastening with a promise of redemption. In the depths of our repentance, when we have at last realized that we cannot save ourselves, we hear again the sound of laughter. No thunder sounds this time, but rather the still, small Voice of God comes gently laughing. And to our amazement, it's the crystal laughter of a Child.

A Child! Could it possibly be that God Himself should crawl upon His footstool and cry to be held? Priests, we had expected; prophets, we had anticipated; but who would have thought that God would appear in flesh? The deepest and broadest "joke" of history—the great Incongruity of all the ages—grips us in awesome wonder; and we can only laugh with delight at the utter unpredictability of the divine wisdom.

Yet the surprise of the Incarnation has much more humor in store: for it blossoms into a gospel of scandalous inappropriateness. The joke has just begun! The King of kings is born in a stable; the Holy One of Israel is befriended by prostitutes; the Lord of lords is acclaimed on a donkey. He shocks the proper people of His day with His consistently inappropriate behavior and His persistently impious teaching.

The mighty and the proud may have laughed at the scandal of the gospel. But the joke was on them. For the Son of God has come to crash the world's masquerade ball, and His prank won't be complete until He's stolen away every last one of their disguises.

The mischief of Jesus inverted the world's values and priorities, because it had to clarify again that God is God and we are beloved dust—beloved enough to be worth the life of His Son. In the eyes of many, the overturned tables in the Temple were simply chaos. But in the act, Jesus truly restored divine order to the house of God.

A vision desperately needed

Those of us who stand laughing at the empty tomb have a vision desperately needed in our day. In G. K. Chesterton's words, human beings laugh because they've "caught sight of some secret in the very shape of the universe, hidden from the universe itself."[5] Only in the gospel, however, is that glorious secret fully unveiled.

A secularized world that has abandoned the hope of everlasting life denies the secret. Instead, it declares this fleeting life to be the final reality, this footstool to be the throne. Yet earth, when it attempts to take the place of heaven, ends up only imitating hell.

Perhaps the clearest example of the truth is the modern worship, in varying modes, of rationalism. Ever since the Enlightenment, reason has tried to usurp the rightful reign of faith. But in its grasping for the scepter of the King, reason has seized instead the rod of the tyrant. When it refuses to serve the Lord of Light, it submits in bondage to the Prince of Darkness. No wonder, then, that our hearts have been darkened; for claiming to be wise, we've become fools, exchanging "the glory of the immortal God for images" of our mortal selves (Romans 1:21-23).

Precisely for that reason, I have a special fondness for engaging occasionally in the humor of nonsense. Our society's groveling before reason is such a repressive burden that I must periodically rebel against the tyranny, breaking for a moment the bonds of ruthless logic. Though reason masquerades as an emperor, in truth it's only a servant in dazzling raiment; and the silly little puppy of nonsense delights in nipping holes in its logical pants.

Through the discipline of godly humor, then, we declare that "the foolishness of God is wiser than man's wisdom" (1 Corinthians 1:25). When we laugh at the foibles of ourselves and others, with a healing mixture of judgment and mercy, critique and forbearance, we pierce through the sham to reveal the reality, maintaining a vision of the earth as God's footstool.

The laughter that results is more than simply pleasure. It's the sign of a joy that comes from seeing God more clearly because we see ourselves and our planet more clearly. We rejoice to know that this flawed world is not the final world; and we delight in borrowing God's footstool for use as a step stool to peek over the veil and into the throne room of heaven.

You who are our laughing Lord, forgive us our blind silliness, and grant us instead the silliness of true sight—a vision of Your majesty, and of our creatureliness. Thank You for the gift of hope to console us for what we are not yet, but will be; and the gift of humor to console us for what we still are, but will not always be.

Remind us, Lord, that even though this world is now Your footstool, that reality isn't final. For the skies will "disappear with a roar . . . the earth and everything in it will be laid bare . . . and the elements will melt in the heat." Then we'll dwell in a new heaven and a new earth that isn't a footstool, but rather a "home of righteousness" (2 Peter 3:10-13).

On that day, Mighty God, You'll have a new and everlasting footstool, the fitting place to rest Your heel: on the head of the Serpent (Genesis 3:14-15). For Your enemies will be made Your footstool, Your feet will crush sin and death forever (Psalm 110:1, 1 Corinthians 15:25-27).

Even now, Lord God, the sight of Your unshakable purpose, the fulfillment of Your promise, gives birth in me to joy, as it did in Sarah. This delight in Your triumph, Lord, is my Isaac; and I, too, can say, "God has brought me laughter, and everyone who hears about this will laugh with me" (Genesis 21:6).

NOTES:
1. Juergen Moltmann, *Theology of Play*, translated by Reinhard Ulrich (New York: Harper & Row, 1972), pages 29-30.
2. Patrick Kavanaugh, "Lough Derg," in *Collected Poems* (London, 1972).
3. Reinhold Neibuhr, "Humor and Faith," in *Holy Laughter*, M. Conrad Hyers, ed. (New York: Seabury Press, 1969), pages 134-135.
4. Quoted in Elton Trueblood, *The Humour of Christ* (New York: Harper & Row, 1975), pages 39-40, 50; C.S. Lewis, *The Screwtape Letters* (New York: Collier Books, 1982), page 50.
5. G. K. Chesterton, *The Everlasting Man* (New York: Image Books, 1955), page 35.

PART 4

THE
FREEZING OF
JOY

My tears have been my food day and night, while men say to me all
day long, "Where is your God?"
PSALM 42:3

□

"You will seek Me and find Me when you search for Me
with all your heart."
JEREMIAH 19:13-14, *NASB*

□

When you have a feast of high joys, feed on it and be thankful! But
when they are taken from you, gape not after them as the disciples did
after Christ at His ascension; but return thankfully to your
ordinary diet of peace.
RICHARD BAXTER

□

God often visits us, but most of the time we are not at home.
JOSEPH ROUX

CHAPTER 23

"WHERE IS YOUR GOD?"

The symphony of the Scripture begins and ends on joyous notes, and a theme of triumphant delight in the goodness of God dominates all its movements. Yet throughout the music an insistent counterpoint can be heard, a melody of mourning that's sometimes subdued, sometimes almost loud enough to drown out all the rest.

The biblical witness to God would of course be unfaithful to human experience without that sorrowing counterpoint. Creation was indeed born in joy, and it shall doubtless find its consummation in joy. But much of what lies between resounds more terribly with noise or silence than with song. Some of us have yet even to tune our instruments to the right key.

For that reason, throughout our discussion thus far I've felt a bit dishonest, as if I were telling the truth, but not the whole truth. The problem, of course, lies in the topic itself: To focus on joy exclusively is like reviewing only those portions of a concert that are played in a major key, while leaving out those that are minor. If taken alone, such a review is worse than incomplete; it's altogether misleading.

Certainly, we've insisted all along that the ground of our hearts is thirsty. And a book of this sort would obviously be unnecessary if Christian commitment led inevitably to perpetual and perfect joy in this life. But now that we've looked at the Fount of joy, and at its floodgates and furrows, we must emphasize a hard truth: Even when we seek a vision of the Lord, we will not—we *can* not—have perfect joy continuously on earth.

Our origin is in joy, and our destiny is in joy; but the road between the two is long and hard. As the Puritan writer Richard Baxter noted when he spoke of "feasting" on "high joys": "No wise man can expect . . . God should diet us with a continual feast. It would suit neither with our health, nor the condition of this pilgrimage."[1]

Even so, I must hasten to qualify Baxter's remark. It's true that in the physical realm, too much of a good thing at the table can ruin our health, because our systems simply weren't made to handle the overload. Yet with regard to having perfect joy in this life, I think the parallel to be drawn here is not with feasting adults who overindulge, but rather with young children whose stomachs aren't ready to cope on a steady basis with those dishes so welcome and nourishing to the mature digestive system.

Our spiritual systems, in fact, *have* been created to handle the rich food of continually perfect delight in God. We were made for nothing less than the glory of rejoicing eternally in His presence. But we've only recently been born into the household of the King; and we can't fully digest such glory until we've grown tall enough to reach the table God has promised to spread on that great Day when He prepares "a feast of rich food for all peoples" (Isaiah 25:6).

Perhaps that's why Baxter added that a diet of continual "high joys" is not fitting for "the condition of this pilgrimage." The day will come when the pilgrimage is over, and the stomach full grown; and then, God willing, we shall feast forever on the fruit and wine of His presence, as fully as we desire. But in the meanwhile, we must be content with something less than continually perfect delight in God, and we must give thanks for those smaller portions of joy we're able to have even now. Our joy may at times indeed be "full" (John 15:11), because it will fill us up to the greatest measure of which we are presently capable. But in heaven, we'll be able to hold infinitely more delight in the Lord than we can now imagine.

Our discussion of joy has made no claim, then, to present the entire menu of our present "diet." Instead, we've sought to identify the kinds of food that best strengthen and mature us so that we can enjoy more and more of the banquet God has so graciously spread. Our goal has been to recommend those particular sources of nourishment as the best way to grow and to whet our appetite for the delights of their taste.

But the time has now come to warn of junk foods, of spoiled foods, and even of poisons. Like small children exploring the kitchen cabinets, we tend to experiment by tasting a number of things that are at best void of nutrition, at worst deadly. When we could be stretching for the table, we're often content to play in the garbage can instead.

The chapters that follow are a stack of warning labels for the spiritual kitchen. The collection is admittedly not complete, so you can add your own according to your further insights from Scripture and experience. Some of the items labeled are like candy: They won't make us sick in small amounts, but in any amount they can spoil our appetite for dinner. Others are like eggs that have been off ice too long: They can make us ill, but once our stomach is emptied of them, we're well again, and wiser. Still others, however—I have in mind especially pride and anger—are so toxic that even a few drops, if allowed to stay in our bloodstreams long enough, can be fatal.

The antidotes for each have been prescribed by many spiritual physicians better trained than I in healing. So we don't do much more here than provide the warning labels, suggesting the particular ways in which they sap our strength, and therefore our joy.

Losing our vision of God

Some of the most thorough and effective spiritual prescriptions I've ever read were written by teachers who lived in the Christian communities of the Near East in the Church's early centuries. From the ancient libraries of Egypt, Palestine, and Syria, among others, we've inherited a collection of books of great wisdom, books that examine in careful detail the "physiology" of sin and sanctification. "For Christ," wrote one of them, "is the Doctor of souls, and he knows everything and applies the right remedy for every sickness."[2]

When those early spiritual physicians wrote about the toxic effects of our disobedience to God, they spoke less of spiritual nausea than of spiritual *blindness*. The recurring theme in many of their works is that certain wrong attitudes and behaviors inevitably lead to a loss of vision. They weaken or injure the eyes of our hearts so that we no longer see God, other people, and ourselves as we should. The result is a loss of love toward God, self, and others as well.

In light of our earlier discussion of the "order of joy," we can understand why a loss of vision would lead to a loss of love; and we can predict as well that a loss of joy would not be far behind. If to see God is to know Him, to know Him is to love Him, and to love Him is to enjoy Him, then anything that obscures our vision of God will inevitably diminish our joy. Whatever blocks out the warm sunlight of God's face, casting our "gardens" into shadow, will chill our hearts until the springs there freeze, and the water ceases to flow.

In each of the chapters about joy's "furrows," we focused on the specific way in which a discipline gives us an angle of vision on God that awakens our delight in Him. In the following chapters on how joy "freezes," we'll focus on the specific way in which a problem *prevents* us from viewing God from a particular angle. I'm convinced that God is always with us, and that most often He can be seen at least in a glimpse—if we only know where to turn our attention to look for Him. So in each chapter we'll also suggest where we might profitably seek God in each type of situation that makes it hard to find Him.

It's important to note here that the problems we'll discuss are not necessarily the result of sin. Fear, doubt, or suffering, for example, may come upon us without warning and without our invitation. They've been included in this section with such obvious forms of sin as pride and ambition, not because of a common cause, but rather because of a common result: the loss of joy.

When our spirits are frozen, or when the only waters flowing in them are the salty tears of sadness, we must learn with the psalmist to ask our hearts, "Where is your God?" (Psalm 42:3). Then our hearts, like David's, must answer, "Seek his face!" (Psalm 27:8). I pray that the thoughts of the next few chapters can point the way for that search.

Like the Wise Men, Jesus, we must "search diligently" for You (Matthew 2:1-10). When the cold darkness of this world's desert night has frozen our joy, and the road to where You are seems long and thirsty, we need to glimpse the brilliant star of Your promise: "You will seek Me and find Me when you search for Me with all your heart" (Jeremiah 29:13, NASB).

Let the light of that promise beckon us on to You, Lord, until we find You in the lowly stable of our everyday lives, smiling out at us from the dry, dusty hay of mundane or difficult moments. The warm light of Your face there will melt the frozen springs within us; and with those ancient seekers in Bethlehem, we too will rejoice with great joy (Matthew 2:10).

NOTES:
1. *The Golden Treasury of Puritan Quotations*, page 160.
2. Dorotheos, *Discourses and Sayings*, page 173.

Your iniquities have separated you from your God; your sins have hidden his face from you.
ISAIAH 59:2

□

When I kept silent, my bones wasted away through my groaning all day long. For day and night your hand was heavy upon me; my strength was sapped as in the heat of summer. Then I acknowledged my sin to you and did not cover up my iniquity . . . and you forgave the guilt of my sin. . . . Rejoice in the LORD and be glad, you righteous; sing, all you who are upright in heart!
PSALM 32:3-5,11

□

Lord, my God, You are not a stranger to him who does not estrange himself from You. How do they say that it is You who absent Yourself?
JOHN OF THE CROSS

□

The glory of a good man is the witness of God that he hath a good conscience; have therefore a good conscience and thou shalt always have gladness.
THE IMITATION OF CHRIST

CHAPTER 24

GUILT:
God Behind Us

King David is honored throughout both the Old and the New Testaments as one who served God wholeheartedly. Samuel called him "a man after God's own heart," a description that was repeated centuries later by the martyr Stephen (1 Samuel 13:14, Acts 13:22). Even the Lord Himself said David had walked before Him in "integrity of heart and uprightness," and had followed Him "with all his heart" (1 Kings 9:4, 14:8).

We shouldn't be surprised, then, to find that this man, who so constantly kept his will turned in love toward God, was also the most joyous of biblical characters. Even if we'd never read the many exuberant psalms that bear his name, we could imagine the depths of his delight in God from his behavior on such occasions as the return of the Ark to Jerusalem (2 Samuel 6). David's joy in God so flooded his soul that at times it overflowed into his body as well. It was a joy so intense and powerful that even those closest to him failed to understand it (verse 16).

Yet the chronicler of the books of Kings reminds us of one episode in David's life that marred both his reputation and his heart. "For David," he said, "had done what was right in the eyes of the LORD and had not failed to keep any of the LORD's commands all the days of his life—except in the case of Uriah the Hittite" (1 Kings 15:5).

The story needs no retelling: David lusted after a married woman, Bathsheba, committed adultery with her, and then ordered her husband murdered to cover up the deed (2 Samuel 11). Worse yet, David failed to repent of his wrongdoing until the prophet Nathan confronted him with his guilt (12:1-14).

This sin was surely not the only one of David's life, but it was perhaps the most personally devastating to him and his family. He not only lost the child who was born to Bathsheba; he also heard the rebuke of God that, in consequence of his sin, the sword would never depart from his house (12:10). So rape, murder, and treason eventually tore apart both his home and his nation (2 Samuel 13-19).

What went on in David's soul during that terrible time? We have some insights into his anguish in Psalm 51, which he wrote after Nathan's rebuke. Of particular importance to us there is his cry: "My sin is always before me" (verse 3).

I think that's an accurate description of our field of vision when we're standing in unconfessed sin. If in loving God we turn our head toward Him, then in disobeying God we turn our heart—and the eyes of our heart—away from Him. To rebel is to turn our backs on God, with the result that our sins, rather than His face, are "always before us." When we're guilty before God, then, He's out of our sight because He's *behind* us.

That's not to say, of course, that when we're guilty we don't feel God's presence. In fact, it's precisely His presence that makes us so uncomfortable at such times. We sense ourselves being judged simply by the burning reality of His holiness. So the presence of God doesn't bring us joy if we've estranged ourselves from Him. As the poet George Herbert observed so strikingly, Judas found his door into hell at the lips of Jesus.[1]

David himself describes this reality well in another psalm: "Day and night your hand was heavy upon me" (Psalm 32:4). That heavy hand of God on our shoulders is the fearful burden of guilt, letting us know that He's there, even though our sin is keeping us from seeing Him. Under that burden, our joy, like our strength, is "sapped as in the heat of summer" (32:4). For with God's face behind us where we can't see it, our delight in Him dries up.

David's prayer for joy to return is one of the most touching in Scripture: "Let me hear joy and gladness; let the bones you have crushed rejoice . . . . Do not cast me from your presence or take your Holy Spirit from me. Restore to me the joy of your salvation and grant me a willing spirit, to sustain me" (Psalm 51:8,11-12).

For David's joy to return, of course, David had to see God's face again; and that meant he had to repent. One of the Hebrew words for repentance means literally to "turn around," and in that root meaning we find again the connection between vision and joy. For David to repent, he had to turn around again to face God, to confess his sin, and to follow Him once more with all his heart. With God in his field of vision again, the king would find the joy of his salvation restored.

We must learn a lesson from David's experience. God won't "cast us from His presence" or "take His Holy Spirit from us" to punish us. But His presence won't be a joyous one if we feel the weight of His hand without seeing the smile of His face.

The Lord is no stranger to us unless we make ourselves strangers to Him. God is standing still; and if He's behind us, we know who it was that turned away.

"O LORD, do not rebuke me in your anger or discipline me in your wrath. For your arrows have pierced me, and your hand has come down upon me. . . . My guilt has overwhelmed me like a burden too heavy to bear. . . . My back is filled with searing pain" because I feel the heat of Your gaze from behind me, Father *(Psalm 38:1-2,4,7). Grant me grace to turn around again. Lord, when all I can see are my sins. "Save me from bloodguilt, O God, the God who saves me, and my tongue will sing of your righteousness. O Lord, open my lips, and my mouth will declare your praise"* *(Psalm 51:14-15).*

NOTES:
1. Herbert, "The Sacrifice," in *Herbert*, page 45.

Why, O LORD, do you stand far off . . . in times of trouble?
PSALM 10:1

□

Deliver me from my enemies, O God. . . . O my Strength, I watch for You. . . . O my Strength, I sing praise to you; you, O God, are my fortress, my loving God.
PSALM 59:1,9,17

□

Courage is fear that has run to God in prayer.
ANONYMOUS

□

Keep your face to the sunshine and you cannot see the shadows.
HELEN KELLER

CHAPTER 25

FEAR:
God in the Distance

A small boat in a storm at sea in the darkest hours of the night: I can think of few other circumstances that could generate in me such nauseating, joy-killing fear. Yet that was the predicament the disciples faced the evening after Jesus multiplied the loaves and fishes (Matthew 14:22-33).

In my mind I can see the engulfing darkness— blackness above, blackness below, blackness all around. Only a few shapes are discernible, all of them terrifying: the helpless sails, the towering waves, the horrified faces of my friends. But worst of all, Jesus is somewhere in the distance on the shore, miles and hours away.

In that moment, I can imagine hearing the disciples screaming the cry of the psalmist: Why, Lord, are you so far away when trouble is so near? (Psalm 10:1). You're on the mountain praying, Lord, while the sea is preparing to swallow us whole. If You don't come in a hurry, You'll be too late!

In that frightening episode, we can find portrayed what I believe is the vision of fear: *God in the distance*. Like the disciples, at times we know that the Lord is around somewhere, and certainly busy doing good. But knowing He's there provides little comfort, because whatever we fear seems so much closer to us than He is. We can affirm that He's out there holding the world together, and keeping the stars on track; but what about this sickness right here in our body; these unpaid bills here on our desk; this struggling marriage here in our home?

No wonder fear robs us of joy. When the things that frighten us seem so much nearer than the Lord, they also seem larger than He is. Their proximity intimidates us and rivets our attention until we can no longer see the God who stands beyond them. As that kind of nearsightedness sets in, the God in the distance becomes a disappearing God, and our delight in Him vanishes as well.

Redirecting our focus and moving closer

Peter's experience that night on the stormy sea illustrates the problem well. When that bold disciple looked beyond the nearby waves buffeting the boat to see the Lord in the distance, what he saw enabled him to step out of the boat and walk across the water toward Jesus. But "when he saw the wind" up close once again, "he was afraid" (Matthew 14:30). When Peter's attention was drawn to the threat close at hand, he began to sink.

I think we might learn from Peter two responses we should take to our fears in order to make room for joy to return. One is to turn the eyes of our heart *away* from what frightens us and *toward* the Lord standing in the distance. The other is to begin moving toward the Lord ourselves. "Come near to God and he will come near to you" (James 4:8).

Just how do we go about turning our attention to God and moving closer to Him? Our earlier discussions of worship and prayer should give us a clue.

First of all, we said that taking time to *worship* the Lord—even though we don't feel like it—can help restore our perspective on Him. If we begin praising God for who He is, and thanking Him for what He's done, the eyes of our heart move their focus from the immediate problem to the King seated on the throne beyond them. We're reminded both of His power and of His willingness to help us, and we call to mind His faithfulness in the troubled times when we've been afraid before.

At the same time, the "view from the Throne" puts whatever frightens us in clearer perspective as well. The things we thought were larger than God turn out to be much smaller and less intimidating in the light of the reigning King.

Second, we said that through *prayer* we draw close to God by taking our concerns in the "hands" of our spirit and holding them up in His presence—all the while keeping the eyes of our spirit on Him. As long as the thing we fear fills our field of vision, we're unable to see God beyond it. So we need to objectify both the thing we fear and the feeling of fear we experience by getting an "analytical distance" on them. That means taking a step back and holding them at arm's length to examine them.

Instead of praying, for example, "Lord, if I lose this job, I'll be ruined!" we can begin to pray, "Lord, right now I feel afraid because my job's threatened. And that fear is blocking my view of You. Show Yourself to me, and show me what it is about this situation that threatens me so deeply." That kind of prayer reverses the previous arrangement: Where before, God seemed distant and the fears close at hand, now we have distanced ourselves from the fears, and we have drawn ourselves closer to God.

If in the midst of the storm we can look for God in the distance through worship and draw close to Him in prayer, our fear will in time give way to courage. After all, courage is simply fear that has taken its stand on the faithfulness of God. Once we're able to stand in that place, joy will flow once more from our vision of the One who is faithful.

Meanwhile, when we refocus our attention on the horizon, we may be surprised at what we see there besides God. Elisha's servant cried to the prophet in panic when he saw that enemy troops had surrounded the city to capture them. But when Elisha prayed that the servant's eyes would be opened, the frightened man beheld a host of horses and chariots of fire God had sent to protect them (2 Kings 6:1-22). When we look beyond our circumstances to God and draw close to Him, we too may discover to our surprise—and our delight—that help is on the way.

Teach me, Lord, to make a gift of my fears to You—to wrap them up in prayer, toss them to You in worship, and leave them at Your feet. Whether or not You immediately change the circumstances that frighten me, You'll be changing me *by drawing me close to You, and stirring up in me the joy of Your presence. Then, faithful Lord, I'll be able to sing with the psalmist:*

"Blessed is the man who fears the LORD, who finds great delight in his commands. . . . He will have no fear of bad news; his heart is steadfast, trusting in the LORD. His heart is secure, he will have no fear; in the end he will look in triumph on his foes" (Psalm 112:1, 7-8).

How long, O LORD? . . . How long will you hide your face from me?
How long must I wrestle with my thoughts and every day
have sorrow in my heart?
PSALM 13:1-2

□

As they talked and discussed these things with each other, Jesus himself
came up and walked along with them; but they were kept
from recognizing him.
LUKE 24:15-16

□

Where is my God? What hidden place
Conceals thee still?
What covert dare eclipse thy face?
Is it thy will?
GEORGE HERBERT

□

In consequence of the loss of faith . . . follows . . . loss of joy in the Holy
Ghost. . . . The fountain being dammed up, those living waters spring
no more to refresh the thirsty soul.
JOHN WESLEY

CHAPTER 26

DOUBT:
God in Disguise

In each year's Easter sermons we tend to focus on the joy that overwhelmed the disciples when they discovered that Christ was risen. It's fitting that we should do so. Joy is the heart and soul of Easter: For on that Morning of mornings, God quaked the earth to bring forth a Spring of living water that would flow out to save a thirsty world.

We rarely stop to realize, however, that the waters of that Resurrection Spring didn't make their way into most of the disciples' hearts until long after the stone had rolled away. The apostles at first thought the testimony of the women was "nonsense" (Luke 24:11); the faces of Cleopas and his companion were "downcast" on their way to Emmaus that evening (verse 17); and poor Thomas remained in sad doubt about the whole affair for a full week afterward (John 20:26).

We could cite a number of reasons for their slowness to accept the miracle of Christ's return from the grave—chief among them, of course, the fact that death is usually final! Yet what is to me the oddest aspect of the disciples' experience in coming to believe in the Resurrection has often been passed over: their repeated failure to recognize Him when He appeared.

Here was their best, most beloved friend, a man with whom they'd lived every day for three years. But Mary Magdalene thought He was the gardener (John 20:13-16). Cleopas and another disciple traveled and talked with Him for perhaps hours without recognizing Him (Luke 24:13-35). Thomas had to touch the nail holes in His hands and feet to be sure of His identity (John 20:26-29). And the disciples in their fishing boat who spoke with Him as He stood on the shore thought He was a stranger (John 21:1-14).

No doubt we're dealing here with a mystery involving the nature of the glorified body of Christ. Yet this much we know: The men on the road to Emmaus "were kept from recognizing" Jesus (Luke 24:16). It was God's own doing. And we might reasonably suppose that this was the case for the others as well.

For reasons known for sure only to Himself, then, the Lord at times actually prevented His followers from knowing that He was with them. Though He walked with them and spoke with them, His identity was hidden from them. He was, in fact, a God in disguise.

A lifetime of disguise

In a sense, of course, we could say that in Jesus, God had been in disguise all along as far as most people were concerned. His mother and stepfather knew who He was, but the innkeeper of Bethlehem never knew that his stable housed a king. A prostitute recognized His authority to forgive sin, but the Pharisees failed to see that He was the God who alone could grant forgiveness (Luke 7:36-50). A Gentile Roman centurion acknowledged Jesus' power, and yet His own brothers disbelieved His claims (John 7:5).

The precedent of God operating in concealment was thus well-established by the time of the Resurrection. Nevertheless, the disciples had in many ways been allowed to see through that cover. They'd watched Jesus heal the sick, raise the dead, multiply food, walk on water, and stand transfigured on the mountaintop. They'd heard Peter's confession—"You are the Christ, the Son of the living God"—and Jesus' confirmation of it (Matthew 16:16-20).

Yet somehow, despite all they knew, the disciples were caught off guard by Christ's post-Resurrection appearances; and we can only say with Luke that in those times God *kept* them from recognizing Him. Their inability to see that the Lord was truly with them left them struggling with doubt and drained them of gladness. Then, when Jesus finally revealed His identity, "The disciples were overjoyed when they saw the Lord" (John 20:20).

Not surprisingly, the situation of those disciples is often ours as well. Our doubts may take a myriad of forms: We may doubt God's care for us; we may doubt our own salvation; we may doubt God's testimony in the Scriptures; we may even under trying circumstances doubt God's very existence. Whatever the specific content of our doubt, however, I believe the basic problem is the same. We're somehow failing to see God because He's in disguise; and until we see Him again, our joy will be frozen as it was for the disciples.

Dealing with doubt

When we look closely at the experience of Jesus' friends after the Resurrection, we find no particular pattern in the ways by which the Lord revealed Himself to them. The men on the way to Emmaus had their eyes opened through the Scripture, and then through fellowship in the breaking of bread together (Luke 24:25-31). Mary Magdalene recognized the Lord when He called her by name (John 20:16). John realized that the stranger on the shore was Jesus when he saw that He was providing for them just as He had in the past (John 21:6-7). Thomas had to have the hard evidence of torn, bloody flesh (John 20:24-29).

My own experience has confirmed that God dispels doubt in a variety of ways, according to our need at the time. Again and again my eyes have been opened to the basic truths of the gospel through both the testimony of Scripture and the testimony of fellowship. At other times I've had the Lord call me inwardly by name to reassure me that He was alive. My faith in God's care has been restored on still other occasions when God proved Himself faithful once again through His abundant provision. And at other times I've had to have hard evidence in my hand that God was in control.

I never know for sure how the Lord will appear; but when I'm facing doubts, I've learned to go looking for Him. Somehow it seems that He rarely wears a complete disguise: When His face is masked, His hands may be showing. When His hands are gloved, His feet may be bare. So once I can determine which channels of vision seem to be covered at the moment, I can search for other angles to view Him.

When, for example, nothing seems to be going right, and I can't see God at work in my life, I may begin to doubt whether He really cares for me. Then I must turn to Scripture for a view of God in black-and-white instead. The testimony to His goodness I read there allows me to view the "hand" of God in the past when I can't see the "feet" of God in the present. In this way my doubt is subdued, and my joy begins to return.

If, on the other hand, I should be assailed by doubt about the testimony of Scripture, I look instead for evidences that God is active in my daily life. I remind myself that, as someone has said, "A coincidence is a small miracle where God chose to remain anonymous." And even though the view of God's hand in the past has been concealed for the time, the view of His feet in the present—especially through the fellow saints who love me—can sustain me by renewing my vision and my joy.

The places where we can look for God are so many—including all the "furrows" we've described in previous chapters, and more—that I soon find at least one view that shows where the disguise ends. It may be a view accessible through worship or prayer; it may be through meditation or Scripture study; it may be through fellowship or service, or through any of the other disciplines. But I'm convinced that one way or another, God wants us eventually to recognize Him again, so that our joy can be complete.

Why God would hide

If God wants us to see Him, however, we might rightly ask why He hides His face in the first place. I doubt that we can know for sure, but I have a guess. It seems to me that whenever God's plan for our lives moves into a new and higher level of fulfillment, operating in a new realm, then we naturally have problems for a while understanding what's going on, and seeing the Lord through new eyes in new circumstances.

Just before His betrayal and death, Jesus told the disciples, "In a little while you will see me no more, and then after a little while you will see me. . . . Now is your time of grief, but I will see you again and you will rejoice" (John 16:16,22). That seems to be the pattern, and they didn't understand it (or like it) any more than we do (verses 17-18).

The disciples rejoiced to see and recognize Jesus in His natural flesh, and then they grieved to see Him taken away. When He returned in a glorified body, they failed to recognize Him at first. Their grief continued until He revealed Himself to them in a different way, when they rejoiced once more. Then once again, when even the Lord's glorified body was taken away at the Ascension, "some doubted" (Matthew 28:17). But when He returned again at Pentecost in a still different way, they were overjoyed once more to see Him acting in power.

A time of testing

Another reason why God conceals Himself at times is suggested by the experience of King Hezekiah of Judah. The chronicler tells us that "when envoys were sent by the rulers of Babylon to ask him about the miraculous sign that had occurred in the land, God left him to test him and to know everything that was in his heart" (2 Chronicles 32:31). Though the exact nature of the situation isn't clear from this one sentence, we're told that in some sense God "left" Hezekiah—that is, withdrew the conscious awareness of His presence—in order to show him what was inside his heart.

I think a similar situation occurred on the road to Emmaus. Jesus may well have concealed Himself because He wanted to reveal the disciples' lack of understanding regarding the Scriptures that concerned the Messiah (Luke 24:25-27). The same principle seems at work in Thomas's situation as well. Perhaps God arranged for Thomas to be absent when the others saw the Lord in order to show that he should have trusted the testimony of his friends (John 20:29).

To put it bluntly, though we don't particularly enjoy having to search for God, the search is good for us. It tests us—not in the sense that a student is tested by a graded exam, but rather in the sense that gold is tested in the furnace. Battles with doubt refine us by bringing our spiritual dross to the surface where we can recognize and confess it, so that the Lord can take it away from us.

We might say, then, that sometimes God covers *His* true identity so that He can *uncover* *our* true identity. We're strengthened by such testing when we persevere in the ensuing search for Him. Once we find the Lord, we'll find, as well, that our faith as been purified, our vision has been broadened—and our joy has been restored.

God of Disguises, You're also a God of Mercy; You elude us for our good. You rouse us out of our sterile slumber to hunt for You. And in the chase, our childish faith is shredded on the brambles of the doubts we struggle through on our way. But just when we've lost every scrap of the covering we should have out-grown long ago, You show Yourself and let us catch You, and You clothe us in more durable fabric. Thus, in Your holy game of hide-and-seek, my Lord, the winner's reward is joy.

God created man in his own image, in the image of God he created him;
male and female he created them.
GENESIS 1:27

☐

You have taken off your old self with its practices and have put on the
new self, which is being renewed in knowledge in
the image of its Creator.
COLOSSIANS 3:9-10

☐

It is certain that man never achieves a clear knowledge of himself unless
he has first looked upon God's face, and then descends from
contemplating Him to scrutinize himself.
JOHN CALVIN

☐

Am I new minted by Thy Stamp indeed?
Mine eyes are dim; I cannot clearly see.
Be Thou my Spectacles that I may read
Thine Image, and Inscription stampt on me.
EDWARD TAYLOR

☐

For if you see nothing else than that you are a sinner, despair will
follow. You must lift up your eyes, then, and behold Christ.
Then joy will follow.
MARTIN LUTHER

CHAPTER 27

DESPAIR:
God in a Broken Mirror

In sifting through the writings of Christian thinkers from many periods and cultures, I've recognized in the last few years a point of agreement that had escaped me before. Perhaps the notion isn't new to you, but it came as a surprise to me to find how many theologians have affirmed that *the knowledge of God and the knowledge of self are tightly intertwined.*

I grew up a typical child in the sixties, when intense introspection was considered normal by many in our society. Not surprisingly, it was also a time of extreme narcissism. After I was apprehended by the Lord, then, I had a healthy reaction against such self-preoccupation. The Christian circles where I moved taught me to focus my attention on the Lord more than on myself, and the results were fruitful.

You can thus imagine my surprise some years later to open the first volume of John Calvin's *Institutes of the Christian Faith*—that great master work on the sovereignty of God—and to find at the head of the first paragraph these words: "Without knowledge of self there is no knowledge of God."[1] All my Christian life I'd been told that Calvin's theology focused above all on the majesty of the Creator, and here he was, beginning his comprehensive statement of faith with talk about self-knowledge!

Before long I came to realize that Calvin wasn't alone. In the early Church the road from self-knowledge to God-knowledge was noted, for example, by Clement, a second-century bishop and teacher of Alexandria. In the late classical period, Augustine pointed in the same direction. In the Middle Ages, Catherine of Siena spoke of "dwelling in the cell of self-knowledge in order to know God's goodness."[2] And the list goes on.

As I read further, however, I discovered that this avenue of knowledge was a two-way street. Calvin went on to say that "without knowledge of God there is no knowledge of self,"[3] and the other writers also emphasized that an exclusive focus on self-knowledge was unhealthy. To my surprise, I even discovered that a derogatory term for narcissists often thrown around in the sixties had actually been coined over five hundred years before by Byzantine Christians. They called people who were caught up in excessive introspection by the disparaging title *Omphaloscopoi*—translated literally, "the navel gazers."[4]

The connection between God-knowledge and self-knowledge
The deeper I delve into Scripture and these Christian teachers, the more I see just how much our understanding of God and our understanding of self influence each other. The connection exists, I believe, for at least three reasons.

The first is simply that we've been made in the "image" and "likeness" of God (Genesis 1:26). In light of that reality, we should expect to find some kind of important parallels between who we are and who God is. To use a metaphor from Catherine and other writers, the soul is the "mirror of God."[5]

The second reason for a connection is what I would call *the incarnational principle*. God's way of dealing with humanity—which finds its clearest expression in the Word taking on flesh (John 1:14)—is to embody the spiritual in the physical, the supernatural in the natural. So we must often look to redeemed human nature to learn what it reflects about God's nature. As George MacDonald noted, "If there be any meaning in the Incarnation, it is through the Human that we must climb up to the Divine."[6]

These two realities give us reason to believe that knowledge of self will give us some knowledge about God. But a third reality makes it abundantly clear that we must also have knowledge of God from some other source to correct our knowledge of self. Though we're made in the image of God, that image has been fractured in the Fall; the mirror has been broken by sin.

This means that the true information about God within us is mixed with a great deal of misinformation. So if we look only at ourselves as we are and assume that all we see is "normal" and according to God's intention, then we'll be misled. Doing that, Calvin said, is like looking at the ruins of an old building and thinking we see an intact edifice.[7]

Worse yet, because we naturally tend to think of God in human terms, we may assume that God looks exactly the same way we do if we don't realize His reflection in the mirror is marred. That mistake can lead to disastrous effects.

My relationship with my daughter provides a clear example of the discernment we need in cultivating self-knowledge and God-knowledge. When Lydia comes to me with a scraped knee or a hurt feeling, I naturally reach out to her in love and attempt to comfort her. I feel her pain inside myself as well, and will do all I can to aid her healing.

The desire to love and protect my child is part of God's

image within me, and parallel to God's reaching out to our hurt in the Incarnation. So knowing that about myself allows me to understand something of the nature of God, because He, too, is a Father. Jesus Himself illustrated this principle in the Sermon on the Mount (Matthew 7:9-11).

On the other hand, I have irritable days and pressured moments when my patience is short. In those times, if Lydia comes to me with a problem I'm (regrettably) more likely to say, "It's no big deal. Stop crying."

Such impatience and irritability is part of the crack in my "mirror." So if I should look at that weakness, or at some similar sin, and say, "That's how God is," then I'm being misled. What I think is an attribute of God is actually a flaw on the surface of the mirror.

Now few of us would come right out and say that we think God has bad days, or that He gets up on the wrong side of the bed some mornings. Yet we tend to draw the conclusion implicitly. I've met countless people who assume that God's patience is rather short, or that His dealings are rather harsh, or that He's negligent and preoccupied. In most cases, their thinking seems to have been influenced by the appearance of those flaws in the human mirror of themselves or someone close to them (especially parents). Consequently, like the third servant in the parable of the talents, they can't view God with joy because they see Him as a "hard man."

The grasshopper God
So what has all this to do with the problem of despair? Over the years I've tried to observe carefully the dynamics of discouragement, and especially of hopelessness. One pattern that seems to have emerged in my observation is that *the people who despair of God's goodness the most frequently are those with the lowest view of themselves.* They're also the ones

who find their joy continually draining away.

Having noted the mutual influence between self-knowledge and God-knowledge, we can see why this might be the case. If those who see mostly cracks in their mirrors assume that the Lord is in some way reflected there, such a distorted image will present them with a God who is difficult to trust, love, and enjoy. Not surprisingly, they'll be more likely to give up on walking with such a God.

Perhaps the best examples of this principle are the ancient Israelites who had come out of Egypt and had finally reached the borders of the Promised Land. When the men they sent to spy out the land returned, they reported that it flowed "with milk and honey" (Numbers 13:27). But then most of the spies added that the inhabitants were giants and lived in fortified cities (verses 28-32).

One man—Caleb—was confident of God's strength, and of his own strength in God. So he called for an invasion (verse 30). But the rest of the spies, except for Joshua, despaired of entering the Promised Land or conquering it. Their reason? "We seemed like grasshoppers *in our own eyes*" (verse 33). They were convinced that the Lord wasn't able to grant such puny people victory (Numbers 14:3).

When the Israelites looked in their distorted mirrors, they saw quite accurately a lack of size, strength, and experience. But they should also have seen there the children of a God who was a Deliverer, a Conqueror, and a Healer. If they'd focused on the good things God had worked into them in the desert instead of the cracks that still had to be mended, they might have gone on to the joy of possessing the Promised Land.

But instead, they looked in their marred mirrors and saw insignificant insects. Consequently, when they looked to heaven, they saw only a grasshopper God who was small, weak, and hopeless. So they despaired at the sight of such a

God, and their gladness at reaching Canaan turned into grumbling and wailing (Numbers 14:1-2).

Correcting the image
Despair freezes joy because its view of God is a fractured one. When we assume that the marred image in the mirror is the ultimate truth about who we are and who God is, then we naturally give up on ourselves and on a God who fails to waken in us a love for Him and a pleasure in Him.

What's the corrective for a broken image? Calvin was convinced that the Scriptures give us what we need for a clear view of both God and ourselves. My experience has confirmed as well that whatever time we spend looking in the mirror should be supplemented by a close look at God in black-and-white. For if we look long enough there, we'll find ourselves in black-and-white, too.

In those scriptural "spectacles" we'll see that we're made in God's image, but that the image has to be restored as we "put on the new self" (Colossians 3:9-10). We'll find that we're "God's workmanship, created in Christ Jesus to do good works" (Ephesians 2:10). We'll learn that "it is God who works in [us] to will and to act according to his good purpose" (Philippians 2:13). And we'll discover that "he who began a good work in [us] will carry it on to completion until the day of Christ Jesus" (Philippians 1:6).

The Puritan writer Thomas Hooker gave his readers what I think is sound advice for the person who is struggling with despair: "Pass no hasty sentence against thyself but according to the evidence of the Word. If thou art to be approved, let the Word of God do it: and let the same Word examine thee, if thou comest to be examined. If this Word speak for thee, no matter, though all men and angels speak against thee, and if it condemn thee, no matter who speaks for thee: by it thou risest or fallest to thine own master."[8]

Certainly the loving fellowship of other Christians who reflect God's image more clearly than we do will correct our vision of God as well. But I'm convinced that above all we must "let the word of Christ dwell in [us] richly . . . giving thanks to God the Father" for who it says He is, and who it says we are in Him (Colossians 3:16-17). When we do, the image of God in our mirror will become more and more like His portrait in the Scripture, and we'll rejoice to see the transformation.

Forgive me, Father, when I've thought of You as a grass-hopper God, when I've made You in my image. How many Promised Lands have I failed to enter because my eyes were on myself and my weakness rather than on Your love and Your power? Make me a Caleb, Lord, following you wholeheartedly, ready to take the hill country that lies ahead (Numbers 14:6-14).

Polish my mirror and fill the cracks; brighten the light that falls on me. Let the day come, Lord, when You Yourself can look in the mirror that I am, and be fully pleased with the reflection You see there.

NOTES:

1. Calvin, *Institutes*, I. i. 1, page 36.
2. Calvin, *Institutes*, pages 36-37; Clement of Alexandria, *Instructor*, iii., page 1; Augustine, *Soliloquies*, I. ii., page 7, II. i., page 1; Catherine of Siena, *The Dialogue*, page 25.
3. Calvin, *Institutes*, pages 36-37.
4. Stephen Runciman, *The Great Church in Captivity* (Cambridge, England: Cambridge University Press, 1968), page 141.
5. Catherine of Siena, *The Dialogue*, page 48.
6. George MacDonald, *Unspoken Sermons* (New York: George Routledge & Sons, 1871), page 73.
7. Calvin, *Institutes*, pages 195-196.
8. Hooker, *The Poor Doubting Christian*, pages 77-78.

You said in your heart, "I will ascend into heaven; I will raise my throne above the stars of God. . . . I will ascend above the tops of the clouds; I will make myself like the Most High."
ISAIAH 14:13-14

☐

"In the pride of your heart you say, 'I am a god; I sit on the throne of a god in the heart of the seas.' But you are a man and not a god, though you think you are as wise as a god."
EZEKIEL 28:2

☐

Pride loves to climb up, not as Zacchaeus to see Christ, but to be seen.
WILLIAM GURNALL

☐

Pride . . . is a lifting up of the heart above God and against God and without God.
THOMAS MANTON

☐

A proud man hath no God.
BENJAMIN WHICHCOTE

CHAPTER 28

PRIDE:
God Below Us

The teachers in the Egyptian church of the early centuries had a wise saying about what Christians should do when they see another person sinning. They were aware of the apostle Paul's warning that it's precisely when we think we're standing firm that we're most likely to fall (1 Corinthians 10:12). So when someone around us falls, they insisted, instead of feeling self-righteous by comparison we should always say to ourselves, "He today; I tomorrow."[1]

I think that realization of our common human predicament sums up the vision of humility. To be humble is to view ourselves as one among many; to see that we're all fallen and prone to sin, but that we're all nevertheless precious to God. Though we have differing gifts, and walk at different points along the road home, all that we are and have comes to us through grace alone.

Paul desired to impart such a vision to the Corinthians, whose church was torn with divisions through the arrogance of its leaders. He told them they needed to see themselves with humility: "Then you will not take pride in one man over against another. For who makes you different from anyone else? What do you have that you did not receive? And if you did receive it, why do you boast as though you did not?" (1 Corinthians 4:6-7). The apostle was convinced that we're all beggars, equally indebted to God's goodness.

Lifting ourselves up in pride
The early Christian monks once told a story of how the devil appeared, disguised as an angel of light, to a humble man who was praying in his cell. "I am the angel Gabriel," the devil said, "and I have been sent to you."

But the monk escaped the deception because of his great humility. Thinking himself no better than any of his brother monks, he answered simply, "See whether you were not sent to someone else. I am not worthy that an angel should be sent to me." Unable to tempt the old man to be proud, the devil vanished.[2]

It's no chance occurrence that Satan chose pride as his lure to try to trap that saint. Pride, after all, was what had made the devil the devil in the first place: It had filled him until it left no room within him for heaven, and no room within heaven for him.

Tucked away in Isaiah is a passage where God condemns the pride of someone called the "morning star, son of the dawn" (Isaiah 14:12). The prophecy is explicitly addressed to "the king of Babylon" (verse 4), but an ancient tradition of the Church interprets this text as a description of Satan's expulsion from heaven. Whether or not that interpretation is valid, we can see in God's rebuke a terrifying portrait of pride that would apply to both the devil and to anyone else who imitates his sin.

This is what the proud heart says: "I will ascend to heaven; I will raise my throne above the stars of God. . . . I will ascend above the tops of the clouds; I will make myself like the Most High" (Isaiah 14:13-14).

I will ascend. Those words are the motto of the proud. In pride, we deny our common position with our brothers and sisters, and try to lift ourselves above them, thinking ourselves better than they are. The word "haughty," in fact, is related to the word "height," just as "humility" is related to "humus," the ground. When our hearts are proud, we follow the Enemy in his quest, as the poet John Milton said, "to set himself in Glory above his Peers."[3]

The inevitable result of such self-elevation is a devastating tumble: "Pride goes before destruction, and a haughty spirit before a fall" (Proverbs 16:18). "How you have fallen from heaven," the Lord told the "son of the dawn! You have been cast down . . ." (Isaiah 14:12). With such a fall inevitably comes misery, for the "morning stars" who sang together in joy can no longer include the fallen one in their happy music (Job 38:7).

Yet even in that lowly position of dishonor, the proud heart strives to stand above others. Thus Milton has the devil declare defiantly as he stands up after his plunge into the pit: "Better to reign in hell, than serve in Heaven."[4]

Seeking a place above God
Evidently Satan sought more than a place above his fellow angels. He wanted to take the very throne of God for himself (Isaiah 14:13-14). Pride drove him until he actually sought to stand above even his Creator. That's why in Jesus' temptation in the wilderness, the price required for power was to bow at Satan's feet. If Jesus had done so, then at last the Enemy would have succeeded in looking down upon God below him (Matthew 4:8-9).

Few of us, even the proudest among us, would admit to envying God His throne. Yet I think pride toward other people actually shoves us sooner or later toward that very ambition in one sense or another. Dorotheos tells us that in the first stages of pride, "a man despises his brother, considers him worth little or nothing, while he puts a much greater value on himself." Unless such a person repents, says Dorotheos, then eventually "he lifts himself up against God, and ascribes what he does right, not to God, but to himself."[5] The throne of God is the throne of grace. Whenever we deny grace by judging ourselves worthy of it, we're seeking to usurp that throne.

C. S. Lewis notes: "In God you come up against something which is in every respect immeasurably superior to yourself. . . . As long as you are proud, you cannot know God. A proud man is always looking down on things and people: and, of course, as long as you are looking down, you cannot see something that is above you."[6]

I agree with that description of pride, and in particular with the observation that the proud heart can't see God. But in another sense, I think we might well invert the picture here. In biblical imagery, proud eyes don't look *down*; they're always looking *up*, away from the "common" people and toward the next rung of the ladder they intend to climb in their ascent (Isaiah 37:23). The neck of the proud is "outstretched," the face turned upward in a posture of disdain (Isaiah 3:16).

Because pride drives us eventually to place ourselves above God—above His law, above His grace, above His authority—then the haughtily upturned eyes of our heart have no vision of the Lord. Turning Lewis's image on its head, we might say that as long as we're looking up, we can't see Someone below us.

But wait, you might say. Despite our distorted view of ourselves, God really *is* above us, our superior in every way. And of course I'd agree. But the great irony and paradox of the gospel is that God has also placed Himself *below* us, in the form of a Servant. That's where the proud heart is unable to see Him.

In Christ the divine humility has stooped to wash feet and cook breakfast, to carve oxen yokes and ride donkeys, to sweat blood and to die (John 12:14, 13:1-17, 21:9-13). Though "being in very nature God," Christ "did not consider equality with God something to be grasped," but came instead to serve (Philippians 2:6-7). So the proud hearts who surrounded Him couldn't see God there, because their eyes disdained to look below them where the humble dwelt. Nor will we ever see Him below us, either, as long as our eyes are lifted up in pride.

Pride's fleeting pleasure

With God below our range of vision, we find little cause for joy. Pride has its own pleasures, of course. Any mountain climber will tell us that looking down from immense heights can be deliciously intoxicating. But the inebriation soon gives way to a hangover, and we find ourselves grasping for still another drink to overcome the pain. So we're driven to climb higher still.

Yet even the false, fleeting comforts of pride are shattered when our time comes to fall. Then even the counterfeits of joy are lost, and we find ourselves waking up in a pit of misery, with the worm of conscience gnawing away at us (Isaiah 14:11).

The hard reality is that those of us who stand in pride have only two alternatives: We must humble ourselves, or else God will humiliate us. The path to joy for the proud heart is thus a difficult one. That path must always be the way that leads to a vision of the Lord. And if we would see the King who laid aside His robe for a wash towel, we must drop to our knees and wash feet with Him.

Once we can find the grace to fall to the ground on our

own, our joy will grow even as our vision of God grows. At the same time, we'll rejoice to discover that many of the snares Satan has planned are powerless with us as they were with that humble monk.

Antony, one of the fourth-century fathers of the Christian monastic movement, once spoke of a vision he had. In it, he saw all the devil's traps laid out across the earth. So he groaned and said, "Who can pass through them all?" And a voice came answering, "Humility."[7]

The Enemy's temptations, I'm convinced, are mostly stationed in high places. Humility alone can pass through all those snares, because humility alone is close enough to the ground to crawl beneath their reach. Given that lowly posture, the humble man or woman may have a dirty face, but it will nevertheless be radiant. For in it will be reflected the joyous light of the humble Servant who was brought low, that we might in good time be exalted to feast at His table.

How often, my God, I have thought in folly that the axe could raise itself above the One who swings it, and the saw could boast against the One who uses it. As if a rod were able to wield the One who lifts it up! (Isaiah 10:15). Forgive me for reaching, Lord, for grasping at Your grace as if it were my due, for playing the prince when I'm only a pauper.

My pride has brought me misery. Yet I can rejoice to know that even though You oppose the proud, You give grace to the humble (Proverbs 3:34). When I see You below me, and at last join You there, then "I will bless the LORD at all times; His praise shall continually be in my mouth; my soul shall make its boast in the LORD; the humble shall hear it and rejoice" (Psalm 34:1-2, NASB).

NOTES:
1. "The Sayings of the Fathers," page 105.
2. "The Sayings of the Fathers," page 171.

3. John Milton, *Paradise Lost*, Merritt Y. Hughes, ed. (New York: Odyssey Press, 1962), page 6.
4. Milton, *Paradise Lost*, page 13.
5. Dorotheos, *Discourses and Sayings*, page 97.
6. C. S. Lewis, *Mere Christianity* (New York: Macmillan, 1973), page 111.
7. "The Sayings of the Fathers," page 156.

Be content with what you have, because God has said, "Never will I leave you; never will I forsake you."
HEBREWS 13:5

□

This is the day the LORD has made; let us rejoice and be glad in it.
PSALM 118:24

□

True contentment is a real, even an active, virtue—not only affirmative but creative. It is the power of getting out of any situation all there is in it.
G. K. CHESTERTON

□

If one accepts each day as a gift from the Father's hand, one may sometimes hear a voice saying, "Open it. I invite you to share with me in these little appointments with myself as we try to unwrap the hidden beauties in an ordinary day."
GERHARD FROST

□

Is my gloom, after all Shade of His hand, outstretched caressingly?
FRANCIS THOMPSON

CHAPTER 29

DISCONTENT:
God Above Us

The word of the Lord once came through the prophet
Zechariah to Zerubbabel, who was rebuilding the Temple
at Jerusalem and evidently having a frustrating time at it.
Little had seemed to go right for a long while (Ezra 4). So
God had to address Zerubbabel's perception that his work
wasn't amounting to much.

On that occasion, the Lord asked the builder a question that I believe He issues to everyone struggling with
discontent: "Who despises the day of small things?" (Zechariah 4:10). Sadly enough, I must often answer, "*I* do, Lord."

The day of small things. The day of grocery shopping
and clothes washing. The day of fixing bike tires and help-
ing the new neighbors move in. The day with hours spent
just making a living or just keeping the kids in line or just
resting a little in the back yard. The day that seems tedious,
flat, insignificant.

We have seasons in life when such days tend to cluster,
accumulating like dust into a gray veil of discontent. With
our nose to the grindstone and our eyes to the ground, we
fail to see the Lord in our daily movements, and so we move

in a joyless routine. What has God to do, anyway, with overgrown lawns and dirty dishes?

Yet the word of the Lord to Zerubbabel is also, I think, the word of the Lord to us. For in the day of small things, we're slowly raising a temple where the Lord can dwell; and the mundane moments we find so tedious are the common wood and stone with which we build.

Sometimes God hides what is precious by placing it so close to us that we can't see it. Thus discontent is actually a form of farsightedness. We search the horizon restlessly for some sign of a spectacular crimson sunrise, while the unspectacular things lying close at hand appear in our vision only as dull, gray blurs.

In those numbing "winters of our discontent," we must hear the rest of Zechariah's prophecy: "This is the word of the LORD to Zerubbabel: 'Not by might nor by power, but by my Spirit,' says the LORD Almighty" (Zechariah 4:6). With those words, God lifted the builder's eyes to focus, not on the distant and inaccessible horizon, but rather on Himself.

There, Zerubbabel saw the God who was above him. That weary laborer discovered that none other than the Holy Spirit was the Overseer who was personally ordering all the arrangements of even the things that seemed no more significant than sawdust. Such a renewed vision of the Lord enabled him to look down once more with different eyes at the everyday circumstances surrounding him. He could thus continue working with a new joy, knowing that God was watching over him.

Discontent in the desert

We see the same need to look above among the ancient Israelites, for whom discontent was the great killer in the desert. (I know you probably think I too often use those poor folks as a foil; but the apostle Paul tells us their troubles "occurred as examples to keep us from setting our hearts on evil things as they did," 1 Corinthians 10:6.)

No sooner had the Israelites crossed the Red Sea than they began to grumble about God's provision (Exodus 15:22-25). They were looking to the horizon for a land flowing with milk and honey, but for the moment all they had at hand was dust and scorpions. So the joyful music of the tambourines gave way quickly to joyless complaints.

Already the people had forgotten to lift up their eyes to see hovering over them the pillar of cloud by day and the pillar of fire by night (Exodus 13:20-22). They journeyed and they camped in the shadow and the light of those pillars. Those pillars symbolized the God who had saved them. But when they kept their eyes down, or only on the distant horizon, they forgot Who was watching over them, and their gladness was lost in discontent.

It's important to note here that we're speaking of a particular kind of discontent: the kind that takes our eyes off the Lord. There's also a godly discontent, a holy urging to move on and apprehend the promises of God. That second kind looks to the horizon as well, but only to keep its feet headed in the right direction through the rocks and sands of the present. And while it walks, it doesn't grumble; it sings.

Godly discontent is thus a healthy dissatisfaction with what we're presently *giving to God*. But ungodly discontent is a destructive dissatisfaction with what we're presently *given by God*. When we walk in sinful discontent, then we're like the Israelites: When the Lord gives us deliverance, we want water; when the Lord gives us water, we want bread; when the Lord gives us bread, we want meat (Exodus 15-16).

According to Catherine of Siena (and many others), the highest joy of heaven is that we will at last behold God face-to-face, while the foremost torment of hell is that the damned are deprived of seeing God.[1] If that's indeed the case, then we can understand how, as Milton said, the mind "in itself can make a Heaven of Hell, a Hell of Heaven."[2] For the eyes of habitual discontent are also deprived of seeing God by their failure to look up.

How do we redirect our gaze to see the Lord and delight in Him again? Many of the disciplines we've discussed can help, but I think three of them are especially useful in this regard: Worship will refocus our eyes upward. Play will help us rediscover God's abundance. And meditation will uncover the handiwork of God in the everyday things around us.

In the final analysis, I believe, whatever helps us remember that the God above us is at work in what is ordinary will teach us the great lesson of joyous contentment: We must not despise the day of small things.

This is the day You have made, Lord. Do we dare refuse to rejoice in it? If we look only to what we have, we'll never be satisfied, for we could always have more. But if we look up to You instead, we'll have our fill. So, my God, "Satisfy us . . . with your unfailing love, that we may sing for joy and be glad all our days" (Psalm 90:14).

NOTES:
1. Catherine of Siena, *The Dialogue*, pages 80, 84.
2. Milton, *Paradise Lost*, page 13.

Refrain from anger and turn from wrath; do not fret—
it leads only to evil.
PSALM 37:8

□

"Therefore, if you are offering your gift at the altar and there remember
that your brother has something against you, leave your gift there in
front of the altar. First go and be reconciled to your brother; then come
and offer your gift."
MATTHEW 5:23-24

□

Anger constantly irritates the soul, and above all at the time of prayer it
seizes the mind and flashes the picture of the offensive person before our
eyes. . . . Anger . . . is calculated to cloud the eye of your spirit and
destroy your state of prayer.
EVAGRIUS

□

It is the great duty of all Christians to put off anger. . . . A man cannot
wrestle with God and wrangle with his neighbor at the same time.
PHILIP HENRY

CHAPTER 30

ANGER:
God Obscured

The Lord's warning in the Sermon on the Mount about "speck-hunting" is familiar to most of us: "Why do you look at the speck of sawdust in your brother's eye and pay no attention to the plank in your own eye?" (Matthew 7:3). According to the traditional interpretation of that passage, Jesus was revealing the hypocrisy of our judging another person's sin when the same sin appears in our own life.

From the context it seems evident to me that this standard interpretation is correct. These words of the Lord appear immediately after His command not to judge, and just before the exclamation, "You hypocrite!" (verses 1-2,5).

Yet I've sometimes wondered whether the Lord's warning might not also uncover an important principle about the nature of anger. Often the sin in another person's life becomes evident to us because we ourselves have been offended or injured by that sin. When that's the case, in our anger at the offender we attempt to "fix" the other person's problem through some kind of "punishment"—physical, emotional, or otherwise.

If we view Jesus' words as a description of anger, then

we might say that the speck of sawdust in the other person's eye is an offense against us. So what, then, is the plank in our own eye? I think we might safely say that the speck and the plank are actually the same thing—that is, they both represent the offense. But the same offense that appears small in the eyes of the offender usually appears much larger to the one who's offended. For the offender, it's only a speck; for the offended, it's more like a plank.

What makes the offense seem so much larger to the one who's offended? In spiritual sight as in physical sight, the closer a thing is to our eyes, the larger it appears. So when we focus our eyes up close on something, it tends to be magnified until it fills our entire field of vision.

That's precisely what happens when we're angry. While the offender may forget what's happened, we who are offended tend to fix the eyes of our heart on the offense, and hold it in the center of our field of vision until we can see little else. So offenses become like flashing lights that demand our attention and our response.

For that reason, anger can distort our view of the world, and it can blind us to the vision of God altogether. When an offense occupies our mental and emotional attention, we have little left over for the Lord. That's one reason, I think, why Jesus insisted that if we want to approach the altar of God, we must be first reconciled to our brothers and sisters (Matthew 5:23-24). Perhaps that's also why Peter told husbands to treat their wives considerately. If they didn't, the break in the marriage relationship would hinder their prayers (1 Peter 3:7).

Anger and joyous prayer are mutually exclusive. Have you ever noticed how hard it is to enter into a spirit of genuine prayer when you're angry at someone? Or how hard it is to become angry with someone while you're in a spirit of prayer? A number of ancient Christian teachers, in particular Evagrius Ponticus of Egypt, noted this problem when they wrote of how anger "clouds the eye of the spirit" and "destroys the state of prayer" because it continually flashes before the mind a picture of the offender.[1] Thus anger saps our joy by keeping us from seeing God.

The example of Saul

King Saul provides the classic biblical example of what anger can do to our vision of God and of others. His jealousy of David caused him to take offense at the young man's popularity (1 Samuel 18:5-9). Though David had proven himself a faithful friend, servant, and comforter, Saul's anger distorted his vision until he could only view David as a threat. In fact, it eventually twisted his view of others as well, until the king came to see even his own son Jonathan as a rebel and a conspirator against him. The anger eventually grew like a cancer into uncontrollable rage, until Saul attempted to kill both David and Jonathan (1 Samuel 18:10-11, 20:30-33).

At the same time, that anger blinded Saul to the hand of God that was so obviously resting on the youth. Where others saw in David a hero the Lord had raised up to deliver His people from their enemies, Saul could only see a shepherd boy whose strength was a personal political threat. The Lord was missing from the picture altogether. When Saul looked at David, David's supposed offense filled his field of vision so that the view of God was totally obstructed. No wonder, then, that Saul's joy had gone, and he was a tormented man.

Suffering from the "torturers"

Jesus told Peter that if he didn't forgive an offender, Peter himself would suffer from the "torturers" (Matthew 18:34). Evagrius called anger an "irritant" of the soul, and I believe that psychological irritation is one form of the torture we suffer when we fail to forgive. Just as a foreign object in a physical eye torments us until we get it out, so anger hurts the eye of the heart until it's removed.

Failure to remove the irritant results in progressive loss of vision and even permanent damage, both in physical and in spiritual eyes. First our sight is simply blurred by the tears that flow when our eye is irritated. But if the object remains long enough, the eye festers, closes, and eventually becomes seriously injured. Anger turns to resentment, resentment to bitterness, bitterness to rage. And as we see from Saul's example, unchecked rage gives birth finally to a desire for the offender to die.

That's why we must first remove the "plank" from our own eye before we can deal with the other person's "speck" (Matthew 7:5). We simply can't see clearly enough to deal with that person redemptively until our own vision is restored. Otherwise, our focus on the offense blinds us in such a way that we stumble and swing wildly with our "tweezers," until we've scratched up the other person's face in a misguided attempt to pluck out the speck.

Healing through forgiveness

In the Rincon dialect of the Zapotec natives of Mexico, the English phrase "I forgive you" is translated by words that mean literally, "My face heals toward you."[2] I believe that beautiful word picture reflects a profound reality: When we've been angered, the only way the eyes of our heart can be restored to health is through forgiveness.

What does it mean to forgive? One of the Greek New Testament words we translate "forgive" means literally "to release, to let go." And that's precisely what we must do. We must let go of the offense that we've held so firmly at the center of our field of vision, and cast it away. Only then does our vision of the Lord, and our joy in the Lord, return.

But how do we go about genuinely forgiving someone? Whether the "debts" people owe us are recent or longstanding, I believe a few basic insights are helpful here.

First, we should remember that Jesus told Peter he was obligated to forgive others because he himself had been forgiven so much by God. Whenever I'm having difficulty forgiving someone, I read once again the parable of the unmerciful servant (Matthew 18:21-35). It never fails to help me get things in godly perspective.

Second, we must remember that if we don't forgive, we keep the offender in an emotional prison that chains our relationship. In the past, many nations had what was called "debtor's prisons," where folks who couldn't pay their bills were jailed until they did. The problem, however, was that their confinement prevented them from earning any money. So the debtors and their families often starved to death.

When we fail to forgive, we're keeping offenders in a similar kind of prison that prevents them from working to restore our relationship. Only when we let them go can things change. And only *we* can let them go.

Third, we must keep in mind that holding on to anger destroys us spiritually in the way we've previously described. For our own sake, as well as for the sake of the offender, we must let go. Bitterness is actually a set of spiritual handcuffs— with one end on the offender's wrist, and one on ours. In light of the Greek word's literal meaning, "Forgive, and you will be forgiven" (Luke 6:37) could just as well be translated "Release, and you will be released."

Fourth, we must recognize that God often allows us to be offended in order to work something into our character. As G. K. Chesterton has said, "We make our friends; we make our enemies; but God makes our next-door neighbor." To take an image from Dorotheos, we tend to act like dogs when we're offended. If someone throws a stick at a dog and it hits him, the dog often angrily bites the stick rather than biting the one who threw it. When someone angers us, we also tend to focus our attention on the "stick"—the offender—instead of looking to God and wondering why He thought we needed the reproof.[3]

Finally, the most important step to forgiveness is to pray for our enemies (Matthew 5:44). Evagrius used to say, "The man who prays for his enemies is a man without rancor."[4] To pray for an offender, after all, is to lift that person up in the presence of God. That's the surest way I know to pluck an offense out of our spiritual eye, and to look once more with joy into the face of the Lord.

Seventy times seven (Matthew 18:22)—have I learned to count that high, merciful Father? No. I know all too well the sting of the torturers. I recognize the heavy plank that boards up my windows, darkens my room, and hides my view of heaven.

I tremble, Lord, to pray sincerely, "Forgive us our debts, as we forgive our debtors" (Matthew 6:12). If You took as long to let go of anger as I do, Lord God, who could stand? Yet only when that's my desire can I go on to pray as well, "Lead us not into temptation, but deliver us from evil." Deliver us, Lord, from the evil of unforgiveness. Plaster our blinded eyes with the mud of humility to restore both our sight and our joy (John 9:6-7).

NOTES:

1. Evagrius Ponticus, *The Praktikos and Chapters on Prayer*, translated by John Eudes Bamberger (Kalamazoo, Mich.: Cistercian Publications, 1981), pages 18, 58-59.
2. *Searchlight on Bible Words*, compiled by James C. Hefley (Grand Rapids: Zondervan Publishing Co., 1972), page 121.
3. Dorotheos, *Discourses and Sayings*, page 147.
4. Dorotheos, *Discourses and Sayings*, page 155, note 14.

The kingdom of God is not a matter of eating and drinking, but of righteousness, peace and joy in the Holy Spirit, because anyone who serves Christ in this way is pleasing to God and approved by men.
ROMANS 14:17

☐

This is what the LORD says. . . . "Forget the former things; do not dwell on the past. See, I am doing a new thing! Now it springs up; do you not perceive it? I am making a way in the desert and streams in the wasteland."
ISAIAH 43:14,18-19

☐

Nothing is so deadening to the divine as an habitual dealing with the outsides of holy things.
GEORGE MACDONALD

☐

Safe? . . . Who said anything about safe? 'Course he isn't safe. But he's good. He's the King, I tell you.
C. S. LEWIS

C H A P T E R 31

LEGALISM:
God in a Box

In the days of Eli, the priest of Israel, God's people were growing spiritually blind and deaf. "In those days," the Scripture tells us, "the word of the LORD was rare; there were not many visions" (1 Samuel 3:1). Evidently, those who could see or hear the Lord were few. For that reason, I suspect that joy in the Lord was a stranger to most of them.

Yet God wasn't willing to turn His back on His people, even though they'd settled into a deadly consistency. So He chose young Samuel to become His prophet. On the evening when the boy's prophetic call was issued, the Lord made an intriguing promise—or perhaps, under the circumstances, it was a threat. "See," He said, "I am about to do something in Israel that will make the ears of everyone who hears of it tingle" (1 Samuel 3:11).

Sadly enough, it seems, in Eli's day God's people had come to consider their blindness and deafness normal, and their routine relationship with God adequate. After all, hadn't they settled down in the land of Canaan as God had promised? They had their traditions. As long as they offered the prescribed sacrifices, wasn't "business as usual" enough?

They were comfortable with a little god they could keep in a box, where he'd stay safe, tame, and predictable.

But God Himself had different plans. He was about to set in motion events that would change the course of history through the establishment of a royal throne. "Business as usual" wasn't good enough for the Lord. The rituals Israel considered adequate were only the beginning of a great and glorious plan that would make ears tingle, not just throughout the twelve tribes, but eventually throughout the whole earth. God was ready to come busting out of His box.

Not safe, but good

The people of Israel had once seen the Lord split a sea in half, rain bread from heaven, call water from a rock, and crumble a city with a shout. If they knew anything about the God of their fathers and mothers, they should have known that He was a God of surprises. His choice of Samuel to "make their ears tingle" wasn't the first time He'd caught His people off guard, and it certainly wasn't the last.

Consider just a few of these "famous last words" we might have heard from some biblical characters:

"I'm past the age of child-bearing."

"We'll trap those slaves at the Red Sea!"

"Virgins don't have babies."

"Roll the stone back; that's the last we'll see of Him."

The historical record of Scripture demonstrates again and again that God is not bound by our expectations. We can't always predict what He'll do.

Is that to say that our Lord is capricious or arbitrary? Of course not! As the apostle James tells us, "the Father of the heavenly lights . . . does not change like shifting shadows" (James 1:17). Jesus Christ, like the Father who sent Him, is the same yesterday, today, and forever (Hebrews 13:8). His character—His love, holiness, and mercy—are unfailing.

We can count on that above all else.

But like Aslan the lion in C. S. Lewis's *Chronicles of Narnia*, God is always showing up unexpectedly. The beaver in that story said it well: He's not by any means "safe." But He's good.[1]

Mistaking the part for the whole

If God's nature and character are sure, then why have His people so often been mistaken about His intentions? Certainly our sin blinds us to much of what we should see in God. But many times even men and women who have genuinely desired to obey Him have been found to be opposing His will, and have missed seeing Him. Why, for instance, would a man like Peter argue with God when He told him to eat unclean animals? (Acts 10:9-16).

The reason, I believe, is this: God's purposes never change. But because we're finite and fallen, we never come to see them *exhaustively*. So we're continually discovering "new" features in our vision of God that were there all along.

Adam and Eve knew from God's promise that her seed would crush the head of the serpent, but the details of that future redemption weren't given at the very beginning of the Fall (Genesis 3:15). Abraham knew that through his descendants all the families of the earth would be blessed, but as far as we know, he wasn't told much more about how that would happen (Genesis 12:3). David knew that his throne would be established forever; Isaiah knew that God would send a Man of sorrows, acquainted with grief (1 Kings 2:4, Isaiah 53). And the Pharisees knew all these prophecies. Yet most of Jesus' contemporaries failed to recognize God when He came to earth.

We may think that matters are different for Christians, now that Christ has come and both Testaments have been given to us. But even though God revealed His fullness in Christ, He's still "able to do immeasurably more than all we . . . imagine" (Ephesians 3:20). The Bible is complete in the sense that no more books can be added to it, but the Bible doesn't tell us everything. If it did, John reminds us, "the whole world would not have room for the books that would be written" (John 21:25). Evidently, the Lord still has surprises in store!

God has always known exactly what His intentions are, but He doesn't let us in on everything. We just can't hold it all. And what we do see, we see "through a glass, darkly" (1 Corinthians 13:12, KJV). Our multitude of denominations, each with its own interpretation of Christ and the Scriptures, is ample evidence of that reality.

Nevertheless, we still tend to cherish a part of the truth we see about God, and insist that it's the whole picture. We may draw detailed blueprints of the Second Coming, for example, when all we have is a dazzling vision from John that lends itself to countless interpretations. Or we may insist that God has restricted His miracles to a certain historical period simply because we've never witnessed a miracle ourselves. Whatever our theological orientation, we probably have some private or traditional box into which we expect God to fit.

Needless to say, when our God is confined that way—when He's hidden inside some box of our own making—our joy is diminished. The less we see of God, the less delight we'll take in Him, and the more often we'll miss the pleasure of seeing Him altogether when He shows up in some place where we insist He can't be. No wonder a grim joylessness has always been characteristic of the legalist.

"The legalist?" you may ask. "But isn't the legalist someone who adheres too strictly to rules, who hopes to earn salvation by externals? Wasn't that the problem of the religious leaders of Jesus' day?"

Yes. I agree that such legalism was their primary problem. But if we look at the heart of that problem, I believe we'll see that its essence was not so much *rules* as it was *rigidity*. Certainly, they hoped to save themselves by law-keeping, but it was a particular kind of law-keeping: the kind that allows only one interpretation of the law, which of course must be its own.

Jesus could heal a woman on the Sabbath, for example, in an act that for Him was not work, but rather a joyous celebration of God's liberating power. So from His perspective, to heal on the Sabbath was not to break the laws against Sabbath labor. But the synagogue ruler counted it as work, and condemned Jesus for His action because it didn't agree with his own rigid interpretation of the law (Luke 13:10-17).

I'm convinced that such religious leaders were obsessed with laws and with externals, not simply because they thought to save themselves by them, but because they saw them as a way to *corral God*—to make Him controllable. What the Lord had given them as limits for themselves they mistook as limits for Him.

If God made the Sabbath, they claimed, then God would not break the Sabbath by healing on it. If God condemned fornication, then God would not go anywhere near a prostitute. Unable to see what God was doing outside of the box where they thought they had Him kept, the legalists couldn't see the Father at work in the Son. They were "blind guides" of the blind (Matthew 15:14).

The inevitable loss of joy that proceeded from their loss of vision showed itself continually. When a man born blind was healed on the Sabbath, he and all who knew him rejoiced to see God's loving power. But the Pharisees could only grumble about the breaking of a rule (John 9:16). When Jesus raised Lazarus from the dead, the whole community was shaken with joyous awe. But the chief priests, the Pharisees, and the Sanhedrin could only worry about what the Romans would do when they heard of such events (John 11).

We, too, have our boxes. Only those of us who will let God out of those boxes will be able to rejoice at seeing all the unexpected things He does. When the seventy-two disciples came back from their mission, Jesus was "full of joy through the Holy Spirit" at what He saw God doing. But He noted at the same time that such joyous realities had been hidden from those who thought they had God all figured out (Luke 10:1-23).

May God deliver us from having Him all figured out! Only if we're willing to look at every place for evidences of God's activity will Jesus be able to say to us as He did to His returning missionaries, "Blessed are the eyes that see what you see."

God of surprises, flatten my boxes! The highest heavens cannot contain You, much less these crates I build (1 Kings 8:27). When I think to trap You in them, I only end up trapping myself, and it's dark and lonely in there.

So let me look for You at work in the most unlikely of places: in the secular scenes of the marketplace; in the dry bones of a religious organization long dead; in a church or denomination other than my own. Wherever I think You've never been, or in the place I think You've abandoned, surprise me, Jesus, by showing up to preach the gospel and heal the sick and raise the dead. Then I, too, will be "full of joy" to know that You're the untamed Lord of heaven and earth.

NOTES:
1. C. S. Lewis, *The Lion, the Witch and the Wardrobe* (New York: Macmillan, 1950), pages 75-76.

But one thing I do: Forgetting what is behind and straining toward what is ahead, I press on toward the goal to win the prize for which God has called me heavenward in Christ Jesus . . . . As I have often told you before and now say again even with tears, many live as enemies of the cross of Christ. . . . Their mind is on earthly things.
PHILIPPIANS 3:13-14,18-19

□

Let us throw off everything that hinders and the sin that so easily entangles, and let us run with perseverance the race marked out for us. Let us fix our eyes on Jesus, the author and perfecter of our faith.
HEBREWS 12:1-2

□

We are half-hearted creatures, fooling about with drink and sex and ambition when infinite joy is offered us, like an ignorant child who wants to go on making mud pies in a slum because he cannot imagine what is meant by the offer of a holiday at the sea.
We are far too easily pleased.
C. S. LEWIS

□

I rejoice, because He gives me to feel in myself "the mind that was in Christ":—Simplicity, a single eye to Him, in every motion of my heart; power always to fix the loving eye of my soul on Him who "loved me, and gave Himself for me"; to aim at Him alone, at His glorious will, in all I think, or speak, or do.
JOHN WESLEY

CHAPTER 32

AMBITION:
God in the Background

"Blessed are the pure in heart," Jesus insisted, "for they will see God" (Matthew 5:8). The promises of the other Beatitudes—to possess the Kingdom, to inherit the earth, to be called children of God—are all precious beyond the telling. But to me, this is the most thrilling promise of all. If we desire more than anything else to have a clear vision of the Lord and the joy that flows from that vision, then we do well to ponder the meaning in this sentence of the word "pure."

Both the English word and the Greek term it translates have as their primary meaning "unmixed." To be pure in heart thus means to have a will that is "unmixed," which is single and unified in its purpose. In the words of the title from Soren Kierkegaard's famous essay, "Purity of heart is to will one thing." This understanding clarifies the meaning of James's warning: "Purify your hearts, you double-minded" (James 4:8).

The pure in heart are simply those who have their wills and their eyes focused singly on the Lord's will. The writer of Hebrews tells us that such singleness of vision is in fact the only way to run the race of faith without faltering: "Let us fix our eyes on Jesus, the author and perfecter of our faith" (Hebrews 12:2).

We can understand, then, why the pure in heart will see God. Those who have totally devoted their wills to God's will, who have turned their hearts lovingly in His direction, will have Him at the center of their field of vision. All else will be in the background, on the periphery, viewed either in the light of its closeness to God or in the shadow of its distance from Him.

We can also see why Jesus would warn, "The eye is the lamp of the body. If your eyes are good, your whole body will be full of light. But if your eyes are bad, your whole body will be full of darkness" (Matthew 6:22). The word translated here as "good" can mean whole, sound, or healthy; but it can also mean single, simple, or clear. The healthy natural eye sees a single, clear image, and so does the healthy eye of the heart. But just as an unhealthy eye hinders vision, so the eye that fails to focus on God—that presents a double or fuzzy image of what it sees—will block the light of God's face from entering and illuminating us.

We've noted before that our eyes can "lead" our hearts in the sense that what we perceive as desirable turns our will toward the object of our desire. Not every turning of our will toward some good is necessarily a turning away from God. But when the good toward which we turn our hearts assumes the center of our field of vision, then God is relegated to the background. Consequently, our view of Him is impaired, and our joy dries up.

The example of Solomon
King Solomon provides us with a clear and tragic example of how our hearts can be led away from God by our eyes. When the Lord first asked the king what he wanted Him to

grant, Solomon asked for wisdom to govern God's people righteously (1 Kings 3:4-15). The eyes of his heart were focused on the will of the Lord, and because of that focus, God was able to give him other good gifts as well—riches, honor, and power as king of Israel (verses 10-13). But the Lord intended those other good gifts in Solomon's life to remain at the outer edge of his field of vision.

Sadly enough, however, the king came in time to turn his primary attention elsewhere. He focused his eyes on power, wealth, and wives, and so married hundreds of women as a seal of political alliances. The result, the Scripture says, was that "his wives turned his heart after other gods, and his heart was not fully devoted to the LORD his God, as the heart of David his father had been" (1 Kings 11:4). With the turning of Solomon's heart away from God toward other desires came the overt worship of idols (verses 5-8).

The distraction of ambition

This redirecting of our heart's primary attention from God to something else could be called by many names. Solomon's experience shows us that in the final analysis, it's the sin of idolatry—worshiping something other than God. Nevertheless, I've chosen to call this impairment of our vision of the Lord *ambition* because of the useful word pictures that lie behind this term.

In the Greek vocabulary of the New Testament, two words are frequently translated by our English word "ambition." The first is always negative (for example, Galatians 5:20), coming from a root word that refers to a hired day-laborer, mercenary, or prostitute. It once meant literally "one who sells him or herself out for profit." The term was also applied to unscrupulous politicians who gained office by buying votes.

In the word "ambition," then, we have a picture of someone whose primary aim is different from what his or her activity might suggest. The hired day-laborer, the mercenary, the prostitute, and the corrupt politician are not interested in the provision of the harvest, the defense of the nation, the good of someone beloved, or the administration of justice. Their goal, rather, is money.

When we allow something other than God to occupy the center of our hearts, then even if we continue in what appears to be spiritual behavior, we too will actually be aiming at something other than what our activities suggest. We may seem to be running "the race marked out for us," but if our eyes aren't fixed on Jesus, we won't be running, as Paul called it, "in such a way as to get the prize." Instead, we'll only be "running aimlessly," because our faces won't be aimed toward the true goal (1 Corinthians 9:24,26).

The root of the English word "ambition" further enriches our understanding here. It comes from the Latin verb meaning "to walk around." The term originally referred to public office seekers who went around canvassing for support.

Eventually, if we've been distracted by ambitions of whatever sort—wealth, power, fame, pleasure—then we'll not only slow down in the race of faith; we'll finally leave it altogether to wander around in circles, chasing after lesser desires. Whatever we allow to be first in our field of vision will ultimately set the course of our direction, and lead us to sell ourselves out for every special interest that comes our way. For that reason, when we lose the singleness of vision, we lose the race.

We lose our joy as well. Countless servants of God who somehow lost their original purity of heart along the way have testified to the numbness that sets in, the loss of delight in the Lord and in His presence that characterizes a wrong direction. The change may have begun in very small ways, or through fondness for some small thing. But slowly, the fondness becomes a love, and the love becomes an idol.

For a while, such an idol can give us what John of the Cross called "vain joys." But the delight we take in anything that usurps the centrality of God in our lives will always show diminishing returns. To maintain the same level of enjoyment, we'll have to seek more of whatever it is we want: more power, more wealth, more fame, more pleasure. The water of joy "stolen" from God may taste "sweet" at first, but in the end it's poison (Proverbs 9:17-18).

We must emphasize here that ambition—not in the narrower traditional sense, but in the broad definition we're assigning it—may be directed either toward things that are themselves sinful (such as unjust economic power) or toward things that are good in themselves (such as the esteem of other people). The writer of Hebrews tells us that as we run the race of faith, we must "throw off" not only "the sin that so easily entangles" but also "*everything* that hinders" (Hebrews 12:1). For that reason, if we discover that something we desire, though good in itself, is hindering us from the race by preoccupying our attention, then we must cast it away.

An additional insight in this regard comes to us from Jonathan Edwards, in his essay *The Nature of True Virtue*. Edwards suggested that many things appear good in themselves—or, as he said, "beautiful" in themselves—when we focus only on them. But if we carefully consider them in the light of the complete picture of life, with God at the center, we may discover that they don't fit harmoniously into the whole. Thus, seen from the perspective of the "single" eye, such things are actually less than beautiful, and are no longer attractive to us.[1]

Ambition or aspiration?

The English New Testament speaks in several places of a second kind of "ambition," translating a different Greek word whose literal meaning is "love of what is honorable or valuable." The kinds of ambition referred to here, such as preaching the gospel (Romans 15:20), are obviously honorable and worthy of our adoption.

Nevertheless, we find that even preaching can be motivated by the other kind of ambition (Philippians 1:17). The activity can seem spiritual enough, yet the heart behind it can be "mercenary." So how can we tell the difference between the two kinds of motivation?

This, I think, is precisely the point at which the connection between vision and joy can be helpful in understanding our own hearts. The kind of "ambition" that contributes to an abiding joy in God's presence is the kind that's "honorable." The thing we seek should find its value only in its ability to point our hearts toward God.

The ungodly ambition, however, will attract attention to itself. It will drain our delight in the Lord's presence. Whatever joy it gives us will be "vain"—only fleeting and hollow. And if we lose it, we'll lose our joy, instead of finding that our joy still flows from the presence of God.

For that reason, I prefer the translation "aspiration" for the second kind of ambition. This English word comes from a root meaning literally "breathing toward," and I think it provides the perfect picture of the runner whose face is toward the goal, who "breathes toward" God as he or she perseveres in the race of faith. An ambition will be characterized by wandering around in search of lesser prizes, and grasping for them. But an aspiration will be characterized by a steadfast focus on the goal of God Himself, and a letting go of whatever else hinders the race.

Whatever lesser goods we desire in life, we must ask of

each one: Is this an aspiration or an ambition? Is it at the center or the periphery of our field of vision? Do we desire it for God's sake or for its own?

If the thing we enjoy leaves us thirsty for more of it, we'd better examine carefully our reasons for wanting it. But if it tastes of God, and leaves us thirsty for more of God, then we can be encouraged that the Lord is in focus, and our joy is not vain.

Forgive me, Lord, for leaving You at the edge of my vision— for daring to make the Creator a mere frame around a picture of one of His creatures. In the light of Your face, Jesus, all else becomes shadow. Next to the precious gold of Your joy, all else is dross. I consider everything a loss compared to the surpassing greatness of knowing You, Christ Jesus my Lord, for whose sake I have lost all things. I consider them rubbish, that I may gain You (Philippians 3:8).

Give me a pure heart so that I can see more and more of You. Let me be content with nothing less than You, Jesus. For whoever has You and everything else has no more than the one who has only You.

NOTES:
1. Edwards, *True Virtue*, pages 2-3.

Rejoice that you participate in the sufferings of Christ, so that you may be overjoyed when his glory is revealed.
1 PETER 4:13

□

Now if we are children, then we are heirs—heirs of God and co-heirs with Christ, if indeed we share in his sufferings in order that we may also share in his glory. I consider that our present sufferings are not worth comparing with the glory that will be revealed in us.
ROMANS 8:17-18

□

The Son of God suffered unto death, not that men might not suffer, but that their sufferings might be like His.
GEORGE MACDONALD

□

Well's them who are under crosses, and Christ says to them, "Half Mine."
SAMUEL RUTHERFORD

□

As sure as God puts His children into the furnace of affliction, He will be with them in it.
CHARLES H. SPURGEON

CHAPTER 33

SUFFERING:
God Beside Us

In the stark and terrifying book called *Night*, author Elie Wiesel recounts the horrors of his experience as a teenager in the Nazi concentration camps of the 1940s. Every page of the work simmers with anger and with anguish, as we might well expect. But what is perhaps the book's most shattering moment comes when Wiesel describes how the Nazi SS sentenced a young child to death by hanging.

As the prisoners watched the execution in horror, a voice came from behind Wiesel asking, "Where is God? Where is He?" Half an hour later, when the child still hung strangling from the rope because he was too light, the same prisoner demanded once more, "Where is God?"

At that moment, within himself Wiesel heard a voice answer: "Where is He? Here He is—He is hanging here on this gallows."[1]

For that author, the death of the small child was the death of God. Wiesel had grown up a devout Jewish believer, but the nightmare days in a concentration camp had strangled his faith. So in that despairing moment, the teenage Wiesel concluded that such terrible things could only happen if there were no God.

I must confess that I've suffered very little in my life-time: some chronic physical pain from the aftermath of a childhood disease; a great deal more emotional pain from my own brokenness, from broken relationships, from the death of those I've loved deeply. But in the shadow of the anguish Wiesel describes, I hesitate to speak at all of suffering. How dare I respond to someone whose pain is probably more than I'll ever know?

Nevertheless, the portrait of joy, however brilliant its colors may be, is incomplete without the muted shades of suffering. So we must speak now about that subject as well, for suffering issues to joy the weightiest challenge of all. As Lewis Smedes has said, "If our joy is honest joy, it must somehow be congruous with human tragedy. This is the test of joy's integrity: is it compatible with pain?"[2]

In view of my limited experience with suffering, then, I must simply echo the witness of the many Christians who have found joy even in the midst of pain. Only a Dietrich Bonhoeffer, an Aleksandr Solzhenitsyn, or a Corrie Ten Boom could answer Wiesel directly, out of the depths of their own anguish. But I believe that those who have both suffered and rejoiced have told others of us enough to catch a glimpse of where God is when we hurt.

God on the gallows

For the Christian, any understanding of God's relation to human suffering must begin at the Cross. At the heart of the gospel is the scandalous and terrifying claim that God Himself has suffered, God Himself has died, God Himself has risen again to conquer suffering and death. We have not suffered alone.

In a sense, then, we must agree with Wiesel: In that awful moment of the child's execution, God was indeed on the gallows. It was nothing less than the spectacle of God's own death. But where we must disagree with Wiesel—while our hearts are chastened by his suffering—is in the conclusion that God's death and the child's death that day were final.

We who bear witness to the crucified God confess with tears that the child's agony was a participation in the agony God Himself underwent so long ago, when He hung, not on a gallows, but on a cross (1 Peter 4:13). Yet that great act of divine suffering and death was not final. Jesus Christ rose again in joy. So we now can affirm that the child's agony also is not final, because it has been taken up into God's own agony (Isaiah 53:5-6). With Christ, that child will someday rise again in joy.

The prisoner's question—"Where is God?"—was actually an echo of Christ's own cry of abandonment from the Cross: "My God, my God, why have you forsaken me?" (Matthew 27:46). In that anguished call, the joy of the Son, who had eternally beheld the face of the Father in love, was utterly lost.

George MacDonald wrote of what Christ experienced in that moment: "Never before had he been unable to see God beside him. Yet never was God nearer him than now. . . . For God was his God still, although he had forsaken him—forsaken *his vision* that his faith might glow out triumphant; forsaken *himself*? no; come nearer to him than ever."[3]

In our suffering as well, God is nearer to us than ever. Yet grief, the ancients agreed, is best described as a "constriction" of the heart. Thus with grief comes a narrowing of our sight, a loss of our heart's peripheral vision. So it's precisely to the periphery that we must turn our attention if we're to see, in our suffering, that God is beside us, nearer than ever, suffering with us.

In His infinite love for us, the Lord feels our pain as His own. "Among lovers," said John of the Cross, "the wound of one is the wound for both, and the two have but one feeling."[4] If we can glimpse our hurting God beside us for even a moment, His face will stir in us a joy in His unsearchable love.

I've often thought of the two thieves who were crucified with Jesus, for they provide a compelling parable of vision and blindness. Both were suffering, both were dying. But one saw God suffering and dying beside him, and the other did not. The one entered with Jesus that day into the joy of paradise; the other remained in his misery. I believe that when we suffer, we too can see what the first thief saw, and rejoice in Jesus' presence despite our pain.

That is, in fact, the lesson we in the United States can learn these days from the countless testimonies of Christians tortured and imprisoned for their faith in many nations around the world. I'm thinking of people like Irina Ratushinskaya and Alexander Ogorodnikov, two Soviet believers who were recently released after a long confinement. They've given independent testimony that at times each one could rejoice actually to feel a physical warmth of God's presence with them in the freezing temperatures of their punishment cells.

Beside Him in glory

The vision of God suffering beside us, however, is only part of the perspective that leads to joy in suffering. For we've been told that we shall also reign beside God in glory. Christ's resurrection has sealed the ultimate victory over sin, suffering, and death.

Though many scoff at such a claim as a deceptive opiate for pain, we can't leave out this part of the scriptural witness if we're to be faithful to the reality God has promised us. As C. S. Lewis has insisted, "Scripture and tradition habitually put the joys of heaven into the scale against the sufferings of earth, and no solution of the problem of pain which does not do so can be called a Christian one."[5]

When Paul or Peter or other New Testament writers talk of suffering, they inevitably talk of glory as well. "For I consider," said Paul, "that our present sufferings are not worth comparing with the glory that will be revealed in us" (Romans 8:18). "But rejoice," said Peter, "that you participate in the sufferings of Christ, so that you may be overjoyed when his glory is revealed" (1 Peter 4:13).

Were suffering and death final, our joy would be but shallow and fleeting. "If only for this life we have hope in Christ, we are to be pitied more than all men" (1 Corinthians 15:19). But part of the good news of the gospel is that this world's pain is *not* final. "Earth has no sorrow that Heaven cannot heal."[6]

For our joy to be complete in suffering, then, we must see not only that God is beside us suffering, but also that we are beside God reigning. Even now, we're "seated . . . with him in the heavenly realms" (Ephesians 2:6), and the day will come when we'll "reign for ever and ever" with Him (Revelation 22:5). Next to that triumphant eternity, the suffering of today or even of a lifetime grows infinitely small; and so the joy of our vision of glory can pour comfort and hope into the thirsty ground of our present pain.

Our sufferings are chips from Your Cross, Jesus. When grief constricts our heart and our vision, turn our head to see You there beside us, and to remember that even though the Father has one Child without sin, He has none—even that One—without sorrow.[7] With that vision I'll know that especially "at night Your song is with me," because my night is the shadow of Your Cross; and with joy I'll be able to sing in the shadow of its wings (Psalms 42:8, 63:7).

NOTES:

1. Elie Wiesel, *Night* (New York: Bantam, 1982), pages 61-62.
2. Lewis B. Smedes, *How Can It Be All Right When Everything Is All Wrong?* (New York: Harper & Row, 1982), page 15.
3. MacDonald, *Unspoken Sermons*, pages 166, 168.
4. John of the Cross, *The Collected Works*, page 460.
5. C. S. Lewis, *The Problem of Pain* (New York: Macmillan, 1962), page 114.
6. From the hymn "Come, Ye Disconsolate, Where'er Ye Languish" by Thomas Moore.
7. The first sentence and the last clause of this paragraph were adapted from the words of Puritan writers Joseph Church and John Trapp, quoted in *Puritan Quotations*, pages 2228, 11.

PART 5

THE
FEAST OF
JOY

But we all, with unveiled face beholding as in a mirror the glory of the Lord, are being transformed into the same image from glory to glory.
2 CORINTHIANS 3:18, NASB

☐

We know that when he appears, we shall be like him, for we shall see him as he is. Everyone who has this hope in him purifies himself, just as he is pure.
1 JOHN 3:2-3

☐

"He will take great delight in you. . . . He will rejoice over you with singing."
ZEPHANIAH 3:17

☐

Seeing holiness is the main thing that excites, draws, and governs all gracious affections; no wonder that all such affections tend to holiness. That which men love, they desire to have and to be united to, and possessed of. That beauty which men delight in, they desire to be adorned with. Those acts which men delight in, they necessarily incline to do.
JONATHAN EDWARDS

CHAPTER 34

THE FRUIT OF JOY:
Becoming God's Portrait

We've spoken now of how joy flows into the garden of our soul from the fount of God's own delight, and through the floodgates of faith, hope, and love. We've talked of digging furrows to channel that joy, and of ways to warm the channels when joy becomes frozen. So we're almost done with our discussion—but not quite yet. And what is last to be said is perhaps most important.

After all, wet soil isn't the goal of irrigation. A garden isn't a garden unless it grows something. And the garden of the soul was created to grow fruit—the fruit of God's Spirit, which is the character of God's Son (Galatians 5:22).

"I am the true vine," said Jesus, "and my Father is the gardener. . . . You are the branches. If a man remains in me and I in him, he will bear much fruit. . . . The Spirit of truth . . . will bring glory to me by taking from what is mine and making it known to you" (John 15:1,5; 16:13-14).

In these and other words of our Lord from the night of His betrayal, we see a beautiful picture of the Holy Trinity's cooperation to make our garden flourish. I'm convinced that joy makes its special contribution to that process of growth by the vitalizing vision it fixes within us of the Father, the Son, and the Holy Spirit. By keeping our eyes so continually on God, it shapes our perceptions, our thoughts, and our behaviors to conform to His. As an ancient philosopher once described it: The habit of our thought will determine the color of our soul, because our soul is dyed by our thought.

No wonder, then, that the sight of God, as Paul tells us, transforms us into His likeness (2 Corinthians 3:18). And John affirms that whoever looks toward the day when we see the Lord face-to-face is even now being purified by that hope (1 John 3:2-3). Thus the water of joy carries a life-changing vision of God throughout the branches of the Vine, spurring them to grow and bear the fruit of holiness.

Motivation

The writer of Hebrews tells us that "for the *joy* set before him," Jesus "endured the cross, scorning its shame, and sat down at the right hand of the throne of God" (Hebrews 12:2). What was the joy set before Him? Since His destination was the throne of God, I believe the delight that urged Him onward was the Father who was waiting for Him at the end of the race. As Catherine of Siena described it, Jesus' clear vision of the Father gave Him such joy that "He ran like one gloriously in love along the way of obedience."[1]

For us as well as for Jesus, joy sends us on our way to the throne by fixing in us *a vision of the Father's welcome as our reward.* Thus joy gives us *motivation* to run the race of our growth in holiness. Dorotheos put it this way: "What, more than anything else, makes a soul do good if not the joy which that good itself will bring?"[2]

Of course, God rewards our faithfulness as well with a "crown of life" (Revelation 2:10). But John's glimpse of heaven reveals that we'll take those crowns and cast them at the feet of the Father (Revelation 4:10). God Himself is the "treasure hidden in a field," and it's because of our joy over Him that we're willing to "sell" all we have to possess Him (Matthew 13:44).

Direction

At the same time that the book of Hebrews tells us to look to the Father, it reminds us to "fix our eyes on Jesus, the author and perfecter of our faith" (Hebrews 12:2). We focus our attention on Christ because He's our example, the great pattern for our lives (John 13:15). In Him we see the fruit of the Spirit embodied in flesh.

The vision we gain in joy, because it's also a vision of Christ, thus has the power to give us *direction*. For in joy we fix our eyes on *the character of the Son as our goal*. The world clamors daily with a myriad of patterns for "human development," each claiming to know the way to "wholeness." But Jesus said, "I *am* the way," and no one can come home to the Father's welcome except through Him (John 14:6). Only when we love as He loved, imitating His pattern, do we bear abiding fruit (John 15:12,16).

As Jonathan Edwards observed, the beauty of Christ's character that we delight in attracts us in His direction: "By the sight of the transcendent glory of Christ, true Christians see him worthy to be followed; and so are powerfully drawn after him."[3] I've often thought of Jesus' goodness as the great magnetic pole of the world in which our lives are compasses. When His holy character exerts its attractive power on the metal of our hearts, we find ourselves turning toward Him, pointing in His direction.

Strength

The runners in a race need more than motivation and a goal; they must also have the energy to persevere until they finish. So we can be encouraged to know that a third way in which joy contributes to our progress in holiness fills precisely that need. When we have *a vision of the Holy Spirit's power as our source*, God's joy becomes our *strength*.

Paul had his eyes firmly fixed on the Spirit, and he wanted his friends at Ephesus to gain the same joyful vision. "I pray," he told them, "that out of his glorious riches he may strengthen you with power through his Spirit in your inner being" (Ephesians 3:16). Paul asked that "the eyes of [their] heart" might be "enlightened" in joy, so that they could see God's "incomparably great power for us who believe" (Ephesians 1:18-19).

When we gain such a joyful view of the Spirit's power and its accessibility, we can draw on God's grace to participate in His holiness. God gave us the oil of joy, said Isaiah, precisely so that we might become strong "oaks of righteousness, a planting of the LORD for the display of his splendor" (Isaiah 61:3). Truly, then, "the joy of the LORD is [our] strength" (Nehemiah 8:10).

The portrait of God

Gregory of Nyssa, a fourth-century bishop and one of the great theologians of the Church, once spoke of our growth in holiness as the painting of a picture. That picture, he said, is a portrait of Christ, in which His beautiful image is perfected in us. Consequently, the colors we must use to paint Him accurately are the virtues we see in the character of Jesus.[4]

Gregory's image provides us with a useful way of understanding how the fruit of holiness leads to a different "order of joy" from the one we've described before. We've spoken, of course, about God's people seeing, knowing, loving, and enjoying Him. But as the transformation of our character proceeds, more and more God Himself is able to look upon us in a way that leads to His own delight. In us, He sees the beauty of holiness; He knows that beauty as the character of His Son; He loves the beauty; and so He takes great joy in seeing Christ's beauty in us.

Thus in the wonderful mystery of salvation, we have the privilege of becoming tributaries for the river of joy that flows between the Father, and the Son, and the Spirit. "The LORD takes delight in his people," declares the psalmist. "Let the saints rejoice in this honor and sing for joy" (Psalm 149:4-5).

Dare we believe it? The Lord "will take great delight in you," said Zephaniah. "He will rejoice over you with singing" (Zephaniah 3:17). We serve the Lord God Almighty, omnipotent Creator and Sustainer of the universe, who's in need of absolutely nothing. Yet He has allowed us nevertheless to give Him something of genuine value to Him; to make a real contribution, however small, to the superabundance of divine pleasure. For it was, after all, for His "pleasure" that we were created (Revelation 4:11, KJV).

I can hardly bear the exhilaration of the thought: for God Himself to be so delighted in us that He would sing for joy! The Lord who once wept over a barren, desolate Jerusalem (Luke 13:34-35) and who planted His own body there as a seed to restore life to its soil, now rejoices at the sight of the New Jerusalem springing up. He tastes with gladness the fruit of our swelling garden. He has sown in tears, and now He reaps with songs of joy (Psalm 126:5).

Even so, the fruit we offer for God's pleasure is only a foretaste of the great Wedding Supper of the Lamb (Revelation 19:9). Though we all eagerly await that Feast of feasts, God's own anticipation of the Day is infinitely greater. For at the consummation of all things, our God will rejoice over us "as a bridegroom rejoices over his bride" (Isaiah 62:5). And not even the heavens, I suppose, will be able to contain the joy of that triumphant Song.

Yet even now, Lord, let my Lover come into His garden and taste its choice fruits (Song of Songs 4:16). Then, on the day when we celebrate the Feast, my soul, too, "will be satisfied as with the richest of foods" (Psalm 63:5). For "you will fill me with joy in your presence, with eternal pleasures at your right hand" (Psalm 16:11).

NOTES:
1. Catherine of Siena, *The Dialogue*, page 328.
2. Dorotheos, *Discourses and Sayings*, page 113.
3. Edwards, "Religious Affection," in *Selections*, pages 252-253.
4. Gregory of Nyssa, "On Perfection," *Patrologia Graeca* (Paris: 1857-1866), Volume 46, page 272.

On this mountain the LORD Almighty will prepare
a feast of rich food for all peoples,
a banquet of aged wine—
the best of meats and the finest of wines.
On this mountain he will destroy
the shroud that enfolds all peoples,
the sheet that covers all nations;
he will swallow up death forever.
The Sovereign LORD will wipe away the tears
from all faces.
ISAIAH 25:6-8

□

"To him who is thirsty I will give to drink without cost from the spring
of the water of life."
REVELATION 21:6

□

For I have found a joy that is full, and more than full. For when heart,
and mind, and soul, and all the man, are full of that joy, joy beyond
measure will still remain. Therefore, the whole of that joy shall not enter
into those who rejoice; rather, they who rejoice shall
wholly enter into that joy.
ANSELM OF CANTERBURY

CHAPTER 35

"WHOEVER IS THIRSTY, COME!"

Today I had a dream in the daylight.

Far above me, I saw the skies tear apart and roll back like a scroll. I saw a Light flooding down from the rupture in such a blaze that the sun itself blackened, and the seas boiled. Then I heard a sound like a whisper from beyond the world's edge that grew louder and louder until I could see that it was a flaming Wind, sweeping the globe.

From every race and nation and tongue, the Wind gathered together a countless host of men and women and children, bringing them to the Light. Some were singing, some half sleeping; most were weeping. But all had strapped to their backs baskets of golden fruit, and all of them had left their shoes behind.

Above the tumult came suddenly a Voice like the sound of many waters. The words spilled over the multitude in sparkling breakers, bowing them, washing them, filling them, lifting them up in its melodious foam. Then the invitation came: "Whoever is thirsty, come; and whoever wishes, take the free gift of the water of life!"

The Wind brightened and quickened to become a

Whirlwind, encircling the multitude and drawing it along in its train. Soon the entire host was turning as one in a vast circle, with eyes lifted to the Light. Then the Voice said, "Let the dance begin!"

In the center of the circle there arose a murmur of delight, and I saw there now a Lamb, frisking and frolicking in the Light. Then a little child took hold of His fleece, laughing; and a woman, once bent over, straightened up and took the hand of the child. Another took her hand, and another his, until all had joined at last in a brilliant, spiral nebula of dancing fire.

The Lamb leapt up, and the dancers followed, whirling in the Firestorm, burning, yet without being consumed. So the spiral dance mounted up on the flames, a promenade that twisted its way laughing into the gaping wound of heaven.

When the last of the procession had entered, they looked over their shoulders to see that the hole through which they had come appeared as a dark abyss. But suddenly it began to crease and close up. The Whirlwind was folding it, smaller and smaller, until at last it was only a black speck, which came hurtling in a gale to the Lamb. Then the Lamb swallowed it, and it was no more.

The multitude came swirling into a vast banquet hall, without ceiling or walls. Each one who came had a place no one else could fill at the great table there. Each setting had for a place card a small white stone, on which a new name was inscribed, which no one could read but the one who sat there. And the napkin at each place was a white linen robe.

So the dancers unloaded one another's burdens, and placed the fruit on the table. Then they began to don their new clothes and throw their old ones onto a heap. But the more clothing they threw on the pile of torn, stained garments, the smaller the pile became, until it had shrunk into a single filthy rag. Then a spark from the blaze of the Whirlwind ignited it, and it was utterly consumed, so that not even an ash remained.

The banqueters sat down. Every place at the table faced the head of the table, where the Lamb reclined. For there were no longer many directions in which they could gaze or move, but only one.

A fountain flowed out from the Lamb to fill the guests' cups to overflowing, and without ceasing. In that flow was every tear they had ever shed on earth, counted and poured into His own. It was a dazzling wine, aged from eternity and therefore crystal clear. And in each cup was reflected the face of the Lamb.

The river that flowed into the cups flowed out again as well into a glassy sea that surrounded them and extended forever. The waters of the Fountain, and of the cups, and of the sea were one; and so I could no longer tell as they drank whether the multitude was within the sea, or the sea within the multitude.

They dined upon the fruit of the tables, all sharing with their neighbors, and finding their neighbors' fruit sweeter than their own. Beside the Lamb stood a fruit-bearing Tree, and He gave its fruit to the banqueters as well. No one could distinguish between the fruit from the baskets and the fruit from the Tree. For it was the same fruit.

Then when all were filled, the Lamb was transformed before their eyes, and His chair with Him. He became a King, and the chair became His throne.

At the sight of Him all hushed with the breathless silence of love. They knew that Face: They had seen Him and delighted in Him a thousand times before. But always before they had looked upon Him only through a dark veil. Now they saw Him in all His glory; and He saw in them His own glory, written on their faces, reflected back from them at countless angles, like the light on a diamond of facets without number.

Then suddenly there came a sweet, tinkling sound, like the melody of a wind chime—for in that place, all that was not silence was music. It was one of the white stones, tossed by a child at the foot of the throne; and it was followed by another, and then another, and then a hailstorm of all the others. When the storm was spent, there stretched out beneath the feet of the King and beyond the horizon a gleaming mosaic pavement, with each stone in its assigned place. And the multitudes bowed down, and sang.

They were joined by innumerable hosts of heaven. All sang with one voice, and yet with a myriad of voices; in ten thousand tongues, yet all understood one another. Each one stood in a place where no one else could stand, assuming a perspective on the King no one else could take. Each saw a feature of the King no one else could see. So they sang praise to Him, and testimony to each other of what they saw.

Then the King stood, and His Father was seated in His place. The royal Son extended His scarred hands, and said: "I am the First and the Last, the Beginning and the End. I chose you to be Mine before the foundation of the world. Now let the Bride come!"

So the multitude rose, and the glory of their joy was their wedding garment, shimmering and ready for the Bridegroom. Then the Wind and the Bride said, "Come!" And all who heard said, "Come!"

Today I had a dream in the daylight, my Lord. But if the glory of that dream so filled me with gladness that I can hardly tell it in words, what will be the splendor of the Reality when it comes?

It will be "the Alpha and the Omega" of all desire, all delight. It will be rapture "immeasurably beyond all we can imagine." It will be, my Lord, "joy unspeakable, and full of glory." Even so, come, Lord Jesus.

A PRAYER OF ANSELM
OF CANTERBURY

O God, I pray, let me know and love You, so that I may rejoice in You. And if I cannot in this life know, love, and rejoice in You fully, let me advance day by day until the point of fullness comes. Let knowledge of You progress in me here, and be made full in me there. Let love for You grow in me here and be made full in me there, so that here my joy may be great with expectancy while there being full in realization.

O Lord, through Your Son You command—or rather, You counsel—us to ask; and through Him You promise that we shall receive, so that our joy may be full. O Lord, I ask for what You counsel through our marvelous Counselor; may I receive what You promise through Your Truth, so that my joy may be full. God of truth, I ask to receive it, so that my joy may be full.

Until then, let my mind meditate upon what You have promised; let my tongue speak of it. Let my heart love it; let my mouth proclaim it. Let my soul hunger for it; let my flesh thirst for it; let my whole being desire it until such time as I enter into the joy of my Lord, the triune God, blessed forever. Amen.

ANSELM, ARCHBISHOP OF CANTERBURY (1033-1109)